AF841090

Insurance Law in Serbia

Insurance Law in Serbia

Vladimir Marjanski

This book was originally published as a monograph in the International Encyclopaedia of Laws/Insurance Law.

Founding Editor: Roger Blanpain
General Editor: Frank Hendrickx
Volume Editor: Herman Cousy

Wolters Kluwer

Published by:
Kluwer Law International B.V.
PO Box 316
2400 AH Alphen aan den Rijn
The Netherlands
E-mail: lrs-sales@wolterskluwer.com
Website: www.wolterskluwer.com/en/solutions/kluwerlawinternational

Sold and distributed by:
Wolters Kluwer Legal & Regulatory U.S.
7201 McKinney Circle
Frederick, MD 21704
United States of America
E-mail: customer.service@wolterskluwer.com

ISBN 978-94-035-0736-1

e-Book: ISBN 978-94-035-0896-2
web-PDF: ISBN 978-94-035-0906-8

The Author

Dr Vladimir Marjanski was born on 14 June 1977 in Zrenjanin, Serbia (former Yugoslavia). He graduated from the Faculty of Law in Novi Sad in 2002, where he earned his Master's (The Legal Nature of Insurance Contracts – 2006) and his Doctorate (Public Offer of Securities – 2010). In June 2003, he accepted a position as a teaching assistant at the Faculty of Law in Novi Sad, where he currently holds the title of Full Professor, specializing in commercial law. He carried out research at the Asser College Europe Institute in The Hague, the Netherlands (2006) and at the Karl Franz University in Graz (2008). The subjects of his scientific interest are insurance law and capital market law.

The Author

Table of Contents

List of Abbreviations

DOZ	Državni zavod za osiguranje – State Institute for Insurance
EU	European Union
FPRY	Federalna Narodna Republika Jugoslavija (1946–1963) – The Federal People's Republic of Yugoslavia (1946–1963)
FRY	Savezna Republika Jugoslavija (1992–2003) – The Federal Republic of Yugoslavia (1992–2003)
GDP	Gross Domestic Product
JZO	Jugoslovenska zajednica osiguranja – Yugoslav Insurance Association
LCC	Zakon o privrednim društvima iz 2011. godine – The Law on Commercial Companies (2011)
LI	Zakon o osiguranju iz 2014. godine – The Law on Insurance (2014)
LMIN	Zakon o pomorskoj i unutrašnjoj plovidbi iz 1998. godine – The former Yugoslav Law on Maritime and Internal Navigation (1998)
LO	Zakon o obligacionim odnosima iz 1978. godine – The former Yugoslav Law on Obligations (1978)
NBS	Narodna banka Srbije – The National Bank of Serbia
OJ RS	Službeni glasnik RS – Official Journal of Republic of Serbia
OJFRY	Službeni list SRJ – Official Journal of Federal Republic of Yugoslavia
SCG	Državna zajednica Srbije i Crne Gore (2003–2006) – The State Union of Serbia and Montenegro (2003–2006)
SFRY	Socijalistička Federativna Republika Jugoslavija (1963–1992) – The Socialist Federal Republic of Yugoslavia (1963–199

List of Abbreviations

General Introduction

Chapter 1. General Background Information

1. The Republic of Serbia is a small Danubian country covering a surface area of 88.361 square kilometres. The greater portion of state territory lies within the central Balkan area, while the smaller one, north of the Danube, geographically belongs to the area of Central Europe. The territory of the Republic of Serbia is administratively divided into provinces, districts, municipalities, and the City of Belgrade. According to the data from official website of Statistical Office of the Republic of Serbia, Serbia (without Kosovo i Metohija) had a population of 6,871,547.[1]

§1. Political System

2. The fundamentals of the political system in the Republic of Serbia have been regulated by the Constitution since 2006.[2] The Constitution lays down that the Republic of Serbia is a state of the Serbian people and all citizens living on its territory, that it is based on the principles of rule of law, social justice and civil democracy, human and minority rights and freedoms, and that it adopts European principles and values.[3]

3. One of the basic principles of the Serbian political system is the principle of separation of powers into legislative, executive, and judicial.[4] The legislative function is carried by the National Assembly. It enacts laws and other general acts, also containing regulations relating to insurance law. The National Assembly is comprised of 250 members of parliament elected in direct elections by means of secret voting in accordance with the statutory provisions.[5] The executive function is carried out by the President of the Republic and the Government. The President proclaims laws by decrees. In essence, his/her role in the regulative sphere is limited exactly to the above circumstance. The Government, according to the Constitution, adopts regulations, decisions, and other acts aimed at the enforcement of passed

1. https://www.stat.gov.rs/en-US/ (accessed 1 Feb. 2022).
2. OJ RS, 88/2006.
3. *See* Constitution of Serbia, Art. 4.
4. *Ibid.*
5. *See* Constitution of Serbia, Art. 100, para. 1.

laws. The Government is responsible towards the National Assembly for the policy of the Republic of Serbia, for the enforcement of laws and other general enactments of the National Assembly, as well as for the functioning of the state administration.[6] The Government consists of the Prime Minister, one or more of his/her deputies and the ministers. The Prime Minister coordinates the Government, provides for the Government's uniform political activities, harmonizes the work of the Government's members and represents the Government. The ministers are accountable to the Prime Minister, the Government, and the National Assembly for their work and the state of affairs within the domains falling into their ministry's competence.

4. The courts protect the rights and freedoms of citizens. They adjudicate pursuant to the Constitution, laws and other general acts adopted by the legislative and executive. The courts are obliged to apply the law, not to create it. This principle is most consistently implemented in the field of penal (criminal and misdemeanour) law. In private law, however, certain specificities do exist: a judge is obliged to render a decision based on a request from a party even when a certain matter is not governed by law. If the statutory lacuna cannot be filled in any other way, he/she will create a rule for the case at hand and thereby overcome the lack of a statutory norm. In such cases, judges take on a role similar to the legislature. However, their decision is only binding on the parties to a particular civil law relationship. The same applies for the rule established by such a decision. In accordance with the principle of separation of powers, it cannot hold the attributes of general legal norms.

§2. Commerce and Industry

5. Serbia has an economy based mostly on various services (63.8% of the Gross Domestic Product (GDP)), industry (23.5% of the GDP), and agriculture (12.7% of the GDP). In the late 1980s, at the beginning of the process of economic transition from a planned economy to a market economy, Serbia's economy had a favourable position, but it was gravely impacted by the UN economic sanctions from 1992 to 1995, as well as the excessive damage to the infrastructure and the industry during the NATO bombing in 1999. After the ousting of former Yugoslav President Slobodan Milošević in October 2000, the country went through an economic liberalization process and experienced fast economic growth. The GDP per capita (nominal) rose from USD 1,160 in 2000 to USD 7,742 in 2020. Furthermore, the Republic of Serbia has been preparing for membership in the European Union (EU), its most important trading partner. At present, its main economic problems are a relatively high unemployment rate (about 10%, 2021) and a large trade deficit (USD 3.9 billion, the first quarter of 2021).

6. Serbia's primary industries include base metal processing, furniture production, food processing, machinery, chemicals, sugar, cars, tyres, clothes, and pharmaceuticals.

6. *See* Constitution of Serbia, Art. 124.

§3. Financial Institutions

7. The most important financial institutions within the domain of Serbia's public finances are the Ministry of Finance under the auspices of the Government of the Republic of Serbia, the National Bank of Serbia (NBS), as well as the Securities Commission that monitors the capital market.

8. The Serbian Ministry of Finance performs tasks related to the state budget, public revenues, public spending, and public debt in the country.

9. NBS is the central bank of Serbia, and as such, its main responsibilities are the protection of price stability, the Dinar exchange rate policy, management of foreign currency reserves, and maintenance of efficient payment and financial systems. The position, organization, authorities, and functions of the NBS, as well as its relationship towards Serbian state organs, and international organizations and institutions are provided for by the Constitution of the Republic of Serbia and the Law on the NBS.[7] The NBS is autonomous and independent in carrying out its tasks established by the Law on the NBS and other enactments, while it is accountable for its work to the National Assembly of the Republic of Serbia. The fundamental purpose of the NBS is to achieve and maintain price stability. Apart from that, without questioning the achievement of its basic purpose, the NBS contributes to the preservation and reinforcement of the financial system's stability. The NBS has the tasks to: determine and implement the monetary and foreign exchange policies; manage foreign exchange reserves; define and implement, within its scope of authority, the activities and measures aimed at maintaining and strengthening the stability of the financial system; issue and revoke operating licences for banks, carry out prudential supervision of bank operations, and perform other activities in accordance with the law governing banks; issue and revoke licences necessary for carrying out insurance operations, exercise supervision over such operations, issue and revoke authorizations for the conduct of specific activities within the field of insurance and perform other activities in accordance with the Law on Insurance; issue and revoke licences for the performance of leasing operations, exercise supervision over such operations and perform other activities in accordance with the Law on Leasing; issue and revoke operating licences of voluntary pension fund management companies, issue and revoke fund management licences, exercise supervision over such operations and perform other activities in accordance with the law governing voluntary pension funds; issue banknotes and coins and manage cash flows; regulate, oversee and promote the payment system's smooth operation; perform statutory tasks or tasks established by contracts for the Republic of Serbia without threatening thereby its autonomy and independence.

10. The Securities Commission is an independent and autonomous organization of the Republic of Serbia established in 1990. The Securities Commission's legal status is provided for by the Capital Market Law.[8] The Securities Commission is

7. OJ RS, 72/2003, 55/2004 and 44/2010, 76/2012, 106/2012, 14/2015, 40/2015 and 44/2018.
8. OJ RS, 31/2011, 112/2015, 108/2016, 9/2020 and 153/2020.

responsible for the statutory functioning of the securities market with the purpose of protecting the investors and ensuring justice, efficacy, and transparency within the above market. In this sense, the Commission supervises the implementation of the Capital Market Law, the Investment Funds Law[9] and the Law on the Acquisition of Stock Corporations.[10] The Commission is accountable for its work to the National Assembly of the Republic of Serbia.

§4. Legislation and Monetary Regulation

11. The official currency in Serbia is the Serbian Dinar – RSD (1 Dinar is the lowest unit), apart from Kosovo and Metohija, where the Euro is used. The Serbian currency is available in both paper notes and coins.

12. The implementation of monetary policy in Serbia is entrusted to the NBS. As already noted above, the main responsibilities of the NBS are the protection of price stability, the Dinar exchange rate policy, the management of foreign currency reserves and the maintenance of efficient payment and financial systems. The NBS is a public institution in charge of safeguarding the value and purchasing power of money. The core purpose of the NBS is to provide monetary and financial stability. Monetary stability means a low, stable, and predictable inflation and confidence in the currency. Financial stability means a sound financial system in which banks and other financial organizations function well and responsibly safeguard their clients' money. The NBS manages money and interest rates so as to accomplish a low, stable, and predictable inflation rate. By safeguarding the value of the national currency, the NBS contributes to the growth of the citizens' living standards. By managing money and loans, the NBS influences the strengthening and maintenance of public confidence in the Dinar. The NBS maintains financial stability, ensuring safety, and efficiency of the payment system, as well as monitoring and supervising the activities of commercial banks, other financial organizations and insurance companies.[11]

---

9. OJ RS, 46/2006, 51/2009, 31/2011 and 115/2014.
10. OJ RS, 46/2006, 107/2009, 99/2011, 108/2016.
11. Regarding the tasks of the NBS, *see* in more detail *supra* n. 9. Furthermore, regarding the supervisory function of the NBS within the insurance sector, *see* in more detail *infra* nn. 127–128.

Chapter 2. Historical Background of Insurance and the Insurance Law Regulation

13. The historical development of insurance law in Serbia is divided into four leading periods which are grouped into several development phases. The first period began in 1835, as the first Serbian Constitution was enacted on 15 February 1835 and lasted until 1918; the second period was from 1918 to 1945, that is, until the end of the Second World War and the creation of the Federal People's Republic of Yugoslavia (which later became the Socialist Federal Republic of Yugoslavia); the third period lasted from 1945 until 1988 when the transitional process from socialist planned to market economy began; finally, the fourth period of insurance law development in Serbia extends from 1988 until the present time.

§1. The Period from 1835 to 1918

14. At the beginning of this period, the Dukedom of Serbia was a new nation state enacting its first Constitution on 15 February 1835. However, at that time, Serbia was a dependent State under Turkish rule until the Berlin Congress of 1878. Still, it should be borne in mind that it was a State with an independent internal administration. Thus, it had the power to enact its own laws and to have its own judicial and administrative authorities. In 1882, it became the Kingdom of Serbia ruled by the domestic dynasty Obrenović. This is the period of development of a legal system, which included the enactment of the Civil Code and many other laws.

15. Even though the rudimentary forms of insurance regulations could be observed before the commencement of this period, at that time, the sources of insurance law were still undeveloped. Insurance activities got relevant significance on the territory of Serbia only during the nineteenth century, which is the reason why the first detailed regulations on insurance law appeared at that time. In line with the above, the origins of insurance law in Serbia date back to 1844 when the Serbian Civil Code was adopted. Predominantly regulating the civil law matter, this Code had only two paragraphs pertaining to insurance law.

16. Apropos of the legal status of insurance companies, that is, the regulations on them, the main source of insurance law in that part was the Insurance Companies Act (1892), which was applicable to foreign insurance companies, while the status of domestic ones was regulated by the Stock Companies Act (1898). This special treatment of foreign insurance companies was justified by the fact that at that juncture the insurance activity was generally performed by foreign insurance companies.

§2. The Period from 1918 to 1945

17. During this period, Serbia was a part of the Kingdom of Serbs, Croats, and Slovenes. The Kingdom of Serbs, Croats, and Slovenes (renamed the Kingdom of

Yugoslavia in 1929) was formed in 1918 with the unification of the ethnic territory of the South Slavic people. In this newborn state, however, a multiplicity of legal systems was in force. That multiplicity characterized the insurance law as well, particularly its contractual part. In line with that, the Serbian Civil Code (1844) and the Serbian Commercial Act (1860) were applicable on the territory of Serbia and the Vardarian part of Macedonia, while the Bulgarian Commercial Act (1898) was in force in other parts of Macedonia. People living in the territory of Vojvodina were using the Hungarian Commercial Act (1875). In Montenegro, the General Property Code for the Dukedom of Montenegro (1898) was in force, in Bosnia and Herzegovina, the Bosnian Commercial Act (1883), while in Croatia, the Croatian-Hungarian Commercial Act (1875). The Austrian Contract Insurance Act (1917) was applicable in Slovenia, and Dalmatia, that is, the area under the jurisdiction of the former Appellation Court in Split.[12]

18. However, during this period several acts relevant for the entire Kingdom were passed. These include: The Law on the Insurance of Crops and Fruits from Hail (1923), the Air Transport Law (1928), the International Motor Traffic Convention Law (1929), and the Regulation on the Supervision of Insurance Companies (1937).[13]

19. Insurance activity was still relatively underdeveloped. Poor organizational structures, lack of professional staff, prevention of negligence, involvement in high-risk investments, and the lack of state control marked this period.[14] In addition, two-thirds of all insurance companies active within the territory of the Kingdom were subsidiaries of foreign insurance companies.[15]

§3. The Period from 1945 to 1988

20. The commercial, social, and legal development of the country after the Second World War inevitably reflected the development of insurance law and introduced radical changes in that matter. In general, this period is marked by frequent changes and experiments in part of the legal status of insurance companies. Within this period several development phases can be differentiated, and they are distinguished primarily according to alterations in insurance companies' legal status.

12. Predrag Šulejić, *Pravo osiguranja* (*Insurance Law*) (Belgrade: Pravni fakultet u Beogradu, 2005), 34.
13. Šulejić, *Pravo osiguranja* (*Insurance Law*), 35.
14. Ivica Jankovec & Zoran Miladinović, *Pravo osiguranja* (*Insurance Law*) (Niš Pravni fakultet u Nišu, 2006), 25.
15. Šulejić, *Pravo osiguranja* (*Insurance Law*), 35.

I. The Development Phase from 1945 to 1961

21. Immediately after Second World War, under the dominant influence of the Soviet Union, the creation of a new order in Yugoslavia began. A new socialist Government passed numerous acts which formally ended the continuity with the legal system of the former Kingdom of Yugoslavia. One of the most important was the Law on the Nullity of Regulations enacted prior to 6 April 1941 and during the Time of Enemy Occupation of1946. Pre-war regulations were no longer enforced. The courts were not allowed to cite previous jurisprudence.

22. In insurance law, especially in the part related to the legal status of insurance companies, a centralized system along with a strict state control was evident. After the enactment of the Government's decision in 1944 all of the enemies' property was confiscated, including the property of Italian, German, and hostile domestic insurance companies. In 1945 the Government passed a decision that enabled the state to merge all confiscated enemies' insurance companies into one – the State Institute for Insurance and Reinsurance, later renamed the State Institute for Insurance (DOZ).[16]

23. DOZ's structural organization was highly centralized. It was run by the Ministry of Finance. Soon after its establishment, the development of the above entity commenced at a smart pace. There were a couple of reasons for that: (1) DOZ was in possession of all property confiscated from insurance companies. (2) All state-owned property had to be insured with DOZ. Thanks to that, DOZ monopolized the insurance business in Serbia. Privately owned and still operational insurance companies were unable to keep up with such a disloyal competition. Apart from the above, a set of subsequently adopted regulations substantially hindered their ability to operate, which resulted in their liquidation and transfer of their insurance portfolio to DOZ.[17]

24. This system had numerous weaknesses, but the principal was the establishment of effective monopoly over-insurance activities. Free market, actually, ceased to exist. Premiums were remarkably high. In the lack of competition, DOZ imposed extremely harsh insurance terms and conditions (e.g., late payment entailed the immediate loss of all insurance rights). In addition, as the necessity for new forms of insurance appeared, DOZ simply failed to implement them.[18]

25. Given that immediately after the Second World War there were no legal regulations in the domain of insurance contract law, the relevant sources of law before the adoption of the Law on Obligations in 1978 (LO) were only autonomous sources (customs, usages, general terms and conditions). Rules from the pre-war civil and commercial acts, valid during the existence of the Kingdom of Yugoslavia, could only be applied if they were in accordance with Article 4.1 of the Law on

16. *Ibid.*, 36
17. *Ibid.*
18. *Ibid.*

Nullity of Regulations Enacted Prior to 6 April 1941 and during the Time of Enemy Occupation (1946), under the condition that in the subject matter to which they were applicable there was no effective rule in the legislation, as well as that it was not contradictory to constitutional principles and existing regulations.

26. During this period, a special system of mandatory insurance was created. Legal relationships in insurance law were established in two ways: through statutory (automatic) mandatory insurance and through contractual mandatory insurance. Statutory (automatic) mandatory insurance was obligatory for travellers and merchandise by means of public transportation. Contractual mandatory insurance was compulsory for the insurance of companies' assets, the export and import of goods, as well as for all socially owned property being governed by state organizations, institutions, commercial companies, and other socially owned enterprises. Mandatory insurances,[19] regardless of whether based on automatism or contract, were prescribed by the set of by-laws (ordinances, decrees, etc.) pertaining to different forms of insurances, policies or types of transportation.[20]

II. The Development Phase from 1961 to 1967

27. The general economic, social, and legal development of the country, which resulted in the abandonment of the administratively governed system, indispensably had its influences on insurance law.[21] The reform of the insurance companies' legal status began with the adoption of the Law on Insurance Institutes and Insurance Communities (1961).[22] The essence of the reform was in the decentralization of insurance activities. Insurance institutes covering smaller territories (such as municipalities) substituted the DOZ and its authority over the whole state territory. Insurance Institutes had the status of legal entities and independently performed their activities over the territory where they had complete territorial monopoly. The management of insurance institutes were comprised of employees (self-management) and policy holders.[23]

28. Insurance institutes were affiliated with Republic Insurance Associations and were parts of the Yugoslav Insurance Association (JZO – Jugoslovenska zajednica osiguranja). Insurance institutes as direct insurers were automatically reinsured with the Republic Insurance Associations, which were then reinsured with the JZO. The latter association classified their policies by different forms of insurances. JZO was adopting unique rules and insurance premium rates, which were afterwards reaffirmed by the Federal Parliament, thus excluding market competition.[24]

19. *Ibid.*, 40.
20. *Ibid.*
21. *Ibid.*, 36.
22. OJ SFRY, 27/1961.
23. Šulejić, *Pravo osiguranja* (*Insurance Law*), 37.
24. *Ibid.*

29. This system had many disadvantages. The basic ones were the lack of market competition, territorial monopoly, and insufficient stimulation of activities. Losses were covered up automatically. Thanks to the above reinsurance policy enabling loss coverage among institutes, the insolvency of insurance institutes was rendered impossible unless all Yugoslav reserves of the particular insurance form were exhausted.[25]

30. Regarding contractual and mandatory insurances, the situation from the previous period was in a *status quo*. The only novelty was that previous ordinances on mandatory insurances in public transportation and insurances of socially owned property were superseded by the Law on Mandatory Transport Insurance[26] and the Law on Mandatory Insurance of Property and Persons of 1965.[27]

III. The Development Phase from 1967 to 1974

31. This period in insurance development began with the new reform pertaining to the legal status of insurance companies. The reform was completed by the adoption of the Principle Law on Insurance and Insurance Organisations (1967).[28] The aim of the reform was to set the insurance law free of non-economic principles.[29] Through the said Act, the territorial monopoly was abolished, the compulsory affiliation to Associations annulled, along with the compulsory reinsurances, unique insurance conditions and insurance premium rates. Insurance companies were organized in forms of insurance institutes and reinsurance institutes. They had the same status as other legal entities.[30] Nevertheless, as insurance activity was recognized as an activity of a special social interest to the state, the legal status of insurance institutes and reinsurance institutes was in some way special. Apart from self-management, which was simultaneously typical for other legal entities, insurance companies were also governed by policy holders and insurance company founders (social-management). Additionally, the Principle Law on Insurance and Insurance Organizations (1967) envisaged for the first time the possibility of establishing mutual insurance companies and companies dealing exclusively with insurance mediation activities, agency activities, loss assessments and similar affairs.[31]

32. Thus the principle of market economy was introduced to the insurance business in 1967. However, this system received criticism over the period of Constitutional amendments from 1971.[32] Stern rebukes were mainly related to the fact that insurance assets had been alienated from those who created them. It was considered that socially owned capital had slipped away from the workers' direct control and

25. *Ibid.*
26. OJ SFRY, 15/1965, 7/1967. 11/1968.
27. OJ SFRY, 15/1965.
28. OJ SFRY, 71/1967.
29. Šulejić, *Pravo osiguranja* (*Insurance Law*), 37.
30. *Ibid.*
31. *Ibid.*
32. Šulejić, *Pravo osiguranja* (*Insurance Law*), 38.

management. Crucial changes to social-economic relations had to happen inevitably influencing insurance law as well. The result was the promulgation of new Socialist Federal Republic of Yugoslavia (SFRY – Socijalistička Federativna Republika Jugoslavija) Constitution (1974)[33] which introduced modifications in the law and marked the beginning of a new era in the development of the legal status of insurance companies.

33. Contractual insurance law also had certain novelties in the period between 1967 and 1974. Since there were no other laws on insurance contracts, the abovementioned Principle Law on Insurance and Insurance Organizations (1967) regulated insurance contractual relations in a few Articles 62–73. It laid down standards protecting policyholders against the Insurance Institutes' arbitrariness. In addition, the Law on Mandatory Risk Assessment in certain Insurance Types (1967) introduced new forms of mandatory insurance. It became inoperative in 1971 as the Constitutional Law entered into force.[34]

IV. The Development Phase from 1974 to 1988

34. As previously mentioned, the new Constitution of 1974 changed the relations in insurance law and marked the beginning of a new era in the development of the legal status of insurance companies. The Constitution laid down that organizations of associated labour, self-management communities of interest, social-political communities and other socially owned entities could establish insurance associations in which they were enabled to accumulate their assets together with other entities. Those rules were introduced in order to secure property and people by decreasing potential damage-causing difficulties. Thus, instead of insurance institutes and reinsurance institutes, the rules provided for the possibility of establishing insurance associations. Mutual relations between founders, the management and the ruling of the Association were regulated by the Self-Management Agreement on the Establishment of Associations, the Association's Statute, and other self-management acts.

35. The above system of insurance company legal status was determined in detail by two federal and several republic laws. The federal laws were: the Law on the Principles of the Insurance System of Property and People (1976),[35] which comprised norms on mandatory insurances previously prescribed by special laws, and the Law on Practicing Economy Abroad (1976),[36] having a special part on the principles of the establishment of insurance and reinsurance companies abroad. Some questions were regulated by federal by-laws. The consequences of implementing the Law on the Principles of the Insurance System of Property and Persons were that

33. OJ SFRY, 9/1974.
34. Šulejić, *Pravo osiguranja* (*Insurance Law*), 41.
35. OJ SFRY, 24/1976.
36. OJ SFRY, 15/1977.

Republics and Provinces were enabled to pass their own rules by means of which they were able to elaborate and provide for details regarding general terms prescribed by the federal law.[37]

36. At that time, the Yugoslav legislation on insurance law was continuously developing. Yet, there was an obvious disharmony between regulations on the legal status of insurance companies and the rules on contractual insurances.[38] Whereas the legal status of insurance companies was based on principles of socialist economy and self-management relations, contractual insurance was primarily founded on rules analogous to developed countries' standards and market economy. The legal lacuna in this part of insurance law was present for a long time, until the enactment of the (LO).[39] This Act, which with minor changes is still in force, thoroughly determined insurance contracts. Regulating contractual insurance in almost seventy articles, this Law diminished the importance of applying customs and commercial laws. Still, this Law remained silent on three important areas: naval insurance, credit insurance, and reinsurance. For this reason, special laws on transport insurance were enacted: the Law on Maritime and Internal Navigation (1977)[40] and the Law on Obligations and Material and Legal Relations in Air Transport (1977).[41]

§4. The Period from 1988 to Present Time

37. The last period in insurance law development began shortly before the dissolution of Yugoslavia with the reform of the SFRY Constitution (1974) by means of the Constitutional Amendments from 1988. In a nutshell, those Amendments led the way to the introduction of private entrepreneurship and private property, which led off to changes within insurance law which once again began to operate on principles of market economy and profit maximization. Within this period, one could notice several distinctive development phases regarding the legal status of insurance companies. However, contractual insurance law was determined by the standards established (1978, last amendments in 1993), along with additional special laws which were, or still are, in force for particular insurance forms (e.g., transport insurance).

38. This period is delineated by the breakup of Yugoslavia, the creation of new states in the Balkans, a difficult economic and political situation, which all had an

---

37. In that manner, they passed the following acts: the Law on the Insurance System of Property and Persons in the Socialist Republic Serbia (1977), the Law on the Insurance of Property and Persons in the Socialist of Republic Croatia (1977), the Law on the Insurance of Property and Persons in the Socialist Republic of Bosnia and Herzegovina (1977), the Law on the Insurance of Property and Persons in the Socialist Republic of Macedonia (1977), the Law on the Insurance of Property and Persons in the Socialist Autonomous Province Kosovo (1977) and the Law on the Insurance of Property and Persons in the Socialist Autonomous Province Vojvodina (1977). *See* Šulejić, *Pravo osiguranja* (*Insurance Law*), 41.
38. Šulejić, *Pravo osiguranja* (*Insurance Law*), 41.
39. OJ SFRY, 29/1978, 39/1985, 45/1989, 57/1989 and OJ FRY, 31/1993.
40. OJ SFRY, 37/1977.
41. OJ SFRY, 22/1977.

influence on the development and evolution of insurance law. Nevertheless, during the last few years (especially since 2004), there has been a significant progress and modernization, so that the Serbian insurance law is being harmonized with the legislation of the EU.

I. The Development Phase from 1988 to 1996

39. The system established by the Constitutional Amendments from 1988 got its final form by enactment of the Law on the Principles of the Insurance System of Property and Persons (1990).[42] The Act's title was the same as the previous one, due to the fact that at the time of its adoption the former SFRY Constitution (1974) was still in force. According to the Constitution, the federation had jurisdiction over the insurance of property and persons.[43] The new Act was organized in the same manner as the erstwhile, so that besides the norms on the legal status of insurance companies, it also contained rules on mandatory insurance. Despite the above, a comprehensive reform within the part of insurance law pertaining to the legal status of entities was initiated by the above Act. The concept of insurance for people's associations was left behind. As private property and private entrepreneurship were slowly introduced, former insurance associations were transformed into independent legal entities and companies.

40. According to the Law on the Principles of the Insurance System of Property and Persons (1990), different forms of legal entities could perform insurance activities. Those forms were: limited liability insurance companies, companies for mutual insurance, public insurance companies, mixed insurance companies, special insurance organizations for other insurance activities, insurance and reinsurance pools and the Yugoslav Bureau for Insurance.

41. Apart from the Law on the Principles of the Insurance System of Property and Persons, other legal sources providing for the legal status of insurance companies which were in force were: the Law on Companies (1988, amendments in 1989 and 1990),[44] the Law on Securities (1989),[45] the Law on Enforceable Reconciliation, Insolvency and Liquidation (1989),[46] the Law on Foreign Investments (1988),[47] the Law on Foreign Trade Business (1989),[48] and so on. Finally, the legal status of insurance companies was furthermore regulated by a set of by-laws.

42. Considering the fact that this period was the period of the breakup of Yugoslavia, that situation inevitably influenced the development of law in general and insurance law as well. The dissolution of the SFRY led to the creation of new States

42. OJ SFRY, 17/90, 82/90.
43. *See supra* n. 35.
44. OJ SFRY, 77/88, 40/89 and 46/90.
45. OJ SFRY, 84/89.
46. OJ SFRY, 84/89, OJ FRY, 37/93 and 28/96.
47. OJ SFRY, 77/88.
48. OJ SFRY, 28/89.

on the Balkans. Four ex-republics, members of the SFRY (Slovenia, Croatia, Bosnia and Herzegovina and Macedonia), became independent States, while Serbia and Montenegro decided to remain together as one common State – the Federal Republic of Yugoslavia (FRY). The Constitution of the FRY was promulgated on 27 April 1992.[49]

II. The Development Phase from 1996 to 2004

43. The next phase in the development of the legal status of insurance companies began in 1996 with the enactment of the Law on Insurance of Property and Persons (1996).[50] This law was founded on the FRY Constitution in 1992.

44. Pursuant to the Law on the Insurance of Property and People (1996), insurance activity was restricted to the following forms of legal entities: joint stock companies, mutual insurance companies and agencies for provision of insurance services. In addition to the above, this Act brought novelties related to the establishment of insurance companies (licences from the authorities, significantly larger financial assets for the initial capital, etc.).

45. Within the domain of contractual insurance law, the LO was still in force. Yet, transport, marine and other forms of transportation insurance which were not standardized by rules prescribed in the LO were in this period regulated by two new laws. Those laws were: the Law on Maritime and Internal Navigation of 1998 (LMIN)[51] and the Law on Contracts and Property Relations in Air Transport (1998).[52] These two acts together with the LO and certain special laws on mandatory transport insurance are still the major sources of the contractual insurance law in Serbia.

III. The Development Phase from 2004 to Present Time

46. The last phase within the development of insurance companies' legal status began in 2004 when the Law on Insurance (2004)[53] was passed by the Parliament of the Republic of Serbia. The Republic had authority to adopt that law, since the Constitutional Charter of Serbia and Montenegro (4 February 2003)[54] put civil and insurance law matters under the jurisdiction of Republics. The Constitutional Charter further provided that previous federal laws could be applied as republic regulations, as long as the Member States did not enact their own general acts within their

49. OJ SFRY, 1/92.
50. OJ FRY, 30/96, 57/98, 53/99 and 55/99.
51. OJ FRY, 12/1998, 44/99, 74/99, 73/2000 and OJ RS, 101/2005, 85/2005 and 73/2010, 87/2011, 10/2013.
52. OJ FRY, 12/1998, 15/1998 and OJ SCG 1/2003.
53. OJ RS, 55/2004, 70/2004, 61/2005, 61/2005, 85/2005, 101/2007, 63/2009, 107/2009, 99/2011 and 119/2012.
54. OJ SCG, 1/2003.

scope of competence. By this Constitutional Charter, FRY changed its name to the State Community of Serbia and Montenegro. Eventually, the State Community split into its two constituent parts, and two independent states were created, that is, the Republic of Serbia and the Republic of Montenegro. As of that moment, the former Member States have attained full formal legislative sovereignty on their respective territories.

47. Crucial changes introduced by the Law on Insurance (LI – Zakon o osiguranju iz 2004) in comparison with previous laws were harsher requirements for the establishment of insurance companies and progressive harmonization with the EU legislation. With the exception of norms related to mandatory insurance, the LI abrogated all other norms set in the former Law on the Insurance of Property and Persons (1996).

48. The reform of Insurance law was continued when the newest LI (2014) was enacted.[55]

49. Besides the LI (2014), there are other laws by which numerous specialized agencies and corporations for different forms of insurances have been established. These laws are: the Act on the National Housing Loan Insurance Corporation (2004),[56] the Law on Bank and Insurance Companies Insolvency and Liquidation (2015),[57] the Deposit Insurance Act (2015),[58] the Law on the Export Credit and Insurance Agency of the Republic of Serbia (2005).[59]

50. Finally, in 2009, the Act on Compulsory Insurance within the Transport Sector[60] was adopted. This law codified rules on mandatory insurances in public transport. It contains mainly *lex specialis* norms on contractual insurance law and together with the above-mentioned LO and special laws on the transportation insurance represents a cornerstone of modern contractual insurance law in Serbia.

55. OJ RS, 139/2014 and 44/2021.
56. OJ RS, 55/2004.
57. OJ RS, 14/2015 and 44/2018.
58. OJ RS, 14/2015, 51/2017 and 73/2019.
59. OJ RS, 61/2005 and 88/2010.
60. OJ RS, 51/2009 and 78/2011, 101/2011, 93/2012, 7/2013.

Chapter 3. Sources of Insurance Law

§1. Legislation

51. The most important sources of insurance law in Serbia are the Acts of Parliament. They can be divided into two major groups: Acts regulating the legal status of insurance companies, including the State's relationship towards them within the sphere of supervising their activities (hereinafter 'Acts pertaining to the legal status of insurance companies') and Acts regulating the obligations within the domain of insurance, that is, the ones pertaining to the contractual relationships within insurance (hereinafter 'Acts pertaining to contractual relationships within insurance').

I. Acts Pertaining to the Legal Status of Insurance Companies

52. The basic statutory source of insurance law pertaining to the legal status of insurance companies is the LI. The LI contains provisions pertaining to the types of subjects in the insurance business, their foundation, management, financial activities, supervision over their work, changes within their legal forms, changes in their status and winding up.

53. Despite the fact that the LI regulates the legal status of subjects in the insurance business fairly in detail, their legal status is subsidiarily, that is, in uncovered parts, regulated by provisions of other acts. The most important among them is the Law on Commercial Companies (LCC – Zakon o privrednim društvima iz 2011),[61] due to the fact that entities being active within the domain of insurance are established in the form of commercial companies (joint stock companies or limited liability companies) or entrepreneurs and because of the fact that their legal status is regulated by the LCC.[62]

54. Apart from the above, other acts bear certain relevance to the regulation of the domain of insurance law pertaining to the legal status of insurance companies. Their number is relatively high, so that only the most important ones are going to be enumerated according to their enactment dates, along with a brief presentation of their domains of regulation, especially bearing in mind their relevance to insurance. First, the Privatization Act[63] of 2014 regulating the privatization procedure of state and socially owned companies, including insurance companies. Second, the

61. OJ RS, 36/2011 and 99/2011, 83/2014, 5/2015, 44/2018, 95/2018, 91/2019 and 109/2021.
62. Joint stock insurance companies and mutual insurance companies can only be established in the form of joint stock companies. Insurance intermediation companies, insurance agencies and agencies providing other insurance services may be established in the form of joint stock companies or limited liability companies. Finally, natural persons may carry out insurance agency operations in the capacity of entrepreneurs.
63. OJ RS, 83/2014, 46/2015, 112/2015, 20/2016.

Foreign Investments Act[64] of 2002 and Law on Investments,[65] which, among others, regulate the conditions under which foreign legal entities and natural persons may establish commercial companies in the Republic of Serbia. Third, the Act on the Registration of Commercial Entities[66] of 2011 regulating the principles and procedure of commercial entity registration, as well as other issues pertaining to their registration. Fourth, the Accounting Law[67] of 2013 representing the basic law in the Republic of Serbia within the domain of accounting. Fifth, the Law on the Insolvency and Liquidation of Banks and Insurance Companies[68] of 2015 regulating the conditions and some issues pertaining to the insolvency and liquidation of banks and insurance companies. This Act represents *lex specialis* in regard to the Insolvency Act[69] of 2009. Sixth, the Capital Market Law[70] regulating, among others, the procedure joint stock company shares emissions, including joint stock insurance companies. Seventh, the Foreign Exchange Operations Act[71] of 2006 regulating, among others, the foreign currency operations of insurance companies. Eighth, the Foreign Trade Law[72] of 2009 regulating, among others, the conditions of performing insurance and reinsurance operations abroad.

55. Finally, in particular, segments of insurance specialized organizations performing certain insurance types have been established directly by laws. Therefore the laws regulating their establishment and legal status also represent a source of insurance law pertaining to the legal status of insurance companies. There are three laws within this group: First, the Act on the National Housing Loan Insurance Corporation of 2004 establishing the National Housing Loan Insurance Corporation, a specialized legal entity for credit insurance based on housing loans approved by banks and other financial organizations. Second, the Law on the Export Credit and Insurance Agency of the Republic of Serbia of 2005 establishing the agency as a specialized legal entity for the insurance of exports and foreign investments of domestic legal entities and entrepreneurs. Third, the Deposit Insurance Act of 2005 establishing the agency as a specialized legal entity for the insurance of savings deposits of natural persons with banks. The agency also carries out tasks of a trustee in bankruptcy or insolvency in banks and insurance companies, the shareholder of which is the Republic of Serbia.

II. Acts Pertaining to Contractual Relationships Within Insurance

56. As already mentioned in the part regarding the historical development of insurance law in Serbia, the most important contractual source of insurance law is

64. OJ FRY, 3/2002 and 5/2003.
65. OJ RS, 89/2015 and 95/2018.
66. OJ RS, 99/2011, 83/2014, 31/2019 and 105/2021.
67. OJ RS, 73/2019 and 44/2021.
68. OJ RS, 14/2015 and 44/2018.
69. OJ RS, 104/2009, 99/2011, 71/2012, 83/2014, 113/2017, 44/2018 and 95/2018.
70. OJ RS, 31/2011, 11/2015, 108/2016, 9/2020 and 153/2020.
71. OJ RS, 62/2006 and 31/2011, 119/2012, 139/2014 and 30/2018.
72. OJ RS, 36/2009 and 36/2011, 88/2011, 88/2015.

the LO. This Act regulates in detail the insurance contract by means of sixty-eight articles (Articles 897–965). However, in spite of the above fact, it does not cover the entire domain of insurance. The provisions of Chapter XXVII contain general rules pertaining to contractual insurance relationships; however, they are not applied to three major domains of insurance: marine insurance, credit insurance, and reinsurance.[73] The above domains of insurance have important characteristics, so that special rules are applicable for them. In case of the absence of special laws, the provisions of the LO can be applied subsidiarily, but only those falling outside of the scope of the mentioned Chapter XXVII.

57. Apart from that, although the application of Chapter XXVII and other provisions of the LO is not excluded within the domain of compulsory insurance in traffic, particular contractual issues are regulated otherwise by special laws.

A. *Special Regulation of Contracts in Marine Insurance and Other Contracts to Which Provisions Pertaining to This Type of Insurance Are Applicable*

58. Although the Law on Navigation and Ports in Inland Waters[74] and the Law on Maritime Navigation[75] have been adopted in the Republic of Serbia in the meantime, the LMIN norms of the former FRY in the field of navigation insurance are still applied. The LMIN regulates the domain of marine insurance, as well as other insurance types to which the provisions of marine insurance are applicable, that is, Chapter IV of the above Law (Articles 728–791). The provisions of Chapter XXVII LO are not applicable to marine insurance contracts or to other insurance contract types to which the provisions of marine insurance are applicable.

59. Insurance contracts in air transport also fall into the group of contracts to which the rules of marine insurance, excluding the norms on ship insurance, are applicable. Apart from the above, a small number of rules specific to insurance contracts in air transport are regulated by a special law. Thus, the Law on Contracts and Property Relations in Air Transport of 2011[76] is primarily applicable to insurance contracts in air transport, more precisely, Chapter IV of the above Act (Articles 115–127). Due to the fact that there is a scarce amount of provisions, failing special regulation, the provisions of LMIN are applicable.

---

73. *See* LO, Art. 899.
74. OJ RS, 73/2010, 121/2012, 18/2015, 96/2015, 92/2016, 104/2016, 113/2017, 41/2018, 95/2018, 37/2019, 9/2020 and 52/2021.
75. OJ RS, 87/2011, 104/2013, 18/2015, 113/2017 and 83/2018.
76. OJ RS 87/2011 and 66/2015.

B. Special Regulation of Credit Insurance Contracts

60. The provisions of Chapter XXVII LO are not applicable to credit insurance contracts.[77] The objects of insurance in these contracts are receivables which also represent an economic value, and this is why they are categorized as property insurance. Nevertheless, credit insurance contracts do have a great number of specificities which justify their separate regulation.

61. Credit insurance contracts are mainly regulated by means of autonomous sources (general terms and conditions, etc.). However, taking into account that particular receivables bear larger social importance, special laws have been passed within the domain of insurance of particular receivables. These are primarily credits based on export transactions of domestic commercial entities. The insurance of receivables stemming from export transactions offers coverage in case of non-payment by foreign customers for delivered goods or rendered services. Credit insurance is a constituent part of the export financing procedure. In order to increase or maintain the existing level of business operations, commercial entities are forced to sell goods at longer repayment periods. Thus numerous exporters incur losses due to untimely payment or the insolvency of their customers. Different instruments of risk protection have been developed in practice. The conclusion of contracts on the insurance of export credits turned out to be one of the best mechanisms of such protection. However, as such risks often transcend the capacities of domestic insurance companies, an agency specializing for the insurance of export credits against commercial and non-commercial risks of domestic commercial entities has been established by means of the Law on the Export Credit and Insurance Agency of the Republic of Serbia.

62. Apart from the above, the National Housing Loan Insurance Corporation has been established in Serbia for the purpose of construction stimulation by means of approving favourable loans for the purchase of real estates. The above has been done by means of the Act on the National Housing Loan Insurance Corporation.

C. Special Regulation of Reinsurance Contracts

63. The provisions of Chapter XXVII LO pertaining to insurance contracts are not applicable to relationships based on reinsurance contracts.[78] Reinsurance contracts are not regulated by means of Acts of Parliament, but exclusively by autonomous sources of law (general terms and conditions, etc.) The above is also justified by the specificities of such contract types.

---

77. *See* LO, Art. 899, para. 2.
78. *Ibid.*

D. Special Regulation of Compulsory Traffic Insurance Contracts

64. According to the fact whether they are mandatory or not, insurance contracts can be divided into voluntary and compulsory insurance contracts. Although the application of Chapter XXVII LO is not excluded within the domain of compulsory insurance in traffic, particular contractual issues are regulated otherwise by special laws. The Act on Compulsory Insurance within the Transport Sector (2009)[79] codifying the rules from the domain of compulsory transport insurance is applicable to contracts on the compulsory insurance within road traffic. The following categories are regulated by the above Act: accident insurance contracts of passengers in public transport, insurance contracts of motor vehicle owners against liability for damage caused to third parties, insurance contracts of aircraft owners against liability for damage caused to third parties and passengers, and insurance contracts of boat owners against liability for damage caused to third parties. Consequently, the Act on Compulsory Insurance within the Transport Sector represents *lex specialis* compared to the LO in the domain of contractual insurance law. Should an issue not be covered by the above Act, the LO shall be applied, particularly its provisions from Chapter XXVII.

§2. Government Regulation

65. It follows from the complexity and dynamics of commercial life that it is impossible to regulate all issues by means of Acts of Parliament. The Government of the Republic of Serbia has the authority to pass by-laws in all domains, including insurance. These by-laws can be delivered in the form of regulations, executive orders, ordinances, and instructions. As regards insurance, these are mainly by-laws determining the starting security fund amounts of insurance joint stock companies, the lowest sum of compulsory traffic insurance, the type of property and persons that may be insured with foreign insurance companies, and so on.

§3. Regulation by Other Governmental Agencies

66. Other state organs and specialized organizations in the Republic of Serbia are usually not authorized to create sources of insurance law. The NBS as the organ supervising the operations of insurance companies and other entities active within the field of insurance, may only exceptionally render certain decisions and ordinances having the character of general enactments. These are usually acts providing for the conditions of particular activities within the domain of insurance (e.g., actuaries, insurance representatives), acts pertaining to financial operations of insurance companies (the form and contents of financial reports, limitations of particular forms of technical reserve deposits and investments, etc.), acts regulating the manners and criteria of mathematical reserve accounting.

79. OJ RS 51/2009, 78/2011, 101/2011,93/2012 and 7/2013.

67. Courts do not create law in the Republic of Serbia. As in other European civil law countries, in Serbia, courts adjudicate pursuant to the rules contained in the Constitution, laws, and other general acts. General legal norms always serve as grounds for judicial decisions. The Courts cannot cite individual norms contained in previously rendered judgments in similar-type cases. This means that judicial practice is not a formal source of law. Nonetheless, case law plays an important role in reality because legal certainty and the uniformity of decisions are recognized as legal values. Pursuant to the Court Organization Law[80] of 2008, the Supreme Court of Serbia has the power to take general legal positions to ensure uniform judicial application of law.[81] Although these general legal positions are binding only upon the court that adopted them, judges of lower courts tend to comply with them. They also tend to follow the rulings of higher courts and even earlier rulings of the courts of the same rank in similar cases.

§4. Autonomous Sources of Law

68. Autonomous sources of law are created by commercial entities themselves and not the state. Similarly, as generally in commercial law, autonomous sources of law bear great importance in insurance law. The following categories are considered autonomous sources of law: standard form contracts, general terms and conditions (general and special rules of insurance), business practices, usages and general acts of companies active within the domain of insurance.

I. Standard Form Contracts, General Terms and Conditions (General and Special Rules of Insurance)

69. Standard form contracts and general terms and conditions are widely used when concluding insurance contracts.

70. Standard form contracts are defined as forms containing a number of prior defined contractual clauses. However, they are used less commonly due to the technicalities of insurance contract conclusion.[82] Their function in insurance contracts is usually replaced by insurance policies or cover notes representing documents on the concluded insurance contract.

71. General terms and conditions, apart from Acts of Parliament, are the most important sources of insurance contract law. General terms and conditions represent the terms under which an insurer concludes insurance contracts. They define the

80. OJ RS, 116/2008, 104/2009, 101/2010, 31/2011, 78/2011, 101/2011, 101/2013, 106/2015, 40/2015, 13/2016, 108/2016, 113/2017, 65/2018 and 88/2018.

81. *See* the Court Organization Law, Arts 31 and 44–47. Similarly, the Commercial Court of Appeals has the authorization to set legal positions for the purpose of uniform application of laws from the jurisdiction of commercial courts. *See* the Court Organization Law, Art. 26, para. 2.

82. Vladimir Marjanski, *Ugovor o osiguranju* (*Insurance Contract*) (Novi Sad: Pravni fakultet u Novom Sadu, 2007), 126.

contracting parties' rights and obligations in advance for an indefinite number of situations.[83] Due to the fact that they contain the rights and obligations of the insurer (and the insured) when concluding a particular type of insurance contract, they are considered sources of insurance contract law.[84]

72. General terms and conditions are often referred to as general and special rules (conditions) of insurance. General rules (conditions) of insurance contain previously drawn up provisions pertaining to insurance contracts in general or particular contract types within the framework of certain insurance categories (e.g., within the domain of property insurance, personal insurance). However, special rules (conditions) of insurance contain previously drawn up provisions pertaining to particular insurance contract types, usually depending on the classes of risks covered by the given contract (e.g., fire insurance contracts, insurance contracts against certain acts of God).[85] General and special rules bear the character of general terms and conditions. They are usually printed on the insurance policy reverse page and constitute the insurance contract along with the policy. They can also be contained in a separate booklet handed over to the insured party, which along with the insurance policy, represents a constituent part of the contract.[86]

A. *Conditions of Application and Interpretation of General Terms and Conditions*

73. General terms and conditions represent constituent parts of insurance contracts exclusively under the condition that the insurer warns the insured that the general terms and conditions (general and special rules) represent constituent parts of the contract and, if not printed on the policy itself, that they are handed over to the insured party.[87] Apart from the above, the fact of fulfilling such an obligation needs to be stated in the policy.[88] As regards their contents, only the general terms and conditions handed over to the insured as such are relevant, irrespective of the fact of containing typing errors or the fact of their anachronism. However, it is legally irrelevant whether the insured party, to whom they have been handed over, has in fact read and understood their contents. The contractual character of general terms and conditions has as a consequence that only the terms handed over as such to the insured party shall be in force in the current insurance period.[89] If the insurance company amends the provisions of general terms and conditions, they are not going to bear any relevance to the current insurance period unless the insured party explicitly adheres to them.[90] This applies even if the amended terms are more beneficial

83. Ivica Jankovec, *Privredno pravo* (*Commercial Law*) (Beograd: Pravni fakultet u Beogradu, 1999), 27.
84. *See* LO, Art. 142, para. 2.
85. Marjanski, *Ugovor o osiguranju* (*Insurance Contract*), 127.
86. *Ibid.*
87. *See* LO, Art. 902, para. 3.
88. *See* LO, Art. 902, para. 4.
89. Marjanski, *Ugovor o osiguranju* (*Insurance Contract*), 128.
90. *Ibid.*

for the insured party than the earlier ones. Their amendments shall be effective only for the next period of coverage but also under the condition that their contents are accepted by the insured party.[91]

74. The provisions of the LO (Articles 99–102) are applicable to the interpretation of general terms and standard form contracts. In the event of concluding a contract with previously printed contents or when the contract has already been drawn up and offered by one of the contracting parties, unclear provisions shall be construed as beneficial to the other contracting party.[92] In the event of inconsistencies between special and general insurance terms and conditions, the special terms (the ones applicable for special contract types) shall prevail upon implementation. Finally, in case of discrepancies between certain provisions of the general terms and conditions of the policy, the policy provisions shall be applicable, while if printed policy provisions are inconsistent with certain handwritten ones, the latter shall be prevailing.[93]

B. Supervision over the Implementation of General Terms and Conditions and Closing the Legal Loopholes

75. The inequality of contracting parties renders the supervision of general terms and conditions created by the insurer as the economically more powerful party inevitable.[94] A provision laying down that general terms and conditions must not be contrary to the purpose of the concluded agreement and to good business practices[95] is not sufficient for that end, nor is the fact that their implementation is possible exclusively under the condition of handing them over to the insured party. The importance of general terms and conditions as sources of law in general, but especially their function of regulating insurance relationships requires the introduction of supervision over their provisions. The supervision of general terms and conditions can be prior and follow-up.

76. Prior supervision means the approval of the general terms and conditions' contents by the competent authorities before they become regulatory sources within the particular field. This type of supervision exists in Serbia only in the domain of compulsory motor vehicle insurance owners against liability for damages caused to third parties.[96]

77. Follow-up supervision means court assessment in potential disputes stemming from relationships created by insurance contracts, the constituent parts of which are certain general terms and conditions. Such type of supervision does exist

91. *Ibid.*
92. *See* LO, Art. 100.
93. *See* LO, Art. 902, para. 5.
94. Marjanski, *Ugovor o osiguranju* (*Insurance Contract*), 129.
95. *See* LO, Art. 143, para. 1.
96. *See infra* nn. 133–134.

in the Serbian legal system. The courts can suspend the implementation of certain general terms depriving the other contracting party of exercising their rights, or terms causing the loss of contractual rights or the non-observance of time limits, or conditions that are inequitable or too harsh for the other party.[97]

78. The nullity of particular contractual provisions and thereby of general terms and conditions normally does not have as a consequence the nullity of the entire contract (Latin: *utile per inutile not vitiatur*).[98] However, by declaring certain provisions null and void, a legal loophole may be created in parts of the contract regulated by the subject provisions. For the purpose of closing such legal loopholes, the court is going to apply the yielding provisions of acts automatically replacing the ineffective contractual clause (i.e., the clause of the general terms and conditions as constituent parts of the contract). In other instances, the real intention of the contracting parties needs to be established, and the loophole is going to be plugged by a solution that corresponds to the parties' intention to the greatest possible extent.[99]

II. Business Practices and Usages

79. Business practices are commercial customs so widely accepted and implemented (generally adopted business practices) that entrepreneurs justly expect their observance by the contracting parties.[100] The importance of business practices as sources of law is substantially diminished due to the highly developed statutory regulation. However, in particular branches of insurance where the autonomous regulation of affairs is emphasized, business practices still represent an important complementary source of law. This is particularly the situation within marine insurance and other types of insurance to which the provisions of marine insurance are applicable.

80. The following rule is in force in Serbia regarding the conditions of applying business practices: if the application of business practices is not explicitly stipulated or if the statutory provisions do not require their application, it is necessary that the issue covered by business practices is not simultaneously regulated by statutory provisions or contracts (existence of a legal loophole).[101] On the contrary, the contractual or statutory provision is going to prevail, even if the provision is of a yielding (*ius dispositivum*) nature. Consequently, if their application is not stipulated or referred to in statutory provisions, business practices may be used only as a complementary source for closing legal loopholes. Their application is assumed in the event of a legal loophole. On the contrary, if the issue regulated by means of business practices is also provided for in a corresponding statutory provision, even

97. LO, Art. 143, para. 2.
98. *See* LO, Art. 105, para. 1.
99. Slavko Carić et al., *Međunarodno privredno pravo* (*International Commercial Law*) (Novi Sad: Centar za privredni konsalting, 2000), 54.
100. Carić et al., *Međunarodno privredno pravo* (*International Commercial Law*), 54.
101. Under the word contract, the general terms and conditions (constituent parts of the contract) are to be understood.

if the rule is yielding, the business practices may be applied only if their observance has expressly been agreed upon.[102] It follows that the application of non-stipulated business practices does not prevail over the application of yielding statutory provisions. Despite the fact that the importance of business practices within maritime and internal navigation is especially underscored,[103] even within the domain of marine insurance the rules of non-stipulated business practices will not prevail over yielding statutory provisions.

81. As opposed to the uncodified business practices, usages are codified commercial customs systematized and collected by various national and international authorities, organizations or business associations.[104] According to the traditional classification, they are divided into general and special usages. General usages are applicable to the economy as a whole, while special usages are applied only to certain industries or sometimes to particular types of goods or services. In Serbia, the General Usages for the Trade of Goods were introduced in 1954 by the Principal State Arbitration,[105] as well as a considerable number of special usages. General usages used to bear great importance before the entering into force of the LO.

82. The following rules are in force in Serbia regarding the conditions of applying usages: The application of general or special usages is usually possible only if the contracting parties expressly stipulated it or if it follows from the circumstances that the parties desired their application.[106] Usages will prevail over yielding statutory provisions only in such instances. Despite being codified, accessible to all, and precisely defined customs, usages apply only if the parties agree on their application, while business practices in the situations of lacunae, apply pursuant to the law itself.[107] Exceptions to the above rule, that is, when the usages may be applied without express stipulation or the previously uttered desire of the parties are situations of loopholes in which the court finds that specific usage rule can be treated as a good business practice. Otherwise, the court is not going to apply them and will proceed pursuant to the general rules applicable for the replacement of lacunae in civil law. Finally, by application of the general and special relations rule, special usages have primacy over general ones in situations of their mutual incompatibility.

---

102. *See* LO, Art. 1107, para. 3.
103. To relationships not regulated by the LMN and other acts passed based on it, the practices in maritime navigation shall be applicable – LMN Art. 3.
104. In the former Yugoslav law, the most important were the General Usages for the Trade of Goods. As the title itself implies, these are usages applicable for the trade of goods and not services. As insurance represents a service based activity, general usages used to contain only a few provisions pertaining to the regulation of insurance contracts. However, until the enactment of the LO in 1978, there was a great legal loophole within the legal system of Serbia regarding the regulation of contractual relationships. Therefore, the General Usages for the Trade of Goods used to have exceptional relevance in the capacity of sources of commercial law in general.
105. OJ FPRY, 16/1954.
106. *See* LO, Art. 1107, para. 3.
107. For a detailed analysis of such a rule *see* Dušan Nikolić, *International Encyclopaedia of Laws – Tort Law, Serbia and Montenegro*, 77 (Alphen aan den Rijn: Kluwer Law International, 2007).

III. General Acts of Entities Active Within the Field Insurance

83. General acts delivered by entities active within the field of insurance also fall into the category of autonomous sources, for they are created by commercial entities themselves and not the state. The fact that the mandatory minimum of their contents is sometimes provided for by statutory provisions (e.g., the mandatory minimum contents of the articles of association are regulated by the LCC) does not change their nature due to the fact that commercial entities themselves or their founders deliver them.

84. As opposed to other autonomous sources aimed at the regulation of contractual relationships in insurance, general acts of insurance companies represent an important source of law pertaining to the legal status of companies. General acts regulate issues connected with the legal status of insurance companies (articles of association and statutes), the system of insurance devices (e.g., rules on the establishment of financial results in insurance, rules on the establishment of mathematical reserves in life insurance, rules on the establishment methods and amounts of reserved insurance damages), acts regulating the issues of prevention (e.g., rules on the use of assets for preventive measures), acts regulating mutual employee relationships, acts pertaining to the work of various ancillary bodies (boards, commissions, etc.). All general acts, irrespective of their mandatory or elective nature, have to be in line with the coercive statutory provisions.

Chapter 4. Dispute Settlement and Arbitration

85. Disputes arising from insurance issues in the Republic of Serbia may be settled before state courts or in an alternative manner. However, dispute settlement before courts is for now the most common avenue of settling cases stemming from insurance relationships.

86. The judicial power in Serbia is with the courts. Courts are separated and independent in their work and should perform their duties in accordance with the Constitution, the Law and other general Acts when stipulated by the Law, generally accepted rules of international law and ratified international conventions. The organization of courts is regulated by the Court Organization Law. Courts in Serbia are either courts of general jurisdiction or special courts. Proceedings in both types of courts are similar and are regulated primarily by the Civil Procedure Act.[108] Within the domain of Civil law, there is a traditional distinction between commercial courts and courts of civil (general) jurisdiction. Commercial courts have original jurisdiction over disputes arising from commercial activities, including those stemming from commercial aspects of intellectual property. Their jurisdiction extends to both legal and natural persons engaged in commercial activities, in cases where both parties are economic operators (when they are parties to commercial contracts). When only one of the parties is an economic operator and the other is not, such disputes are decided by courts of civil (general) jurisdiction and not by commercial courts. As an exception, in bankruptcy proceedings, commercial courts have jurisdiction over all disputes where an economic operator is in bankruptcy in relation to other economic or non-economic operators. All of the above is valid for insurance disputes too.

87. Although the disputes stemming from insurance relationships are usually settled before the courts of the Republic of Serbia, their alternative settlement is also possible under certain conditions. There are several means of alternative dispute resolution, yet only two have found their way into the commercial practice of Serbia and have been regulated by law. These are mediation and arbitration.

88. The mediation procedure, as an alternative method of dispute resolution enables the parties to find their mutual interest, which may never be contrary to the public order, coercive statutory provisions and good business practices. Their common interest is to be based on mutual negotiations and agreements aimed at the fastest possible resolution of the disputed relationship and satisfying the interests of both contracting parties along with cost and time minimization. Apart from general dispute resolution by mediation regulated by the Intermediation and Mediation Act,[109] according to Serbian insurance law there is a special alternative dispute resolution method by mediation before a mediator nominated by the NBS. The above

108. OJ RS, 72/2011, 49/2013 and 74/2013, 55/2014, 87/2018 and 18/2020.
109. OJ RS, 18/2005.

special mediation procedure is regulated by a particular piece of secondary legislation: the Decision on the procedure for the compliant of the insurance service user,[110] which by-law is in compliance with the Intermediation and Mediation Act.

89. The resolution of disputes stemming from insurance relationships before arbitration is a rare phenomenon. However, the possibility to resolve such disputes before arbitration is indeed afforded. Irrespective of the type of arbitration, a basic procedural precondition for such a manner of dispute resolution is a valid arbitration agreement (contract or arbitration clause). Arbitral proceedings can take forms of ad hoc proceedings or proceedings before an institutional court of arbitration. Ad hoc proceedings are governed by the Law on Arbitration,[111] modelled after the UNCITRAL Model Law on International Commercial Arbitration, while institutional proceedings are governed by their Rules[112] (which have to be in compliance with the mandatory provisions of the Law on Arbitration and could be filled in with the rules that arbitrators deem appropriate as long as they are in accordance with the general principles of the Law on Arbitration). Currently, there is only one arbitral institution in Serbia for the resolution of disputes with foreign elements – the Foreign Trade Court of Arbitration (FTA) under the auspices of the Serbian Chamber of Commerce. The FTA is a permanent arbitration body that provides conciliation and arbitration services for the settlement of international commercial disputes when the parties agree upon its jurisdiction in accordance with its rules. Its awards have the effect of final judgments of domestic courts and are enforced in accordance with the provisions of the Law on Enforcement and Security.[113]

110. OJ RS, 87/2021.
111. OJ RS, 46/2006.
112. The Rules of the FTA Attached to the Serbian Chamber of Commerce, OJ RS, 52/2007.
113. OJ RS, 106/2015, 106/2016, 113/2017, 54/2019.

Chapter 5. Consumer Protection

90. Consumer protection law is relatively new and undeveloped in the Republic of Serbia. The domain of consumer protection is regulated by the Consumer Protection Act[114] of 2021 and the Law on the Protection of Financial Services Consumers[115] of 2011. According to Article 5 of the Consumer Protection Act, a consumer is a natural person acquiring goods or services on the market for purposes other than their business operations or other types of commercial activities. Sometimes policyholders and insurance beneficiaries can be counted into such a widely set definition of consumers. In the Republic of Serbia, there is no special enactment regulating consumer rights within the domain of insurance. However, certain provisions of the above Acts may be applied for the protection of consumer interests within the field of insurance (policyholders or insurance beneficiaries). These are mainly provisions pertaining to offers for the conclusion of contracts,[116] the interpretation of consumer contracts and unfair contractual terms,[117] provisions on unfair and aggressive business practices,[118] provisions on providing information to consumers on the subject of services,[119] and so on.

91. Although there is no special law regulating only consumer protection within the field of insurance, the laws, both the ones pertaining to the status of insurance companies, and those pertaining to contractual relationships, do contain provisions aimed in different ways at the protection of consumer interests within insurance (policyholders, insurance beneficiaries and third-party claimants).

92. The LI as the basic law regulating the status of insurance companies affords the right to policyholders, insurance beneficiaries or third-party claimants to file a complaint to the NBS exercising supervisory powers within insurance on the work of insurance companies and other entities active within the field of insurance. The NBS acts as a mediator in resolving damages in order to prevent insurance litigation, considers the complaints of policyholders, insurance beneficiaries and third-party claimants and protects the rights and interests of such parties. By means of the Decision on the procedure for the compliant of the insurance service user the NBS provided for a closer way and procedure of protecting the rights and interests of such persons.

93. Apart from the above, it needs to be pointed out that consumer interests (of policyholders, insurance beneficiaries and third-party claimants) within the field of insurance are protected by the nature of provisions regulating insurance contractual relationships in Serbia. Namely, even if the provisions of the LO are mainly of a yielding character, the provisions regulating the insurance contract (those from

114. OJ RS, 88/2021.
115. OJ RS, 36/2011, 139/2014.
116. *See* Art. 3, para. 4 of the Consumer Protection Act.
117. *See* Arts 45–48 of the Consumer Protection Act.
118. *See* Arts 20 and 25 of the Consumer Protection Act.
119. *See* Arts 11, para. 2, and 16, para. 1 of the Law on protection of financial services consumers.

Chapter XXVII LO) are usually mandatory. Article 900 paragraph 1 LO provides for an assumption that norms regulating contractual relationships within insurance are of a mandatory nature unless the possibility of deviating from them is expressly afforded and if they do not offer the possibility for contractual parties to act arbitrarily. Such a character of the above norms follows primarily from the necessity of protecting the economically weaker contracting party (the policyholder). The economic inequality of contractual parties does as a rule lead to legal inequality. The insurer, governed by his/her own interests, usually drafts in advance the conditions of contract conclusion and a great part of contractual terms, thus leaving the other party with the option to either accept those rules or not, not rarely without affording him/her the possibility of adjusting the contractual terms to his/her needs. Due to the fact that the provisions of the LO pertaining to the insurance contract are usually of a mandatory nature, standard form contracts, and general terms and conditions prepared by the insurer may not contain terms contrary to those provisions.

94. A distinctiveness of insurance contracts in comparison with other contracts regulated by the LO is that apart from purely imperative and yielding norms, a third category of provisions is introduced – the so-called semi-mandatory norms. Semi-mandatory norms within the contractual insurance law of Serbia are the ones that may be deviated from only if it is in the best interest of the policyholder or the insurance beneficiary (the consumer).[120] Thus the possibility has been opened up to deviate from mandatory norms when concluding a particular insurance contract if it is in the indisputable interest of the policyholder or the insurance beneficiary. However, in the above cases the deviation to the consumer's benefit depends on the will of the insurer preparing the contract (the policy or the general and special terms of insurance).

95. Similarly, as the LO, the provisions of the Act on Compulsory Insurance within the Transport Sector are usually of a mandatory nature. By means of such provisions, in case of compulsory liability insurance contracts the interests of third-party claimants are protected, that is, persons with whom the insurer is not in a contractual relationship.

96. Apart from norms specific to insurance contracts, the LO contains within its framework of general norms pertaining to all contracts a couple of rules aimed at protecting weaker party interests, that is, those of the contracting party not drafting the standard form contracts or the general terms and conditions. These are norms regulating the interpretation of standard form contracts and general terms and conditions, as well as those pertaining to the supervision of their implementation.[121]

120. *See* LO, Art. 900, para. 2.
121. *See supra* nn. 75–78.

97. Finally, it needs to be emphasized that for the purpose of improving the consumers' position within the domain of insurance and for the purpose of harmonizing Serbian law with EU Directives,[122] it is necessary to introduce provisions on the special obligation of insurers to inform the policyholders prior to conclusion of insurance contracts. EU law shows a strong tendency of enabling policyholders to choose a contract corresponding to their necessities. Therefore such contracts need to contain all the necessary information. Accordingly, the insurer's obligation to provide information to the other contracting party prior to contract conclusion does not mean only the obligation to enter all legally required elements into the insurance policy[123] and informing the policyholder on the general and special terms of insurance,[124] as is the case in Serbia, but also to get the insured party acquainted with a great number of details (e.g., their right to be informed on the applicable law in case of disputes, on the mechanisms of deciding on the complaints to the insurer's decisions), which could be decisive to the opposing party whether to enter into the contract.

122. Council Directive 92/49/EEC of 18 Jun. 1992 on the coordination of laws, regulations and administrative provisions relating to direct insurance other than life assurance and amending Directives 73/239/EEC and 88/357/EEC (third non-life insurance Directive), Directive 2002/65/EC of the European Parliament and of the Council of 23 Sept. 2002 concerning the distance marketing of consumer financial services and amending Council Directive 90/619/EEC and Directives 97/7/EC and 98/27/EC, Directive 2002/65/EC of the European Parliament and of the Council of 23 Sept. 2002 concerning the distance marketing of consumer financial services and amending Council Directive 90/619/EEC and Directives 97/7/EC and 98/27/EC, Directive 2002/83/EC of the European Parliament and of the Council of 5 Nov. 2002 concerning life assurance (recast), Directive 2002/92/EC of the European Parliament and of the Council of 9 Dec. 2002 on insurance mediation.
123. *See* LO, Art. 902, para. 1.
124. *See* LO, Art. 902, para. 3.

Chapter 6. Compulsory Insurance

98. Insurance is generally not compulsory in Serbia. The principle of party autonomy is universally applicable in contractual law. It means that all parties may freely decide whether they are going to conclude a contract, with whom they will do this and under what conditions (the only limitation pertains to the fact that the contractual provisions must not be contrary to mandatory provisions, the public order and the norms of business moral).[125] The same rules are applicable to insurance contracts. However, as an exception, within the domain of insurance contracts in Serbia there are a certain number of contracts concluded under the principle of compulsion.[126] By far the most common ones within the above category are compulsory insurance contracts of motor vehicle owners against liability for damages caused to third parties, accident insurance contracts of passengers in public transport, as well as contracts on the compulsory leasing subject insurance against risks provided for by the leasing contract.

99. Therefore, compulsory insurance contracts are contracts, the conclusion of which by certain categories of persons is required by statutory provisions, failing which they are in breach of law.

125. *See* LO, Art. 10.

126. Compulsory insurance contracts within the Serbian legal system are the following: accident insurance contracts of passengers in public transport, compulsory insurance contracts of motor vehicle owners against liability for damages caused to third parties, compulsory insurance contracts of aircraft owners against liability for damages caused to third parties, compulsory insurance contracts of boat owners against liability for damages caused to third parties (*see* the Act on Compulsory Insurance within the Transport Sector), compulsory insurance contracts of natural person deposits with banks and other financial institutions, compulsory insurance contracts of mediators against liability for damages caused during insurance mediation activities compulsory insurance contracts of auditing companies against liability for damages that might be caused by the expressed opinion of authorized auditors (*see* Accounting and Auditing Law, Art. 33), compulsory insurance contracts against liability of nuclear ship operators (*see* LMIN, Art. 852), compulsory insurance contracts against liability of mainland nuclear plant owners (*see* Nuclear Damages Liability Act from 1978, Art. 15), compulsory insurance contracts of owners or users of dangerous materials transported through the territory of the Republic of Serbia against liability for damages caused to third parties or for environmental contaminations caused in the course of transport (*see* the Act on the Transport of Dangerous Materials from 1990 and the Regulation on the Transport of Dangerous Materials in Road and Railway Transport from 2002), contracts on the compulsory leasing subject insurance against risks provided for by the leasing contract (*see* the Financial Leasing Act from 2003, Art. 34), contracts on the compulsory insurance of actuaries against liability for damages that may be caused by their issued opinions (*see* the Decision on the Detailed Conditions to be Fulfilled by Persons Listed in Art. 39 LI, the Manners of Fulfilling such Requirements, as well as the Necessary Organizational, Cadre and Technical Capabilities of Joint Stock Insurance Companies, OJ RS, 86/2004), compulsory insurance contracts against liability for damages caused by environmental contamination (*see* the Environmental Protection Law of the Republic of Serbia from 1991, Art. 87). Apart from the above compulsory insurance contracts there have been proposals to introduce others as well. These would primarily include contracts pertaining to the insurance against liability of certain categories of persons carrying out professional activities within particular domains (e.g., solicitors, physicians) or compulsory insurance contracts against certain risk types, such as floods or earthquakes that come about frequently in some regions.

100. The compulsory nature of their conclusion follows from the necessity of protecting the public interest. In such instances party autonomy is limited not only because of the mandatory being of their conclusion, but also regarding their contents. Namely, despite the fact that the insurance relationships stemming from them do come about through contracts, there is a statutory obligation to conclude such agreements under conditions pertaining to their most important aspects that are previously set by laws. However, party autonomy is not absolutely excluded. It exists in relation to the persons, with whom the insured party is going to enter into the compulsory insurance contract. In accordance with the above, the contracting party has a freedom of choosing the insurance company, with which it will sign the compulsory insurance contract.[127] Furthermore, the insured party's obligation to conclude the insurance contract corresponds to the insurer's obligation active within the particular domain of insurance to accept the offer to conclude a contract, under the condition, of course, that it fulfils the conditions under which the subject insurance company provides such insurance services.

101. Should the obligation of contract conclusion not be observed, a certain type of relationship (even without a contract) may still come about based on the law itself and under the condition of fulfilling certain statutory presumptions.[128] For instance, if a third party incurs damage from a motor vehicle, the owner of which failed to conclude a compulsory insurance contract against liability, if the damage is caused by unknown vehicles or if insolvency proceedings are instituted against the insurance company obliged to indemnify the injured party, the damages are going to be paid by a guarantee fund.[129] Such a rule was introduced because of the emphasized necessity to protect certain categories of persons within the field of compulsory insurance (persons injured by the use of motor vehicles, persons injured in public transport, etc.).

127. Šulejić, *Pravo osiguranja* (*Insurance Law*), 67.
128. Marjanski, *Ugovor o osiguranju* (*Insurance Contract*), 109.
129. *See* the Act on Compulsory Insurance within the Transport Sector, Art. 74.

Part I. The Insurance Company

Chapter 1. The Insurance Company: Its Form

102. Insurance business shall comprise insurance including coinsurance, reinsurance, insurance brokerage and insurance agency activities.[130] The activity of insurance in its narrower sense is comprised only the conclusion and performance of life and non-life insurance contracts, except contracts on compulsory social insurance.[131] According to Serbian law, insurance activities in their wider sense may be carried out by insurance companies (joint stock insurance companies and mutual insurance companies), reinsurance companies, insurance intermediation companies, insurance agencies, entrepreneurs carrying out agency activities, agencies providing insurance services, as well as specialized organizations (agencies) established by the state for certain insurance operations.[132] However, insurance activities in their narrower sense may be carried out only by a much smaller circle of subjects, that is, exclusively insurance companies – insurance joint stock companies and mutual insurance companies,[133] as well as specialized organizations (agencies) established by the state for certain insurance operations.

§1. Mutual and Premium Insurance

103. According to the manner of insurance organization in the Republic of Serbia for now, there are two types of insurance: premium and mutual insurance. Other types of insurance organization are not present in Serbia.

104. Premium insurance, the most widely represented type functions in practice in a manner that insurance against certain risks is provided upon the payment of premiums to the insurer, that is, the subject carrying out professional insurance activities as a business operator. Premium insurance operations may be carried out in Serbia exclusively by joint stock insurance companies seated in the Republic of Serbia. These may be established only in the form of joint stock companies.[134]

---

130. *See* LI, Art. 2.
131. *See* LI, Art. 5.
132. *See infra* n. 110.
133. *See* LI, Art. 3.
134. *See* LI, Art. 3, paras 1 and 2.

105. Joint stock insurance companies are typical commercial entities carrying out business operations for the purpose of generating profit. Basically there are no greater differences between regular joint stock companies and joint stock insurance companies. Apart from the LI, in segments not regulated by it, the provisions of the LCC (regulating among others the legal status of joint stock companies) are applicable to the legal status of joint stock insurance companies.[135] The specificities of joint stock insurance companies compared to regular joint stock companies (not active within the field of insurance) are the provisions pertaining to their establishment (a system of permits is applicable in the course of their foundation,[136] a larger amount of minimum paid up share capital necessary depending on the type of insurance operations the company wishes to carry out,[137] etc.), shareholder categories (rules on qualified participation in the capital of companies active within the field of insurance[138]), persons that may become members of company organs (e.g., necessary approval of the NBS for members of management and supervisory boards,[139] specific limitations regarding the election of such members),[140] as well as the ones pertaining to the rights and obligations of management and supervisory board members.[141] Apart from the above, certain specific provisions are in force in respect of change of their business name, their seat (an approval of the NBS being necessary),[142] as well as the termination of joint stock insurance companies.[143]

106. As opposed to premium insurance, by means of mutual insurance the potential risks to the object of insurance are secured in a manner that the risk community members associate within the mutual insurance company by paying certain amounts (contributions) thus establishing a fund, from which payments shall be made in the event that the risks come about on the object of insurance, that is, on the economical or personal good of a member (policyholder).

107. A mutual insurance undertaking shall be a legal person with its head office in the Republic, which is registered with a competent authority based on its licence to carry on insurance activities issued by the NBS.[144] A mutual insurance undertaking carries on insurance activities solely in the interest of its members (the insured), abiding by the principles of reciprocity and solidarity.[145] A mutual insurance undertaking may engage in all insurance activities, except reinsurance activities.[146] The

135. *See* LI, Art. 18, para. 1.
136. *See* LI, Arts 42–47.
137. *See* LI, Art. 27.
138. *See* LI, Arts 31–37.
139. *See* LI, Art. 61.
140. *See* LI, Art. 62.
141. *See* LI, Art. 65.
142. *See* LI, Art. 66.
143. The termination of insurance companies is regulated by the Law on the Insolvency and Liquidation of Banks, and Insurance Companies. Regarding issues not regulated by the above Act, the provisions of the Insolvency Act (insolvency proceedings) and the LCC (liquidation proceedings) are applicable.
144. *See* LI, Art. 70, para. 1.
145. *See* LI, Art. 70, para. 2.
146. *See* LI Art. 70, para. 3.

name of the mutual insurance undertaking shall contain the letters 'd.u.o.' (i.e., 'mutual insurance undertaking').[147] Even though sources containing rules on joint stock insurance companies may be applicable for mutual insurance companies, their nature is indeed specific. Mutual insurance companies operate according to the principles of mutuality and solidarity with the purpose of covering the risks imperilling their members. As opposed to other commercial companies, mutual insurance companies have a non-profit character. The funds gathered through contributions (not premiums) are accumulated only in the amount necessary for the operation of the company itself, e.g., for the coverage of obligations towards their members (policyholders) and the provision for necessary reserves. Surplus of accumulated funds may be returned to members at the end of a business year, but the members may also be called upon to pay up the differences, should the funds not be sufficient. In accordance with the above, mutual insurance companies may be established as unlimited contribution companies or limited contribution companies.[148]

108. Unlimited contribution mutual insurance companies have the right to demand from each of their members (policyholders) without limitations the payment of additional contributions necessary for the coverage of unexpected risks and other expenditures.[149]

109. A mutual insurance undertaking founded as a limited contribution undertaking may request each member (the insured), to pay additional contributions that do not exceed the total amount of their previous contribution from the same year, if the claim compensations and other expenditures exceed the contributions previously paid and other revenues of the undertaking.

110. Norms regulating the legal status of mutual insurance companies in the Republic of Serbia show that these are commercial and not civil law associations. Mutual insurance companies are commercial entities that must meet the general requirements applicable for all legal entities: they have to be registered; they must have assets by means of which they are responsible for obligations within legal traffic (minimal paid up part of the share capital,[150] a reserve fund, technical reserves, irrespective of the fact that incomes from contributions should cover the expenditures stemming from the realization of risks), management bodies similar to those in regular joint stock companies; they cease to exist in a same manner as other commercial entities (within liquidation or insolvency proceedings), and so on.

§2. Public or Private Nature

111. The insurance companies described above are private companies. However, the state of Serbia does provide insurance in a limited number of instances where

---

147. *See* LI Art. 70, para. 4.
148. *See* LI, Art. 72, para. 1.
149. *See* LI, Art. 72, para. 2.
150. *See* LI, Art. 73.

the private insurance market is not able to completely meet the interests of insured parties. Retirement and health insurance fall into this category, which represent constituent parts of social security. This domain is going to be analysed in detail within a separate chapter (Part VI – Social Security) along with other insurance types attracting the state's special interest. For this purpose, specialized organizations performing certain insurance types have been established directly by laws in particular segments of insurance. First, by means of the Act on the National Housing Loan Insurance Corporation (2004) the National Housing Loan Insurance Corporation, a specialized legal entity for the insurance of credits based on housing loans approved by banks and other financial organizations has been established. Second, by means of the Law on the Export Credit and Insurance Agency of the Republic of Serbia (2005) the agency as a specialized legal entity for the insurance of exports and foreign investments of domestic legal entities and entrepreneurs has been established. Third, by means of the Deposit Insurance Act (2015)[151] the agency as a specialized legal entity for the insurance of savings deposits of natural persons with banks has been established.

§3. Factual Data

112. The tasks of collecting official data and their statistical processing within the insurance sector in the Republic of Serbia are carried out by the central bank – the NBS. According to the Communication of the NBS (Insurance sector in Serbia – Third Quarter Report 2021),[152] at the end of the third quarter of 2021, the insurance market in Serbia comprised twenty insurance companies. Sixteen companies engaged in insurance activities only and four are specialist reinsurance companies. Of the insurance companies, four are exclusive life insurers, six exclusive non-life insurers, while six provide both life and non-life insurance. The participation of invoiced premiums according to insurance types in the course of the third quarter of 2021 within the total insurance portfolio in Serbia was the following:

(1) Non-life insurance (78.2%):
  - compulsory insurance of motor vehicle owners against liability for damages caused to third parties (31.1%);
  - full coverage motor vehicle insurance (10.1%);
  - property insurance (20.1%);
  - other non-life insurance (16.9%).

(2) Life insurance (21.8%).

151. OJ RS, 14/2015, 51/2017, 73/2019.
152. The Report was published in October 2021 by NBS.

Chapter 2. Access to Business

113. In order to establish companies carrying out insurance operations in their widest possible sense (joint stock insurance companies, reinsurance companies, mutual insurance companies, insurance intermediation companies, insurance agencies or agencies providing other insurance services), it is necessary that certain requirements are fulfilled. Some of these requirements pertain to all companies active within the field of insurance (general requirements), while others are specific to particular types of companies (special requirements).

§1. General Requirements for the Establishment of Companies Carrying out Insurance Operation in Their Widest Possible Sense

114. Due to the fact that the concession principle is applicable for the incorporation of insurance companies in Serbia, a licence of the NBS is always necessary for their establishment.[153] Apart from the fulfilment of general statutory requirements for their foundation (depending on the type of company to be registered), the NBS has the authority to assess whether the establishment of the particular company is justified or not. Such a solution is widely criticized in literature for it opens up possibilities for arbitrary treatment in the course of incorporation licensing, despite the fact that numerous tough requirements have already been provided for by the law that need to be fulfilled if a company wishes to apply for a permit. Without regard to the type of insurance company, the founders may be domestic or foreign legal entities or natural persons.[154]

115. The only general limitation regarding founders pertains to the possibility of qualified participation in the insurance company's capital. For the purpose of preventing that certain persons by means of multiple memberships in insurance companies influence the operations of particular companies the LI provides certain limitations regarding the acquisition of shares in the capital of insurance companies, their subsidiaries, as well as the conditions of acquiring qualified shares in the capital of insurance companies.[155] A person wishing to acquire a qualifying holding in a joint stock insurance undertaking or increase it in such a way that it equals or exceeds 20%, 30% or 50% of the voting rights or core capital of that undertaking, and/or that it becomes the parent undertaking of that undertaking – shall seek prior approval of the NBS for such acquisition and/or increase.[156]

116. Other requirements are specific to each particular type of company active within the field of insurance (special requirements). Therefore, these are going to be presented separately for each particular type of insurance company. In some, there are only a few special requirements.

153. *See* LI, Art 3, para. 1.
154. *See* LI, Art 23, para. 1.
155. *See* LI, Arts 31–38.
156. *See* LI, Art. 31, para. 1.

§2. Special Requirements for the Establishment and Business Operations of Joint Stock Insurance and Reinsurance Companies

117. Apart from the above general conditions pertaining to all companies carrying out insurance operations, when establishing a joint stock insurance or reinsurance company, certain special requirements need to be fulfilled.

118. The establishment procedure is regulated by the LCC. It is practically the same as with other joint stock companies not active within the field of insurance (articles of association, registration, etc.). However, certain specificities do exist regarding joint stock insurance companies. These are provided for by the LI. Certain differences regarding the foundation of joint stock companies not active within the field of insurance were described within the general requirements for the establishment of all insurance companies (foundation approval of the NBS, approval for the acquisition of qualified shares). As regards special requirements, the basic difference compared to the foundation of a 'classical' joint stock company is the necessity to secure a substantially higher minimal amount of the share capital's pecuniary part than is the case with other joint stock companies not carrying out insurance or other financial activities. The amount of the share capital's minimum pecuniary portion depends on the group and type of insurance operations the joint stock company wishes to carry out.[157] Finally, there is a distinctiveness regarding the joint stock insurance company's name too, which must contain the letters 'A.D.O.' (j.s.i.c., that is, 'joint stock insurance company'),[158] as opposed to other joint stock companies that need to be labelled only as 'A.D.' (j.s.c., that is, 'joint stock company').[159]

119. A joint stock insurance company may engage only in activities in one or more classes of insurance within the same insurance group (e.g., life insurance)[160] or only in reinsurance activities.[161] Insurance companies may not engage in life and non-life insurance simultaneously.[162] Joint stock insurance companies may engage in activities directly connected with insurance activities such as insurance intermediation and agency, risk and damage assessment and establishment, sales intermediation and sale of damaged insured goods, as well as providing other intellectual and technical services connected with insurance.[163] The above limitation exists in regard of reinsurance companies too, for reinsurance activities may only be carried out by companies licensed and registered for such activities, excluding companies carrying out insurance activities.

157. *See* LI, Art. 27.
158. *See* LI Art. 23, para. 1.
159. *See* LCC, Art. 22, para. 4.
160. *See* LI, Art. 24, para. 2.
161. *See* LI, Art. 24, para. 4.
162. *See* LI, Art. 24, para. 1.
163. *See* LI, Art. 24, para. 3.

§3. Special Requirements for the Establishment and Business Operations of Mutual Insurance Companies

120. Mutual insurance companies are the second type of entities that according to the LI may carry out insurance operations in their narrower sense. They are also to be incorporated in the form of joint stock companies, so that the norms regulating joint stock insurance companies are accordingly applicable for them in parts not provided for by special norms. There are, however, certain specificities in comparison with joint stock insurance companies. These pertain to the minimum number of founders (at least 250 natural persons if the mutual insurance company is founded to engage in life insurance, and/or a minimum of 300 natural persons or legal entities if the company is founded to engage in non-life insurance)[164] and the status of founders and members (they may have the status of founders or members with limited or unlimited contributions),[165] Finally, the obligatory name of mutual insurance companies is also specific. It has to contain the letters 'd.u.o.' (m.i.c., that is, 'mutual insurance company').[166]

§4. Special Requirements for the Establishment and Business Operations of Entities Active Within the Field of Insurance Intermediation and Agency

121. Intermediation and agency operations within insurance may be carried out exclusively by subjects fulfilling certain requirements – insurance intermediation (brokerage) companies, insurance agencies and natural persons licensed for agency activities in insurance (hereinafter 'insurance agents'). Their legal statuses are regulated by the LI and the LCC.

122. Insurance brokerage activities include insurance and reinsurance brokerage activities.[167] Insurance brokerage activities shall be activities related to introducing the insured and/or policyholder to an insurance/reinsurance undertaking for the purpose of negotiating the conclusion of an insurance/reinsurance contract, preparation for the conclusion of these contracts, as well as providing help in exercising the rights arising from such contracts, in particular in settlement of claims for damages.[168] Insurance brokerage activities shall be carried on, as an exclusive activity, by an insurance brokerage undertaking with its head office in the Republic, registered with the competent authority based on its licence to carry on such business issued by the NBS.[169] Insurance brokerage companies may usually not carry out insurance agency activities.[170] Insurance brokerage companies are incorporated as

164. *See* LI, Art. 71, para. 2.
165. In this regard *see* in detail the discussion pertaining to mutual insurance companies in Ch. 1, Title 'The Insurance Company – Its Form'.
166. *See* LI, Art. 70, para. 4.
167. *See* LI, Art. 85, para. 1.
168. *See* LI, Art. 85, para. 2.
169. *See* LI, Art. 86, para. 1.
170. *See* LI, Art. 86, para. 2.

joint stock companies or limited liability companies, subject to the law determining the legal status of companies.[171] There are only a few specific provisions different compared to the incorporation of 'classical' joint stock or limited liability companies. These are provided for by the LI. The distinctive provisions pertain to the minimum amounts of the share capital's pecuniary portion,[172] the business name (it must include the activity description 'insurance brokerage'), the obligatory conclusion of a contract against liability for damages arising from insurance brokerage activities or unconditional bank guarantees accepted by the NBS and the licensing conditions of the NBS for carrying out insurance intermediary activities.[173] In parts not regulated by special norms, the provisions of the LI regarding joint stock insurance companies apply accordingly to issues relating to the licensing and approval granted to insurance brokerage companies by the NBS.[174] Regarding contractual relationships established by means of insurance intermediation contracts, the provisions of the LO shall be applicable.

123. Insurance agency activities shall be the activities of initiating, proposing or carrying out the tasks of preparation and conclusion of insurance contracts on behalf and for the account of an insurance undertaking. Insurance agency activities are conducted by legal entities (insurance agencies) or natural persons (insurance agents) pursuant to insurance agency agreements on behalf of insurance companies, under the condition that they obtained a licence to engage in insurance agency activities. As an exception, insurance agencies and/or agents can represent more than one insurance company based on their written consent. Insurance agency, as an exclusive activity, shall be carried on by: (1) an insurance agency undertaking with its head office in the Republic, registered with a competent authority based on its licence to carry on insurance agency activities issued by the NBS; (2) a natural person – entrepreneur (hereinafter 'insurance agent') with its head office in the Republic, registered with a competent authority based on its licence to carry on insurance agency activities issued by the NBS. A bank, with its head office in the Republic and established in accordance with the law governing banks (hereinafter 'the Bank'), a financial leasing provider with its head office in the Republic and established in accordance with the law governing financial leasing and the public postal operator with its head office in the Republic and established in accordance with the law governing postal services may, as a supplementary activity, carry on insurance agency business on the basis of prior approval of the NBS for carrying on these activities. An insurance agency undertaking shall not engage in insurance brokerage

---

171. *See* LI, Art. 88, para. 2.
172. If an insurance brokerage company is incorporated as a joint stock company, the pecuniary portion of the share capital must not be lower than EUR 25,000 in its RSD counter-value according to the middle exchange rate of the NBS on the day of payment. If an insurance brokerage company is incorporated as a limited liability company, the pecuniary portion of the share capital must not be lower than EUR 12,500 in its RSD counter-value according to the middle exchange rate of the NBS on the day of payment. If, as an exception, an insurance brokerage company also performs insurance agency operations the above minimum pecuniary portion of the share capital is to be raised by 50% (*See* LI, Art. 88, paras 3–4).
173. *See* LI, Art. 89.
174. *See* LI, Arts 89–94.

activities.[175] There are only a few specific provisions differing from the establishment of a 'classical' joint stock company or limited liability company. These are provided for by the LI. The distinctive provisions pertain to the minimum amounts of the share capital's pecuniary portion[176] that needs to be paid up upon incorporation, the business name (it must include the activity description 'insurance agency/agent')[177] and the licensing conditions of the NBS for carrying out insurance agency activities.[178] In parts not regulated by special norms, the provisions of the LI regarding joint stock insurance companies apply accordingly to issues relating to the licensing and approval granted to insurance agencies by the NBS.

124. Insurance representatives (agents) are entrepreneurs, that is, a natural person – entrepreneur (hereinafter 'insurance agent') with its head office in the Republic, registered with a competent authority based on its licence to carry on insurance agency activities issued by the NBS.[179] Their legal status is regulated by the LCC (Articles 83–92). There are only a few specific provisions regulated by the LI. According to one, at establishment, insurance agent must hold the cash amount in RSD equivalent of EUR 1,500 calculated at the middle exchange rate of the NBS on the date of payment, originating from the applicant's own funds, and in the course of the insurance agent's business must maintain the liquid assets (cash assets, short-term securities and other short-term investments and receivables) at the level of at least 75% of that amount.[180] Other specific provisions pertain to the application for a licence by the NBS for the provision of insurance agency services.[181]

125. Insurance agencies and/or agents must remit to the insurance company all monies, other payment instruments and collaterals collected and/or taken over from policyholders and/or insurance contractors on behalf of the insurance company, by the following workday from the date of collecting or taking over the latest. They are furthermore obliged to hand over other payment instruments or collaterals to the insurance company within the same time limit.[182] Insurance agencies and/or agents collect insurance premiums according to the insurance company's rules and regulations.[183] Until the day of payment and/or remittance to the insurance company, insurance agencies and/or agents are obliged to keep at a safe place the collected monies, payment instruments and collaterals.[184]

175. *See* LI Art. 98, para. 3.
176. If an insurance agency is incorporated as a joint stock company, the pecuniary portion of the share capital must not be lower than EUR 25,000 in its RSD counter-value according to the middle exchange rate of the NBS on the day of payment. If an insurance agency is incorporated as a limited liability company, the pecuniary portion of the share capital must not be lower than EUR 12,500 in its RSD counter-value according to the middle exchange rate of the NBS on the day of payment (*See* LI, Art. 101).
177. *See* LI, Art. 100.
178. *See* LI, Art. 102.
179. *See* LI, Art. 98, para. 1.
180. *See* LI, Art. 103, para. 4.
181. *See* LI, Art. 105.
182. *See* LI, Art. 106, para. 1.
183. *See* LI, Art. 106, para. 2.
184. *See* LI, Art. 106, para. 3.

126. The insurance company or the insurance agent is liable for the acts performed in the course of insurance agency activities.[185] The insurance agency and/or agent is liable towards the policyholder for damages caused by false impersonation or malpractice of the insurance agency and/or agent, and/or due to the fact that the insurance agency and/or agent failed to inform the policyholder on their acting in the capacity of representatives.[186] The general manager of the insurance company and/or the specially authorized official signing the agency contract is liable towards the insurance company for damages caused by such contracts.[187] The provisions of the LO are applicable regarding the contractual relationships established by insurance agency contracts.

---

185. *See* LI, Art. 107, para. 1.
186. *See* LI, Art. 107, para. 2.
187. *See* LI, Art. 107, para. 3.

Chapter 3. Supervision

127. The features of insurance seek special supervision over the operation of subjects active within the field of insurance. Exceptionally, affiliated legal entities of insurance subjects are also subject to supervision (affiliates). Supervision is of utmost importance because of the fact that a substantial period of time may pass from the conclusion of an insurance contract to the insurer's potential obligation to indemnify the policyholder. Supervision may be external and internal. External supervision is carried out by the NBS. Internal supervision overinsurance operators is performed by actuaries and internal audits. In the widest possible sense, there are two supervision types in insurance: the solvency control of insurance operators and the supervision of general terms and tariffs established and passed by those subjects. The supervision overinsurance terms and tariffs is limited to only one type of contract – compulsory insurance contracts of motor vehicle owners against liability for damages caused to third parties.

§1. Solvency Control

I. Contents

128. Solvency control is performed in the phase of incorporation, in the course of business operations, in the event of potential status changes (mergers, demergers and acquisitions of companies active within the domain of insurance) and changes within the legal form (e.g., from an insurance company to a mutual insurance company), as well as during the termination of companies carrying out insurance operations.

129. Solvency supervision in the incorporation phase comprises the control whether the requirements for incorporation are met (e.g., whether the minimum pecuniary portion of the share capital has been paid up), which is manifested in the issuance of operating licences by the NBS, as well as the subsequent control of the fact if the whole incorporation procedure has been carried out in accordance with the pertaining statutory provisions.

130. Solvency control in the course of business operations comprises supervision over: conducting insurance activities in compliance with the granted licence; the liquidity and solvency of companies engaging in insurance activities; technical reserve definition methods; the performance of obligations arising from insurance contracts; deposits and investments of insurance funds according to the law; internal audit methodology; personnel and technical equipment of insurance companies, and so on. Such type of supervision may be direct or indirect. Direct supervision (on site-examination) is performed by insurance inspectors authorized by the NBS.[188] Direct control includes the examination of general acts and business policy

188. *See* LI, Art. 190, para. 1.

acts of companies serving as a base for determining whether the inspected insurance company operates in accordance with the pertaining statutory provisions.[189] Indirect supervision (of site-examination) is carried out through the submission of reports and other data to the NBS (e.g., annual business reports, reports on the performed audits, mutual insurance and reinsurance reports, reports on changes within the capital structure).[190]

131. Supervision within the phase of status changes, changes in the legal form and liquidation of insurance companies means that all status changes and changes in the company's legal form may exclusively be performed upon approval of the NBS.[191] The NBS has an important role in the phase of insurance company liquidation. When the statutory requirements are met, the NBS is authorized to withdraw operating licences of insurance companies and institute liquidation or insolvency proceedings against them.[192]

II. Measures of the NBS

132. The NBS has authority to introduce appropriate measures if the supervision procedure identifies illegalities and irregularities within the operations of entities carrying out insurance activities in their widest possible sense. Measures imposable by the NBS can be categorized to those taken towards insurance operators and to those taken towards management and supervisory board members, persons with special authorizations, as well as qualified shareholders.

133. In the course of supervision of an insurance undertaking, the NBS may: (1) issue a letter of warning; (2) publicly disclose information about the insurance undertaking's failure to meet its obligations or failure to meet them in a timely manner, or about the undertaking's non-compliance with the regulations, at the expense of the undertaking; (3) order measures to eliminate illegalities and irregularities in the operation of the undertaking; (4) order measures for failing to act in line with risk management regulations; (5) order that members of management be dismissed and suspended; (6) order interim measures; (7) place an undertaking into receivership; (8) order that the insurance portfolio be transferred to another insurance undertaking; (9) revoke the licence to carry on specific or all classes of insurance business.

§2. Supervision of Tariffs and Insurance Conditions

134. In Serbia, the supervision of tariffs and insurance conditions is regulated only within the domain of compulsory insurance of motor vehicle owners against

189. *See* LI, Arts. 191–194.
190. *See* LI, Arts 195–196.
191. *See* LI, Arts 227–230.
192. *See* LI, Arts 220–221.

liability for damages caused to third parties. Insurance companies carrying out operations in the area of motor third-party liability insurance shall be obliged to implement joint insurance terms, a premium system with an identical insurance premium basis for these operations and a minimum tariff, also containing the bonus malus system.[193] The NBS issues a pre-approval to the joint terms, the premium system and the tariff adopted by the Association of Serbian Insurers, as well as a pre-approval to their amendments and supplements (prior supervision).[194] By means of supervision over the insurance tariffs, that is, the premium rates collected by insurance companies, a continuous harmonized relationship between premiums and damages is trying to be reached. The prior supervision of insurance terms and tariffs with this particular type of insurance has been established due to the especially emphasized public interest within the sector. This is the most widely represented insurance type entered into by a large number of persons due to the fact that the conclusion of such contracts is a precondition of motor vehicle registration, so that there is a particularly underscored public interest to protect the rights of policyholders, as well as third-party claimants. Insurance companies are obliged to calculate the premium for each compulsory insurance premium system tariff group on the basis of relevant data for each tariff group. The data for calculation of each tariff group premium consists of information from concluded insurance contracts, reported, resolved, paid and reserved claims, costs related to resolving and payment of claims, as well as other information necessary for risk estimation and premium calculation. Insurance companies are obliged to submit the above data to the Association of Serbian Insurers, within the period prescribed by the Association.

135. In other fields of insurance, there is no prior supervision of insurance terms and tariffs because this is considered as a limitation to the development of the insurance sector. Furthermore, the public interest with other insurance types is not as evident as with the compulsory insurance of motor vehicles, so that there is no particular need of establishing such prior supervision.[195]

---

193. Joint insurance terms are delivered by the Association of Serbian Insurers.
194. *See* the Act on Compulsory Insurance within the Transport Sector, Arts 108 and 43.
195. Regarding the subsequent supervision of general and special insurance terms *see supra* nn. 75–78.

Chapter 4. Technical Reserves and Investments

§1. Technical and Guarantee Reserves

136. At the end of the reference period, an insurance undertaking shall be required to determine or calculate technical provisions sufficient to cover all liabilities stemming from insurance contracts, in the manner and within the timeframe laid down by the LI.[196] Technical provisions shall be determined by class of insurance, separately for life insurance and non-life insurance. An insurance undertaking shall calculate the technical provisions prudently, reliably and objectively, by applying actuarial principles, rules of insurance profession and relevant data about the characteristics of insurance portfolio and the risks that are being accepted.[197] When calculating technical provisions, an insurance undertaking shall take into account the rights the insured or insurance beneficiaries may have under the insurance contract, in particular all payments related to concluded insurance contracts and their expected increase.[198] An insurance undertaking shall be obligated to verify whether the technical provisions are sufficient and/or adequate to cover all liabilities stemming from insurance contracts and to submit the results of that verification at the request of the NBS together with the documents and information used to calculate adequacy of technical provisions.[199] The NBS shall prescribe the criteria, methods and deadlines for calculating technical provisions.[200] The NBS shall prescribe the criteria, methods and deadlines for calculating technical provisions.[201]

137. Depending on the class of insurance it carries on, an insurance undertaking shall determine the following technical provisions: (1) unearned premium reserves; (2) unexpired risk reserves; (3) reserves for bonuses and rebates; (4) outstanding claims reserves; (5) mathematical reserve; (6) reserves for insurance where the investment risk is borne by the insured; (7) risk equalization reserves.[202] Unearned premium reserves shall be formed by transferring pertinent amounts from total insurance premium at the end of the current period, separately for each insurance contract, in proportion to the period of insurance.[203] Unearned premium reserves shall constitute a part of the premium which is used to cover the insurance liabilities arising in the following period.[204] Unexpired risk reserves shall be determined as the amount in excess of unearned premium reserves to cover insurance liabilities arising in the following period in connection with insurance contracts in force during the current period.[205] Unexpired risk reserves shall be calculated in order to provide for expected amount of claims and expenses in the following period if the

196. *See* LI, Art. 116, para. 1.
197. *See* LI, Art. 116, para. 4.
198. *See* LI, Art. 116, para. 5.
199. *See* LI, Art. 116, para. 6.
200. *See* LI, Art. 116, para. 7.
201. *See* LI, Art. 116, para. 8.
202. *See* LI, Art. 116, para. 2. and LI, Art. 117–123.
203. *See* LI, Art. 117, para. 1.
204. *See* LI, Art. 117, para. 2.
205. *See* LI, Art. 118, para. 1.

expected amount exceeds the amount of unearned premium reserves and any premium receivables underinsurance contracts. Reserves for bonuses and rebates shall be determined as the amount the insured are entitled to through: (1) share in profit, or other rights underinsurance contracts, unless mathematical reserve is determined for those classes of insurance; (2) future partial reduction of premium; (3) partial refund of premium for unused duration of insurance due to early termination of insurance.[206] Outstanding claims reserves shall be determined as the estimated amount of liabilities for reported but unpaid claims and for incurred but unreported claims in the current period.[207] Mathematical reserve shall constitute technical provisions of insurance undertaking intended to settle the present value of future liabilities under life insurance contracts and under long-term non-life insurance contracts where savings and funds for risk coverage in later years are being accumulated and to which probability tables and calculations used in life insurance are applied.[208] Reserves for insurance where the investment risk is borne by the insured shall be determined as the amount to which the insured are entitled, and which is directly linked to the value of the investment.[209] Risk equalization reserves shall be used for temporal equalization of the course of claims in certain classes of insurance.[210]

138. An insurance undertaking shall be obligated to establish a guarantee reserve for the purpose of continued settlement of liabilities and risk assumption, in the manner set out in this Law.[211] The guarantee reserve shall include core capital and supplementary capital, less deductibles.[212]

§2. Deposit and Investment

139. Under the conditions of rapid monetary value changes, one of the basic problems of insurance companies is how to ensure the real value of monetary assets taking into account their purpose and their spending over a longer period of time.[213] For this reason, the conditions and limitations of reserve deposits and their investment aimed at maintaining their real value is provided for by insurance regulations in Serbia. Simultaneously, heed is paid to the circumstance that the insurer must able to dispose of certain funds at all times in order to meet its obligations towards policyholders.[214] The LI provides for a couple of limitations in regard of making deposits and investing reserves.[215] Technical provisions may be deposited with banks having a head office in the Republic of Serbia or kept as cash in the insurance

206. *See* LI, Art. 119.
207. *See* LI, Art. 120, para. 1.
208. *See* LI, Art. 121, para. 1.
209. *See* LI, Art. 122, para. 1.
210. *See* LI, Art. 123, para. 2.
211. *See* LI, Art. 124, para. 1.
212. *See* LI, Art. 124, para. 2.
213. *See* Jankovec & Miladinović, *Pravo osiguranja* (*Insurance Law*), 174.
214. *Ibid.*
215. *See* LI, Art. 131, para. 2.

undertaking's cash box or in its bank account.[216] Apart from the statutory limitations, the NBS may by means of a decision limit particular forms of reserve deposits and investments.

216. *See* LI, Art. 131, para. 3.

Chapter 5. Accountancy

140. The basic statutory source of law within the field of accounting in Serbia is the Law on Accounting (2019[217]). This law shall regulate the subjects of application of this law, the classification of legal persons, organization of accounting and accounting documents, conditions and manner of bookkeeping, recognition and valuation of positions in the financial statements, drafting, submission and publication of financial statements and annual report on operations, Register of financial reports, National Commission for Accounting, as well as supervision over the implementation of the provisions of this law.[218] The above Law governs the manner of keeping books of account; the recognition and appraisal of assets and obligations, incomes and expenditures; preparing, presenting, submitting and disclosing financial statements; the requirements for and manner of auditing financial statements, as well as internal auditing. Its provisions apply to commercial subjects (companies, entrepreneurs, etc.) and consequently to insurance companies and other entities engaged in insurance operations. The above entities are obliged to keep their books of account; perform the recognition and appraisal of assets and obligations, incomes and expenditures; prepare, present, submit and disclose their financial statements; and perform their internal audits in compliance with the legislation, professional and internal rules (Regulations). The legislation means primary legislation (The Law on Accounting), as well as secondary legislation (by-laws) passed for the purpose of implementing primary legislation.

141. Besides that, important source of law are professional rules too. Professional rules mean the Framework for the Preparation and Presentation of Financial Statements, the International Accounting Standards (IAS), the International Financial Reporting Standards (IFRS), the interpretations that are constituent parts of the Standards, the International Standards of Auditing (ISA) and the Code of Ethics for Professional Accountants. Internal Regulations shall, in terms of this Law, mean constitutional documents issued by a legal person or a sole proprietor that contain specific instructions and guidelines for the organization of accounting and bookkeeping, accounting policies for guidelines for the organization of accounting and bookkeeping, accounting policies for the recognition, valuation of assets and liabilities, income and expenses, as well as the recognition, valuation of assets and liabilities, income and expenses, as well as other issues of bookkeeping and preparation of financial statements for which this law stipulates that they shall be regulated by constitutional documents of a legal person or a sole proprietor.[219]

142. Legal persons, in terms of this law, shall be classified as micro, small, medium and large, depending on the average number of employees, business income and average value of operating assets determined on the day of drafting of the regular annual financial statement for the business year.[220]

---

217. OJ RS, 73/2019, 44/2021.
218. *See* the Law on Accounting, Art. 1.
219. *See* the Law on Accounting, Art. 2, para. 13.
220. *See* the Law on Accounting, Art. 6, para. 1.

The importance of classification into micro, small, medium, and large legal entities lies within the obligatory nature of yearly financial statement auditing. Large and medium legal entities, as well as small ones issuing securities according to public offers, or the securities of which are traded with on regulated stock markets have an obligation of auditing their yearly financial statements. All insurance companies are deemed to be large legal entities irrespective of their number of employees, their total annual income and the value of their assets and of the fact whether they made a public offer regarding their securities and/or whether their securities are traded with on regulated stock markets.[221] The above means that insurance companies, as well as all other large legal entities are obliged to have their yearly financial statements audited. Other entities carrying out insurance operations in their wider sense (e.g., insurance agencies or insurance intermediation companies) are classified into micro, small, medium or large legal entities in accordance with the criteria set out in Article 6 of the Law on Accounting.

143. There are two types of auditing within Serbian insurance law: internal and external.

144. Internal auditing is performed by particular bodies of the insurance company specially established for that purpose. It is performed as a preventive measure against possible undesired consequences for the insurance company due to the breach of statutory provisions pertaining to insurance. By means of internal audits the adequacy and application of prescribed risk control policies and procedures, the accounting procedures and the organization of accounting activities, the reliability and timeliness of financial and management information, and so on are supervised and assessed. An insurance company is obliged to organize an internal audit which is autonomous and independent in carrying out its tasks.[222] A special purpose department within the company specified in the Articles of Association conducts the insurance company's internal audits.[223] The internal audit unit of the insurance company reports directly to the supervisory board of the insurance company.[224] Insurance company bodies and its employees must not prevent, limit or impede the reporting on the findings and assessments of the persons in charge of internal audit activities in the insurance company.[225] Internal audit activities of an insurance company are defined by the rules of procedure on internal audit rendered by the board of directors of the company.[226] The insurance company must have at least one employee for the purpose of carrying out internal audit activities.[227] Insurance companies shall define the conditions for the nomination and dismissal of internal auditors as well as the organizational position of other internal audit department employees.[228] The persons in charge of internal audit cannot conduct any other

---

221. *See* the Law on Accounting, Art. 6, para. 12.
222. *See* LI, Art. 154, para. 1.
223. *See* LI, Art. 154, para. 2.
224. *See* LI, Art. 154, para. 3.
225. *See* LI, Art. 154, para. 4.
226. *See* LI, Art. 154, para. 5.
227. *See* LI, Art. 156, para. 1.
228. *See* LI, Art. 156, para. 2.

activity in the insurance company, are not authorized nor liable for preparing acts or other documentation which can be a subject to internal audits, nor can they be members of the management or the supervisory board of the company.[229] The internal auditor drafts a report on each completed internal audit.[230] The tasks of internal audits, the contents and submission schedules of reports are regulated by the LI.[231]

145. Apart from internal audits, external ones are also obligatory. They comprise the auditing of annual financial statements of insurance companies; for these are, according to accountancy provisions, categorized as large legal entities. External audits are performed by auditing companies fulfilling the requirements set out in the Accounting and Auditing Law. Audits are performed according to contracts concluded between subjects of auditing and auditing companies until the end of a particular calendar or business year the latest. External supervision over the activity of insurance companies and other entities carrying out insurance operations, including among other the auditing of adopted financial statements, is performed by the NBS.

229. *See* LI, Art. 156, para. 3.
230. *See* LI, Art. 156, para. 4.
231. *See* LI, Arts 157–160.

Chapter 6. Taxation of the Company

146. In accordance with the general rules established regarding all legal entities, insurance companies in the Republic of Serbia are obliged to pay corporate tax established by means of the Corporate Profit Tax Law.[232] The corporate tax base is the legal entity's taxable profit.[233] The principle that the business balance sheet governs the tax balance sheet is applicable to the determination of the taxable profit, which means that the tax base is calculated by adjusting the profit posted in the profit and loss statement in a manner that incomes and expenditures are recognized in the amounts established in the profit and loss statement, in accordance with the International Accounting Standards and the Accounting and Auditing Law, apart from incomes and expenditures for which the Corporate Profit Tax Law provides another type of determination. The principle of accrual accounting is usually used for the purpose of determining business results and the taxable profit, according to which it is deemed that profit is generated upon the creation of the right to receive income, while costs are created when the obligation for their payment is incurred.[234] The taxable period in which corporate tax is accounted is a business year. This usually corresponds to a calendar year. The corporate tax rate amounts to 15%.[235]

232. OJ RS, 25/2001, 80/2002, 43/2003, 84/2004, 18/2010, 101/2011, 119/2012, 47/2013, 68/2014, 91/2015 and 112/2015, 113/2017, 95/2018, 86/2019, 153/2020, 118/2021.
233. *See* the Corporate Profit Tax Law, Art. 6, para. 1.
234. For details *see* Dejan Popović, *Poresko pravo* (*Tax Law*) (Belgrade: Pravni fakultet u Beogradu, 2008), 4, regarding incomes and expenditures within the profit and loss statement, adjustments within the tax balance sheet, the tax law treatment of business losses, as well as the tax base in case of the taxpayer's liquidation or insolvency. For exceptions *see* the Corporate Profit Tax Law, Arts 38 and 34, paras 3 and 4.
235. *See* the Corporate Profit Tax Law, Art. 39, para. 2.

Part II. The Insurance Contract: General

Chapter 1. Generalities

147. Insurance contracts in Serbia are statutorily regulated, bilateral, mutually binding (synallagmatic), aleatory, continuous and in most cases successive legal transactions.

148. Insurance contracts are statutorily regulated, which means that the provisions relating to them are laid down in primary legislation. The general definition of insurance contracts is given in the LO. Insurance contracts are defined in the following manner: By a contract of insurance, a contractor of insurance shall assume the obligation to pay a specific amount to an insurance organization (insurer), while the organization shall assume the obligation, should an event take place which represents the case covered by insurance, to pay to the insured person, or to a third party, compensation, the stipulated amount, or to do something else.[236]

149. Insurance contracts are bilateral legal transactions. The bilateral being means that this legal transaction comes about by the concurrence of wills of two contracting parties. Only organizations (i.e., legal entities that are simultaneously subjects of commercial law) meeting the requirements for engaging in insurance operations in their narrower sense set out in mandatory provisions may have the capacity of insurers. However, all legal entities or natural persons meeting general requirements for contract conclusion may have the capacity of insured parties.

150. Insurance contracts are mutually binding (synallagmatic) legal transactions. This means that there is a mutual dependence of contractual obligations between the contracting parties (both of them are creditors and debtors simultaneously), so that the obligation of one party represents the basis of the other party's obligation. The insurer is a debtor regarding the payment of compensation or the contracted sum of money, while the insured party is a debtor in relation to the payment of premiums, and vice versa. Their obligations are mutually bound with the proviso that the performance of the insurer's obligation always depends on the occurrence of the peril covered by insurance.[237]

---

236. *See* LO, Art. 897.
237. Oliver Antić et al., *Leksikon građanskog prava* (*Civil Law Lexicon*) (Belgrade: Nomos, 1996), 750.

151. From the viewpoint of their legal nature, insurance contracts are aleatory transactions. At the point of aleatory contract conclusion the prestations of one or both contracting parties or the extent of their rights and obligations are not precisely determined but are contingent upon the occurrence of an uncertain circumstance or event agreed upon by the contracting parties.[238] The aleatory being of insurance contracts lies within the fact that at the point of their conclusion the parties are uncertain as to whether and/or when the insured risk, and thus the insurer's obligation and the insured party's right to claim compensation or the contracted sum, is going to come about.[239] If the insured loss does not occur, the insurer is not going to be obliged to perform its basic obligation from the insurance contract. At the point of contract conclusion, the insured party does not know whether it will be economically viable to enter into such a contract and pay the premiums in order to be insured against the potential occurrence of the contracted loss. If the insured loss does occur, the choice will turn out to have been justified. The fact that the policyholder seeks remedy against uncertainties does not mean that insurance contracts do not have an aleatory character. Policyholders tend to protect themselves from contingent occurrences but whether the event is going to happen or not, at what time-point and to what extent, if the policyholder is accordingly going to pay more for premiums than the amount of compensation and whether they are going to receive anything at all, remains uncertain.[240] However, the aleatory nature of insurance contracts does differ from that of gambling contracts. Insurance contracts do not enable policyholders to receive more than actually lost by the occurrence of the insured loss.[241] By means of insurance contracts policyholders are only protected against consequences of risk realization. From the viewpoint of insurers, the aleatory nature of insurance contracts means that at the point of contract conclusion they are aware of the fact that compensation or the contracted amounts will need to be paid for the received premiums. If particular contracts are examined, the insurer's obligation is dependent on a suspensive condition. Consequently, it is contingent due to the fact that the obligation itself and its extent will depend on the fact and time of loss occurrence. In contracts where at the point of their conclusion, it is certain that the insured loss is going to occur (e.g., insurance contracts of persons against death and survivorship) the aleatory nature is manifested in the uncertainty as to when the loss is going to occur. The amount of compensation due by the insurer is also dependent on this fact.

152. Insurance contracts are continuous legal transactions. Continuous contracts are those where the parties' obligations spread over the whole contract duration.[242] In the course of the whole contractual relationship, the insured party is obliged to

238. O. Antić et al., *Leksikon građanskog prava* (*Civil Law Lexicon*), 771.
239. Vladimir Jovanović, *Osiguranje u privredi* (*Commercial Insurance*) (Zagreb: Informator, br. 11–12, 1962), 66.
240. Vladimir Jovanović, *Prava osiguravača prema trećem odgovornom licu* (*The Insurer's Rights towards Third party Responsible Persons*) *doctoral dissertation* (Belgrade: Pravni fakultet u Beogradu, 1956), 89.
241. This rule is consistently implemented only in contracts where the principle of indemnification is applicable.
242. Jovanović, *Osiguranje u privredi* (*Commercial Insurance*), 66.

inform the insurer on all circumstances relevant for risk assessment. However, the insurer must at all times be ready to pay the compensation and is therefore obliged to have certain reserves accumulated in the course of the whole contractual relationship.[243] A consequence of the contracts' continuous nature is that withdrawal from the contract has an *ex nunc* effect, that is, from the point of withdrawal. Contract termination pertains to the future and does not have any effect whatsoever to already performed prestations. For example, in case of withdrawing from the contract the policyholder has a right of compensation for damages incurred before the withdrawal.[244]

153. Apart from their continuous being, insurance contracts often have a successive (periodical) character. Successive contracts are performed by repeated payment of prestations within a given payment schedule.[245] Insurance contracts are successive when the policyholder is obliged to pay premiums that mature within equal time limits. Due to the influence of time to the performance of such contracts and the peculiar manner of their performance, certain specific rules are applicable to them:[246] First, the rules on contract modification and termination due to changed circumstances may be applicable to them. However, general rules (Article 133 LO) are not applicable to insurance contracts but special ones regulating only this contract type.[247] Second, in successive insurance contracts where the insured party's obligation is the premium payment in equal time frames, due to foreign currency exchange rate fluctuations, in legal systems adopting the principle of nominalism (Serbia being one of them), it is possible that additionally to court valorization the rules on contractual valorization are also applied (index, foreign currency and gold clauses). Third, statutes of limitation of particular prestations may be an issue with successive contracts. According to the rule set out in the LO, certain periodical claims expire within a period of three years from becoming due.[248]

154. Insurance contracts are bona fide legal transactions. The above means that the principle of good faith (Latin: bona fides; German: *Treu und Glauben*) is one of the basic underlying principles of insurance contracts. Within insurance transactions the above means an open, honest and reliable attitude within mutual relationships before, during and after contract conclusion up to the contract performance.[249] Although the LO and the LMIN do not expressly provide for such a property of insurance contracts, the good faith principle is a general principle of contract law[250] applicable to insurance contracts as well. The principle of good faith is particularly important in provisions of the LO pertaining to the obligation of

243. *See supra* n. 138.
244. Drago Pavić, *Ugovorno pravo osiguranja – Komentar zakonskih odredaba* (*Contractual Insurance Law – Commentary to the Statutory Provisions*) (Zagreb: Tectus, 2009), 59.
245. O. Antić et al., *Leksikon građanskog prava* (*Civil Law Lexicon*), 708.
246. *Ibid.*
247. *See* LO, Arts 914–916.
248. *See* LO, Art. 372.
249. Pavić, *Ugovorno pravo osiguranja – Komentar zakonskih odredaba* (*Contractual Insurance Law – Commentary to the Statutory Provisions*), 60.
250. *See* LO, Art. 12.

reporting circumstances important for risk assessment.[251] Apart from acting in good faith, the insurer as a subject of commercial law is obliged to carry out insurance operations in accordance with professional rules and customs (care of a prudent businessman).[252]

155. In order for the insurance contract to be legally effective, all important elements determined by the legal nature of such transactions need to be fulfilled. Important elements of insurance contracts stemming from the nature of such transactions are: the insurable risk, the insured event, the object of insurance and the insurance premium for all insurance contract types, as well as the insured sum with insurance contracts where the principle of compensation is not applicable (e.g., life insurance contracts).

156. Risk, as an important element of insurance contracts, represents the possibility that a contingent event occurs, which is not dependent on the exclusive will of an interested party and the coverage of which is legally permitted, that is, it is in accordance with the law, the public order and the principles of ethics. Risks covered by a particular insurance contract are described as insurable risk both in practice and in literature.[253]

157. An insured event is the occurrence of the insured risk that according to the law or the insurance contract is suitable to trigger the performance of the insurer's main obligation.

158. The object of insurance is either property or personal categories (e.g., life, health, physical integrity) imperilled by the potential occurrence of the insurable risk.

159. The premium is the insured party's consideration consisting of monies paid to the insurer as the price of insurance for their undertaking of obligation performance (risk coverage) and the potential performance of obligations stemming from the insurance contract (performance is conditional on the occurrence of the insured event). The premium is simultaneously part of the insurer's total fund from which compensations are covered.

160. Apart from the above four important elements, with insurance contracts where the principle of compensation is not applicable (e.g., life insurance contracts) an important element that must be fulfilled is the insured sum. The insured sum is the pecuniary amount provided for by the contract or law, which simultaneously represents the maximum amount, that is, the upper limit of the insurer's obligation in insurance contracts where the principle of compensation is not applicable. In such contracts, the insured sum represents a material contractual element due to the fact that on the contrary the upper limit of the insurer's obligation would not be known.

251. *See* LO, Arts 907–911.
252. *See* LO, Art. 18, para. 2.
253. *See infra* nn. 161–180.

The reason for the above is the fact that subjects of such insurance contracts are personal categories (life, health, or physical integrity) that do not have an economical market 'price', so that the material value of the insured interest is not determinable. If in insurance contracts where the principle of compensation is not applicable the insured sum is not determined by the contract or is not at least determinable so that its minimum amount is set out in a mandatory provision (as with accident insurance contracts of passengers in public transport, for instance), there is no way for establishing the extent of the insurer's obligations, which circumstance inevitably renders such contracts void.

161. The insured sum is established in the policy according to the agreement of contracting parties.[254] Although, taking into account the important being of this contractual element, the insured sum is determined according to the parties' agreement, in practice the insured party usually chooses the amount of the insured sum in accordance with its financial possibilities. This is understandable due to the fact that the amount of the insured sum, apart from the risk, is the most important element determining the insurance premium amount due for payment by the insurance contractor. With insurance contracts where the principle of compensation is applicable (all property insurance contracts and certain contracts on the insurance of persons)[255] the insured sum may be agreed upon but does not represent an important contractual element. If not agreed upon, the contract is going to be valid and in the event of risk occurrence the insurer is going to be obliged to pay compensation in the amount of the damages incurred by the insured party. Such insurance contracts are also called unlimited coverage insurance contracts. They, however, are very rare in practice.

254. *See* LO, Art. 942.
255. For example, health insurance contracts where medical treatment costs are reimbursed in accordance with the principle of compensation.

Chapter 2. Insurable Risk

§1. Insurable Risk: General

162. Insurable risk is an important element of insurance contracts. Within insurance law risk represents the possibility that a contingent event occurs, which is not dependent on the exclusive will of an interested party and the coverage of which is legally permitted, that is, it is in accordance with the law, the public order and the principles of ethics. Risks covered by a particular insurance contract are defined as insurable risk both in practice and in literature.[256]

163. Insurable risk needs to be differentiated from the insured event because these two concepts are often confused. While risk means only the possibility that a certain contingent event occurs, the insured event represents the loss after which the insurable risk is materialized on the object of insurance.[257] It follows that the insured event is the materialized insurable risk suitable to trigger the performance of the insurer's main obligation (e.g., the payment of compensation).[258] The LO, however, erroneously does not differentiate between these two concepts. Insurance events are defined in the following manner by the LO: An event serving as a ground for concluding insurance (an insurance case) must be a future event, uncertain and entirely independent of the contracting party's will.[259] A concept defined in the above manner, despite the fact that it is labelled as insured event, in reality represents only insurable risk due to the fact that only the occurrence of insurable risk on the object of insurance can represent an insured event.

§2. Important Elements of Insurable Risk

164. Risk consists of four elements. These are the possibility of its occurrence, the uncertainty of its occurrence, its independence of the interested party's will and its legality. All of these elements require additional explanations.

I. The Possibility of Risk Occurrence

165. The event consists of two elements: cause and effect. Causes of a certain effect may be various. They may comprise human factors (e.g., the infliction of damages), as well as natural occurrences (such as droughts, earthquakes, storms). The human factor consists of both actions and omissions.[260] The effect itself may

---

256. Marjanski, *Ugovor o osiguranju* (*Insurance Contract*), 15.
257. *Ibid.*
258. For example, in the event of property insurance against fire, the risk is the possibility of a fire. When the insured subject is in reality burnt down, the fire, from the aspect of insurance relationships, represents the insured event.
259. *See* LO, Art. 898, para. 1.
260. Marjanski, *Ugovor o osiguranju* (*Insurance Contract*), 16.

be triggered by one or more causes. For instance, an insured object may be damaged by crashing, fire, and so on in the course of carriage. In such a situation a general rule is applicable, according to which the insurer covers all causes triggering the effect, apart from causes explicitly excluded by the contract or a general norm (e.g., in the event of insurance against lightning the damage itself may be caused by fire, collapse). However, a cause does not always have to be present and is thus not an obligatory constitutive element of the event. Namely, cause (or an event in its narrower sense) may consist of a change in a certain situation (when a cause is an inevitable requirement for the effect to take place), as well as of the prolongation of a certain situation (when there is no cause).[261] The effect does not have to be explicitly provided for by the insurance contract. It may follow from a cause stipulated by the contract. For instance, in case of theft insurance, only the cause (theft) is mentioned, while the effect is self-evident.

166. An event representing a constituent element of risk must be possible. Only possible events may be covered by insurance.[262] On the contrary, if the event's occurrence is impossible, the insurance contract providing for its coverage shall be void. It is therefore of utmost importance to determine, what events are impossible. Impossible is an event that cannot occur according to the rules of logic. However, the narrow likelihood of its occurrence does not render it impossible.[263] Apart from the above, it is necessary to differentiate between absolute and relative impossibility of occurrence of a particular event.[264] Absolutely impossible are events that cannot occur under any circumstances. In relation to absolute impossibility of the occurrence of a particular event two legally relevant situations are possible:[265] First, if the absolute impossibility of occurrence of a particular event is present at the contract conclusion, it shall be deemed that the contract has not at all come about due to the fact that the requirements for its legal effect are not met.[266] Second, if the absolute impossibility of event occurrence comes about while the insurance contract is effective, the contract shall cease to exist for the future.[267] However, a relatively impossible event is a per se possible event, which cannot occur under the specific circumstances of the contractual relationship.[268] Consequently, a relative impossibility of event occurrence means that the contract providing for such coverage is inevitably void.

---

261. An example of a change of situation: damage to the insured property, death, bodily harm of a certain person, etc. An example of prolongation of a situation: the fact that a person accomplishes a certain age in life insurance.
262. Marjanski, *Ugovor o osiguranju* (*Insurance Contract*), 17.
263. *Ibid.*
264. *Ibid.*
265. *Ibid.*
266. *Ibid.*
267. *Ibid.*
268. Article 928, para. 1 LO reads: 'Should an insured object or object whose use is the ground of concluding a liability insurance is lost in course of the insurance period, due to an event not provided for in the insurance policy, the contract shall cease to be valid for the future, while the insurer shall be obliged to restitute to the contractor of insurance part of the insurance premium, proportionate to the remaining time period.' For example, for the insurance of ships within the Mediterranean the

II. The Uncertainty of Risk Occurrence

167. Event occurrence must be contingent, that is, it must not be certain. Certain is an event that will surely occur. However, in order for an event to be deemed certain from the viewpoint of insurance contracts, it is sometimes necessary to know not only if the event is going to occur, but also when it is going to happen.[269] For instance, although it is certain that all people are going to die, life insurance does represent risk coverage due to the fact that it is not known when death is going to approach. Furthermore, as low probability does not render an event impossible, increased probability does not render it certain. It is enough that the possibility for event occurrence exists, so it can be considered uncertain. Another question is, whether the insurer is going to accept the coverage of such risk and under what circumstances.[270]

Uncertainty means the impossibility to establish whether, under regular circumstances, an event is going to occur or when it will occur. Uncertainty is an important element of insurable risk. It is never certain that possible events are surely going to occur. Therefore, uncertainty is an element of insurable risk different from the possibility of event occurrence (although it necessarily supplements it). Uncertainty is inherent in the nature of insurance contracts. Covering an event that is surely going to occur at a certain time-point would mean the elimination of the aleatory nature of insurance contracts, which is one of their elementary features.[271] Insurance contracts covering events that are surely going to occur at a certain time-point shall be null and void due to the fact that they are contrary to mandatory regulations, the public order and the rules of ethics. However, uncertainty is a relative concept. It may exist in relation to:

(1) the occurrence of an event caused by a risk (destruction or loss of the insured object in case of fire, theft, etc.);
(2) the time of occurrence of an event, the happening of which is sure (e.g., it is certain that the insured party is going to die, but it is not known when);
(3) the amount of damage that is going to be caused by a future certain event or, in case of already occurred events, if the amount damages caused by it is unknown.[272]

168. The uncertainty of event occurrence is determined in a negative manner by the LO. The LO regulates instances where it is deemed that the uncertainty of event occurrence is not present. Situations where, according to the LO, uncertainty does not exist are classified into four groups:

---

event of the boat crushing into an iceberg is impossible due to the fact that there are no icebergs in the Mediterranean. The ship could, however, crush into an iceberg if it navigated to waters where such risks are present.

269. Marjanski, *Ugovor o osiguranju* (*Insurance Contract*), 18.
270. *Ibid.*
271. *See* in details *supra* n. 166.
272. Marjanski, *Ugovor o osiguranju* (*Insurance Contract*), 17.

(1) Uncertainty does not exist if the risk occurred prior to contract conclusion. Risks occurring prior to contract conclusion usually may not be covered by insurance. The LO provides for the nullity of insurance contracts if, at the moment of their conclusion, the risk (the insured event) has already materialized.[273] There are, however, certain exceptions to this rule. Thus, the LO provides for the possibility of encompassing a specified period of time preceding the conclusion of contract only if, at the moment of its conclusion, the interested party was not aware that the risk (the case covered by insurance) had already taken place, or that even then the possibility of its taking place had ceased to exist.[274] It follows that, according to the general rule, the subjective relationship of the interested party towards the risk before contract conclusion is decisive. However, the interested party's knowledge that the insurable risk had materialized, does not represent a hindrance for its coverage within marine insurance. Within marine insurance it is possible that in spite of the parties' awareness that the risk had materialized prior to contract conclusion, the insurance contract remains in full legal effect. The above-described uncertainty in these situations must relate to the amount of damage caused by the materialization of such insured risk.[275]

(2) Uncertainty does not exist if there is no possibility for the risk to occur. Impossible risks may not be covered by insurance contracts. In such situations one of the important elements of contract conclusion would be missing: the uncertainty of event occurrence.

(3) Uncertainty does not exist in situations where damages are not yet incurred, but the risk is in the phase of materialization at the time of contract conclusion (e.g., if a landslide of the grounds where the insured building is situated had commenced, irrespective of the fact that no particular damage has yet been incurred). In such situations, there is no uncertainty as to the materialization of the insurable risk, which renders the contract covering it void.

(4) Uncertainty does not exist in situations where, under regular circumstances, the materialization of risk is inevitable. For instance, if due to extremely high water-levels floods are imminent, a concluded crop insurance contract against floods would be null and void under such circumstances, regardless of the fact that it is economically unsustainable for the insurer.[276]

---

273. *See* LO, Art. 898, para. 2.
274. *See* LO, Art. 898, para. 3.
275. *See* LMIN, Art. 751.
276. Marjanski, *Ugovor o osiguranju* (*Insurance Contract*), 18.

III. The Independence of Risk Occurrence of the Interested Party's Will

A. The Concept of an Interested Party

169. An interested party is a person that has or may have certain economical interests from the concluded insurance contract. These are above all the policyholder, and every other person that has or may have certain interests from the concluded insurance contract (insurance contract beneficiaries, mortgagees, owners of insured objects, etc.).[277] If an interested party deliberately causes the materialization of risk (occurrence of the insured event), the insurer is usually not going to be responsible for the consequences due to the fact that the event covered by insurance must come about independently from the will of interested parties. The LO lays down that the insurer shall not be liable for damages caused by wilful misconduct of the contractor of insurance, the policyholder or the beneficiary of the insurance.[278] This is a mandatory provision and insurance policy clauses specifying such liability of the insurer shall be void. The will of other parties not having interest in the materialization of the insurable risk does not have an effect to the insurer's liability from the insurance contract.

B. The Interested Party's Degree of Fault and Its Influence on the Materialization of Risks Covered by Insurance

170. As already pointed out, the risk must be independent from an interested party's exclusive will. An interested party's exclusive will exists if the risk materialization was caused by his/her intent. Coverage of events caused by wilful misconduct or fraud is prohibited by means of mandatory provisions.[279] However, if the contract has already been entered into and the interested party intentionally causes the realization of risk, the insurer is not going to be liable for the performance of its basic obligation from the insurance contract.[280] Insurance policy clauses specifying such liability of the insurer shall be void. This rule is applicable to all types of insurance.[281] However, if the insured event occurs in compulsory liability insurance contracts, the insurer shall be liable for payment of compensation for third-party claimants even if the insured event was caused by an interested party's intent. Of course, the tortfeasor is not going to be protected, for the insurer has a right of redress towards him/her.

171. Gross negligence is the failure to act with the level of care that a person of average physical and intellectual capabilities and moral properties would employ in the same situation and under the same or similar circumstances. Gross negligence differs from intent in that in such cases there is no consciousness nor will to cause

277. Marjanski, *Ugovor o osiguranju* (*Insurance Contract*), 20.
278. *See* LO, Art. 929, para. 2.
279. *See* LO, Art. 920.
280. *See* LO, Art. 929, para. 2.
281. *See* LO, Arts 950–951.

certain consequences.[282] Therefore, gross negligence is a legal standard that may be defined in different manners, but it will at the end be assessed by courts, whether in a particular case a gross or simple (light) negligence has been present. The level of one's will in causing the risk to happen is a lot lower than with intent, and it is not of an exclusive character. As opposed to causing the insured event intentionally, which is prohibited by mandatory statutory provisions, causing the insured event by gross negligence depends on the type of insurance contract, as well as on the particular contractual provisions.[283] However, in the great majority of insurance contract types, gross negligence is not covered by insurance. Causing the insured event by gross negligence is usually covered only in voluntary liability insurance, while it is obligatory only in compulsory liability insurance contracts.[284]

172. Simple negligence is a failure to exercise caution that would be employed by an exceptionally conscientious person, a person with above-average capabilities or a person professionally carrying out certain activities. It is general practice that simple negligence as a degree of fault in causing the insured event is covered by all types of insurance.[285]

173. Whether the interested party caused the insured event through gross or simple negligence or intentionally is established separately in each particular case.

IV. The Legality of Risk

174. One of the important elements of insurable risk is its legality. A legal risk is a risk not contrary to mandatory provisions, the public order and the ethical rules of a particular society. The risk needs to be legal in order to be covered by an effective insurance contract and to thus become an insurable risk. For instance, the coverage of risks intentionally caused by interested parties is expressly prohibited by law. This has already been discussed above. However, although there is no express provision in Serbian law prohibiting the conclusion of insurance contracts for the coverage of consequences to property of criminal, misdemeanour, disciplinary liability or liability in commercial offences, such insurance contracts would be contrary to the basic principles of public order, the purpose of sanctions, as well as to the listed types of liability aimed at personally effecting such actors. Ultimately, such insurance contracts would be contrary to the moral concepts of our society.[286]

175. Illegal risks need to be differentiated from excluded risks. While illegal risks cannot be covered by insurance because they are contrary to mandatory provisions, the public order and the ethical rules of a particular society, excluded risks

---

282. Marjanski, *Ugovor o osiguranju* (*Insurance Contract*), 21.
283. *Ibid.*
284. *Ibid.*
285. Marjanski, *Ugovor o osiguranju* (*Insurance Contract*), 21.
286. Marjanski, *Ugovor o osiguranju* (*Insurance Contract*), 22.

are permitted to be insured, but they are excluded from the insurance according to yielding statutory provisions, the rules of insurance or particular contractual provisions.[287]

§3. Risk Individualization

176. Risk individualization means the determination of the risk's important elements in a particular case. This is carried out through a number of elements necessary to determine the amount of risk transferred to the insurer. Three elements are necessary for risk individualization: the event itself, and the place and time of its occurrence.

177. Events consist of two elements: cause and effect. They may be individualized in three manners. First, they may be individualized through the effect itself regardless of causes (e.g., when the destruction of property is insured irrespective of the cause of destruction). Causes excluded by law or by the contract are not going to be covered in the above instance. Such risk determination is quite rare due to the fact that insurance companies almost never provide such a wide coverage. Second, risks are determinable according to the cause itself, irrespective of the consequences. For instance, when all damages, apart from those excluded by law or by the contract, caused by lightning are covered by the contract. The third way of individualization is when the risk is determined by both cause and effect. For example, death caused by working accidents is covered by personal insurance. The death caused by accident is the effect, while the working accident is the cause.[288]

178. The place of risk occurrence is also an element of its individualization. However, the determination of the risk's place makes sense only if the objects of insurance are persons or movable property. If the object of insurance is real property, the place of risk is always assumed. The place of risk occurrence has the gravest importance within carriage insurance. The particular journey covered by the insurer is always determined in such insurance types. In marine carriage insurance, the carrier ship is usually precisely determined, so that coverage is provided only for risks to the freight while on the particular ship.[289] Unless agreed otherwise or unless something to the contrary follows from the contractual provisions or the general or special rules of insurance, the insurer covers risks to the object of insurance, irrespective of where it is situated. As regards statutory provisions, they do not directly limit the place of a particular risk. A limitation can be provided for only indirectly, for instance, when the movement of a particular vehicle is limited by regulations in force. Infringement upon such limitations will free the insurer of its liability regardless of a contractual provision to the contrary. The situation of risk may have an influence on the object of insurance too. Thus it may be contracted that

---

287. *Ibid.*
288. Branko Jakaša, *Pravo osiguranja* (*Insurance Law*) (Zagreb: Informator, 1972), 121.
289. Jakaša, *Pravo osiguranja* (*Insurance Law*), 121.

all or a part of certain objects or persons in a particular place are going to be covered by the insurance contract. Once the objects or persons are not in the contracted place, they are not going to be covered by insurance.[290]

179. Time as an individualization element represents the time period in which the insurer assumes a particular risk. This element in most cases corresponds to the term of contract, for the insurer usually covers a risk for the duration of the insurance contract. However, the term of contract and the duration of coverage do not have to correspond.[291] For example, conclusion of an insurance contract on the future transport of merchandise. The contract enters into force at the time of its conclusion, while the insurer covers the risk only while the insured merchandise is being carried. Therefore, the coverage of risk may commence at a later time-point and end before contract expiry. The duration of contract is, however, the maximum period in which the risks are covered by the insurer. In particular insurance types, it is possible to cover risks that occurred prior to contract conclusion (so-called putative risks),[292] but it is never possible to cover risks occurring after the termination of the contractual obligation. The period of insurance coverage is sometimes provided for by mandatory provisions. If the period of insurance coverage is laid down by a contract, it can be determined or determinable. If the contract does not provide for anything in that matter, in the absence of mandatory statutory provisions, the insurer is going to be obliged to cover the risk for the entire duration of the contractual relationship. Furthermore, it is possible to contractually determine the precise day of commencement and end of risk coverage. It is also possible to lay down a condition, the fulfilment of which is necessary for the insurer's obligation relating to coverage to come about (e.g., from the point of premium payment). In particular cases, the duration of risk coverage may follow from the other two elements of individualization. For example, in warehousing, insurance risk coverage commences from the point of placing the merchandise into the warehouse, and it ends when the merchandise leaves the warehouse.

§4. Risk Modification

180. By means of insurance contracts the insurer covers the insured risks. However, it is inevitably possible that in the course of the contractual relationship the insured object becomes exposed to the same risks to a lower or higher extent, or even that the risk itself ceases to exist. The above instances are described as risk modifications. A modification may be expressed by the increase, decrease or termination of risk. Each of the above changes may be caused by the policyholder's will, the will of persons for whom policyholders are responsible, the will of third parties, chance or acts of God. The legal consequences of such modifications depend on

290. *Ibid.*, 122.
291. *See infra* nn. 210–212.
292. Such situations are present in marine insurance.

their causes.[293] Risk changes and their legal consequences are going to be discussed in detail in the part pertaining to the contracting parties' obligations.

§5. EXCLUDED RISKS

181. Excluded risks are risks not covered by the insurance contract. Excluded risks need to be differentiated from illegal risks. As already pointed out above, while illegal risks cannot be covered by insurance because they are contrary to mandatory provisions, the public order and the ethical rules of a particular society, excluded risks are permitted to be insured, but they are excluded from the insurance according to yielding statutory provisions, the rules of insurance or particular contractual provisions of the particular policy.[294] A risk may be excluded from insurance in three manners: through yielding statutory provisions, through the rules of insurance or through particular contractual provisions. When a risk is excluded through yielding statutory provisions, it is deemed that it is not covered by insurance unless the parties agreed otherwise. Such yielding provisions are laid down by the LO.[295] However, if an insurer wishes to be exempt from liability, the insurer shall prove that the damage is caused by some of these risks. Due to the fact that these are yielding statutory provisions, the risks comprised by them may be included in particular insurance contracts if so agreed by the parties. In practice such risks are insured for the payment of higher premiums. Apart from the exclusion of risks through yielding statutory provisions, insurers often exclude certain risks by means of the policy or the rules of insurance. If an insured event occurs as a consequence of an uncovered risk, the insurer is going to be exempt from its basic obligation from the insurance contract. Risks frequently excluded in such a manner have surfaced in business practice.[296] Otherwise, within insurance rules or policies risks may be defined in a positive manner through their description, and/or in a negative manner, by listing the risks not covered by insurance. Risk exclusion is never assumed; moreover, it needs to be provided for expressly and concretely.[297]

293. Marjanski, *Ugovor o osiguranju* (*Insurance Contract*), 25–26.
294. *See* LO, Arts 930, 931 and 952.
295. *See* LO, Art. 931, para. 2.
296. Apart from political and war risks, as well as risks stemming from natural properties or deficiencies of merchandise that are in the majority of legal systems excluded by means of yielding statutory provisions, through the provisions of policies or rules of insurance, categories often excluded from insurance include damages caused by nuclear energy, theft, etc.
297. *See* LO, Art. 953.

Chapter 3. Formation of the Insurance Contract

182. As with all other contracts, insurance contracts are concluded by the concurrence of expressed wills of the contracting parties. Serbian insurance law contains only a couple of provisions specially regulating the manner of insurance contract conclusion (LO, Articles 901–906). To all other issues not regulated by means of the above special provisions, the general rules of the LO on contract conclusion are applicable (LO, Articles 26–45).

§1. Offer and Acceptance of Offer

183. An offer is a proposal for entering into a contract made to a specific person and containing all essential constitutive elements of the contract, so that its acceptance would amount to the entering into contract.[298] Exceptionally, a proposal to conclude a contract made to an unspecified number of persons (general offer) and containing essential constitutive elements of contract envisaged by the proposal, is valid as an offer, unless something else follows from circumstances of the case or usage. The person making the offer to conclude a contract is the offerer. In insurance contracts, both the insurance contractor and the insurer may be the offerers depending on the circumstances of the particular case. In business practice, usually the insurance contractor (often the insured party itself) is the offerer when visiting the insurer's or its representative's offices. Due to the fact that insurance contractors do not normally know what all the essential elements of an insurance contract are, the offer is made by filling out a special form already drawn up by the insurer or its representative. However, the insurer may also take the role of the offerer. For instance, when the insurer or its representative visits potential policyholders and make offers for the conclusion of particular contracts. However, sending premium price lists or tariffs[299] presenting[300] or handing over general terms and conditions shall be considered only as an invitation to make an offer (Latin: *invitatio ad offerendum*). Furthermore, presenting and handing over general terms and conditions[301] does not constitute an offer due to the fact that these standard forms (usually printed on the policy) leave enough space for the negotiation of various, usually essential elements of insurance contracts (e.g., the insured sum, the object of insurance). In the same manner, the contractor may take up the offerer's role if in their reply to the received offer a modified[302] or a late acceptance[303] is made, or if a general offer is made to an indefinite number of persons containing all essential elements of the

298. *See* LO, Art. 30.
299. *See* LO, Art. 35, para. 1.
300. A great variety of their presentation is possible. Lately the presentation of an excerpt from the general terms and conditions on the insurer's web-page has been very popular.
301. The act of handing over the general terms and conditions to the future policyholder is one of the conditions for them to become constituent parts of the contract, but does not represent an offer on its own. For details *see supra* nn. 69–72 on general terms and conditions.
302. *See* LO, Art. 41, para. 1.
303. *See* LO, Art. 43, para. 1.

insurance contract,[304] if upon the invitation to offer of a certain person an offer is made or, for instance, if the contract is entered into by purchasing a ticket (accident insurance contracts of passengers in public transport, or baggage insurance).

184. In order for a particular expression of will to be considered an offer, certain requirements need to be met. The expression of will needs to be free (not made under threat, coercion, etc.) and serious[305] (intended for the conclusion of contract), simultaneously containing all essential contractual elements, made by an authorized person in a form prescribed for the particular contract type. It has been pointed out above that the essential elements of insurance contracts, in accordance with their nature, are the insurable risk, the insured event, the object of insurance, the premium and the insured sum (in contracts where the principle of compensation is not applicable). Apart from the above, the parties may condition the contract's full effect on other elements. These are considered essential elements according to the parties' will. In such instances the contract needs to contain these elements too.[306]

185. An offerer is bound by an offer meeting the requirements of contents and form. Consequently, the offer has certain legal effects for the offerer even before the acceptance unless the obligation to honour the offer is excluded, or unless such exclusion may be implied from the circumstances of the business transaction involved.[307] The offer's effect lies within the fact that the offerer is obliged to keep the offer under the offered circumstances until it is binding for the offerer, as well as to enter into the contract under the particular terms if the other contracting party accepts the offer in its entirety. The same is applicable for the insurance contractor and the insurer if they are the offerers, under the condition that the offer needs to be in writing if made by the insurance contractor.[308]

186. The following rules are in force regarding the time limit in which the offerer is bound by the offer. An offer with an indication of the time limit for its acceptance shall be binding on the offerer until the expiration of that time limit.[309] However, there is an exception to this rule when the offerer is an insurance contractor. A written offer made to an insurer to enter into a contract of insurance shall be binding on the offerer – unless he/she has determined a shorter time limit, for eight days after the offer has reached the insurer, and should medical examination be necessary, then in course of thirty days.[310] If, however, no time limit for accepting the offer has been set, the time in which the offerer is bound by the offer depends on the fact whether the negotiations are conducted between present or absent parties. In the

---

304. *See* LO, Art. 33.
305. *See* LO, Art. 28, para. 2.
306. They are usually provided for by general terms and conditions of the insurance. For example, an obligatory physician's report in life insurance contract with a physician's examination.
307. *See* LO, Art. 36, para. 1.
308. *See* Art. 901, para. 2.
309. *See* LO, Art. 37, para. 1.
310. *See* LO, Art. 901, para. 2.

event of negotiations between present parties,[311] the offer needs to be accepted immediately. On the contrary, it is deemed that the offer is rejected. An offer made to an absent person, without indication of the acceptance time limit, shall be binding for the offerer in the course of a period usually needed for the offer to reach the person offered, for his/her considering it, for making his/her decision, and for the answer confirming the acceptance to reach the offerer.[312] An exception to this is the already mentioned provision of Article 90 paragraph 2 LO.

187. The LO's general provisions are applicable regarding the possibility of offer revocation. An offer may be revoked only if the offeree receives the revocation prior to receiving the offer, or simultaneously with it.[313]

188. An acceptance is the other party's consent to conclude a contract. If the acceptance meets all necessary requirements it shall trigger the conclusion of contract. The following requirements need to be fulfilled in that regard: The offer needs to be accepted by an authorized person; the acceptance needs to correspond to the offer (primarily regarding its essential elements according to the nature of transaction and to the parties' will); it needs to be timely (a late acceptance is deemed a new offer); it must be given seriously, e.g., with the intent to enter into the contract; and it needs to be in the form provided by the law[314] or the parties. Silence of the offeree shall not mean the acceptance of an offer.[315] However, there is an exception to this rule when the offeree is an insurance contractor. If the insurer does not reject the offer made by the insurance contractor within a time limit shorter than eight days, or if a longer time limit or no time limits have been established, within eight days or, should medical examination be necessary, in course of thirty days,[316] and which offer does not differ from the usual terms under which insurance contracts are concluded by him/her, it shall be deemed that the offer has been accepted and the contract concluded.[317] In such case, the contract shall be considered as concluded at the moment of the offer reaching the insurer.[318] However, the insurance contractor's silence usually cannot be deemed as acceptance, unless certain additional requirements are met.[319]

§2. The Form of Insurance Contracts

189. The principle of informality of contract conclusion is applicable within Serbian commercial law. In order for a contract to be entered into, it is enough that the

311. Not only persons being physically present on the negotiations are considered as present parties, but also authorized persons talking over the telephone, etc.
312. *See* LO, Art. 36, para. 2.
313. *Ibid.*
314. *See* LO, Art. 38 and 901.
315. *See* LO, Art. 42, para. 1.
316. *See* LO, Art. 901, para. 2.
317. *See* LO, Art. 901, para. 3.
318. *See* LO, Art. 901, para. 4.
319. *See* LO, Art. 42, paras 3 and 4.

wills of contracting parties concur (the principle of consensuality), without limiting the contract's full effect with providing for a special form. However, there are certain exceptions to the principle of informality laid down the law providing for a special form necessary for the full legal effect of certain contracts (the *ad solemnitatem* form following from the law itself). Apart from the above, even if the law does not provide for a special form for the full legal effect of a certain contract type, the parties may stipulate such necessity (the *ad solemnitatem* form following from the parties' will).

190. Within the Serbian legal system insurance contracts fall into the category of contracts where there is an exception to the principle of informality provided for by the law and their full legal effect is dependent on a particular form. However, due to the fact that there are numerous exceptions to this rule, it cannot be stated that insurance contracts are in all instances formal contracts. The LO lays down that an insurance contract is concluded after the contracting parties have signed the insurance policy or the cover note.[320] It follows that an insurance contract is concluded only if the contracting parties sign the insurance policy or the cover note. Failing the above, such contracts will not have legal effect.[321] If a contract is considered formal, the general provisions on formal contracts shall be applicable.[322]

191. There are numerous exceptions to this rule. These exceptions may be provided for by the law or follow from the application of general provisions on the convalidation of contracts lacking the prescribed form. Statutory exceptions follow both from the LO's provisions, as well as the fact that the application of its provisions in case of particular insurance contract types is substantially limited. First, the LO (which introduced the principle of formality in insurance contracts) provides for cases when a contract is deemed to have been regularly concluded although the contracting parties did not sign a policy or a cover note. If a written offer is made to an insurer to enter into an insurance contract containing all the necessary elements, it shall be deemed that the insurer accepted the offer and the contract is concluded unless the insurer declines the offer within a period of eight days (or thirty days if medical examination is necessary).[323] Similarly, it may be set out in the rules of insurance that an insurance contract is concluded upon payment of the premium – the so-called real contract form.[324] Furthermore, the law indirectly allows departure from the provisions on the form of contract conclusion if this is in the obvious interest of the person insured.[325] The fast provision of coverage to the insured party is thus being promoted. Although the LO introduced the principle of formality of entering into insurance contracts, the application of its provisions is limited. In the part pertaining to sources of law, it has been mentioned that its provisions are not

320. *See* LO, Art. 901, para. 1.
321. *See* LO, Art. 70, para. 1.
322. *See* LO, Arts 68–72.
323. *See* LO, Art. 901, paras 2–3.
324. *See* LO, Art. 903.
325. *See* LO, Art. 900, para. 2.

applicable to marine insurance, credit insurance and reinsurance. The principle of informality (consensuality) is applicable within these domains. Of course, the full legal effect of contracts may be limited according to the parties' will in these contract types too. Finally, departure from the principle of formality is also possible according to the general rules of civil law. A contract, the conclusion of which is made dependent on a particular form shall be considered valid although not entered into in such form, after the contracting parties have performed, entirely or substantially, the obligations arising from such a contract, unless something else obviously follows from the purpose of prescribing the form.[326] This is a case of convalidation of contracts lacking the prescribed form.

192. However, in spite of the above exceptions to the principle of formality, insurance contracts are in 95% of cases entered into in a written form, through forms or policies, the contents and form of which are laid down in advance by the insurer according to the law. In cases of exceptions to the principle of formality in insurance contracts, the policy serves only to prove easily the existence and contents of the concluded contract.[327]

§3. Insurance Policies and Cover Note

I. The Insurance Policy

193. Among the great number of documents that could follow the conclusion of insurance contracts, the most important is the insurance policy.[328] Regardless of the fact whether an insurance contract is formal or not, the policy is a document that is usually issued upon the conclusion of insurance contracts. However, it is not possible to give a general definition of insurance policies for their features (functions) depend on statutory provisions, the insurance contract type and the function assigned to it by the parties.[329] Thus, insurance policies represent beyond doubt the most important evidence on the existence and the contents of the concluded contract, but they may also represent the obligatory form of insurance contracts conditioning their full legal effect (Latin: *ad solemnitatem*), identification of documents, debt instruments, while their presentation may serve as evidence on the performance of obligations (e.g., a purchase with a CIF clause (Cost Insurance Freight)) or the realization of rights from another legal transaction (e.g., payment by a documentary letter of credit). Due to the fact that there are numerous functions of insurance policies, the legal relevance of which is various, it is of utmost importance to

326. *See* LO, Art. 73.
327. Marjanski, *Ugovor o osiguranju* (*Insurance Contract*), 142.
328. A conclusion of an insurance contract may be followed by the issuance of numerous documents apart from the insurance policy, such as lists of coverage, certificates on the concluded insurance contract, cover notes, slips.
329. Special properties are usually assigned to it by the insurer. Therefore, the insurer may assign the property of a debt instrument to the policy, which is going to be discussed at a later point.

indicate all of these functions and explain their contents. Finally, after the analysis of insurance policies, the legal nature of these documents within the Serbian legal system is going to be presented.

A. *The Insurance Policy as Evidence*

194. It can be laid down with certainty for all policies that they are the most important but not always the only evidence on the existence and contents of insurance contracts. For the sake of higher transparency and greater accuracy, insurance policies are discussed as those proving the existence of contracts and those proving the contents of concluded contracts.[330]

195. Insurance policies may be the only or one of the evidences on the conclusion of insurance contracts.[331] If the insurance contract is informal, the policy is going to be one of the evidences of contract conclusion. In such cases, the contract conclusion may be proved by other evidence (cover notes, the correspondence between the insurer and the insured, orally, through witnesses, etc.). If the insurance contract is formal, the signed policy or cover note[332] represents the exclusive evidence on its existence, that is, the insurance contract has been entered into.

196. As regards the contents of insurance contracts, the policy is the most important but not the only evidence on the rights and obligations of contracting parties. This is due to the fact that apart from the policy provisions there are certain regulations in the general terms and conditions (general and/or special rules of insurance) which, along with the policy, represent constituent parts of the concluded contract. Similarly, provisions on the rights and obligations of contracting parties are also contained in other sources of law: statutory provisions, business practices and usages, for instance. It is practically impossible to cover all rights and obligations of the contracting parties by the insurance policy. However, this is not the only reason why the insurance policy is not the only evidence regarding the contents of the contract. Even if the insurance contract is formal (Latin: *ad solemnitatem*), subsequent verbal amendments regarding secondary matters not mentioned in the formal contract, shall be valid, unless contrary to the purpose of prescribing the form.[333] Subsequent verbal agreements, by means which obligations of one or the other party are reduced or discharged shall be valid, should the specific form be prescribed only in the interest of contracting parties.[334] A contract, for the conclusion of which a specific form is agreed upon (Latin: *ad solemnitatem* according to the parties' will) may also be amended or altered in some other way by an informal agreement.[335] Apart from the above, it needs to be pointed out that insurance poli

330. Marjanski, *Ugovor o osiguranju* (*Insurance Contract*), 144.
331. *Ibid.*
332. *See* LO, Art. 901.
333. *See* LO, Art. 67, para. 3.
334. *See* LO, Art. 67, para. 4.
335. *See* LO, Art. 69, para. 2.

cies represent refutable and not absolute pieces of evidence on the contents of the concluded contract. It is possible to prove that their contents are inaccurate. However, the party stating the contrary must substantiate such claims.

B. The Insurance Policy as the Form of Insurance Contracts

197. As already pointed out, insurance policies may take up the form of insurance contracts, either pursuant to statutory provisions or according to the will of the contracting parties. The LO treats insurance policies as forms on the concluded insurance contracts. The LO lays down that an insurance contract is concluded after the contracting parties have signed the insurance policy or the cover note.[336] As the application of the LO's provisions pertaining to insurance contracts is limited, this rule does not apply for all types of insurance contracts. However, in types of insurance where the application of Chapter XXVII LO is excluded, the contracting parties may accept the policy (or another type of document) as the written form conditioning the full legal effect of insurance contracts.[337]

198. In cases when the policy represents the form of contract (Latin: *ad solemnitatem*), the general provisions of contract law on formal contracts are applicable for them (Articles 68–72 LO).[338] Furthermore, the policy in such instances needs to have all the essential elements provided for by the law, for these are considered as constituent parts of the form. The absence of some of these elements will render the contract invalid. The LO provides for the elements that need to be indicated in insurance policies. These are the contracting parties, the insured object, or insured person (the object of insurance), the risk covered by insurance, the duration of insurance and the period of coverage, the amount of insurance or an indication that the insurance is unlimited, the insurance premium, the date of issuing the policy, and the signatures of contracting parties.[339] In addition to the elements constituent in every insurance policy, life insurance policies need to include the name and last name of the person whose life is insured, his/her date of birth and the event or time limit being a prerequisite for requesting payment of the amount insured.[340]

C. The Insurance Policy as an Identification Document

199. Identification papers are written documents containing a certain obligation of their issuer, and in most cases they are issued as bearer documents.[341] Their role is to identify the creditor within a legal transaction, and the principle of

336. *See* LO, Art. 901, para. 1.
337. Within marine insurance, as well as in other insurance types where the provisions pertaining to marine insurance are applicable, policies do not have the character of insurance contract forms, unless the parties agree otherwise. *See* LMIN, Art. 935, para. 3.
338. Šulejić, *Pravo osiguranja* (*Insurance Law*), 195.
339. *See* LO, Art. 902, para. 1.
340. *See* LO, Art. 943, para. 1.
341. O. Antić et al., *Leksikon građanskog prava* (*Civil Law Lexicon*), 313.

incorporation[342] is not applicable for them, just as with securities.[343] It is interesting, however, that according to the LO only non-transferable instruments are considered as identification documents.[344] Although identification documents are not primarily meant for transfer, such a provision may trigger an erroneous conclusion that transferable documents (such as an insurance policy) are not to be considered as identification documents. This does not have much sense, for all identification documents issued as bearer documents (not indicating the creditor's name) may always be transferred by simply handing them over (*traditio*). Insurance policies within the Serbian legal system are registered identification documents (the creditor is indicated). By means of insurance policies, persons having certain claims stemming from an insurance contract are identified towards the insurer.

200. Issuers (insurers) may, upon agreement with the insured party, however, enter an identification clause into insurance policies, after which a policy will take up a so-called quasi-negotiable function. By means of such clauses it is in fact made known that the obligation from the policy may be performed towards a certain person (indicated in the policy) or any other holder of the policy instead of the original person indicated (with a freeing effect).[345] By performance towards a bona fide holder of the policy (legal policyholder),[346] insurers shall be freed from their obligations. The insurer is not obliged to materially identify the holder of a policy having the quality of an identification paper. However, the insurer has the right to materially identify such a policyholder, despite the fact that all policyholders are formally authorized by bearing the policy itself to demand the performance indicated in the policy.

201. The conditions of commerce made it inevitable that identification clauses are entered into insurance policies for the purpose of their easier circulation (especially within transport insurance). Thus insurance policies, as already mentioned, may take up a so-called quasi-negotiable function. The transferability of insurance policies is, however, not 'real', that is, it is not the same as with real[347] securities. Namely, in the vast majority of cases, before an insured event comes about there is no real – independent negotiability (transferability) of policies free from the necessity of fulfilling certain requirements falling outside of their scope. This is one of the arguments against insurance policies being securities.[348] The subject issue is

342. The principle of incorporation applicable in securities means that the right indicated in the security may be realized only by means of possessing the security, as well as that such a right may be transferred by simultaneously transferring the security itself.
343. Jankovec, *Privredno pravo* (*Commercial Law*), 761.
344. *See* LO, Art. 257.
345. Šulejić, *Pravo osiguranja* (*Insurance Law*), 196. Within Serbian law life insurance policies may not be bearer policies.
346. The debtor shall be liable for damages if an obligation is performed towards a party for which it was known or should have been known that it is not a bona fide party and thus a legal bearer of an identification paper.
347. The term 'real securities' is used due to the fact that a viewpoint is present in literature, according to which insurance policies are securities in their wider sense (so-called quasi securities).
348. Marjanski, *Ugovor o osiguranju* (*Insurance Contract*), 146.

going to be addressed in detail within the title dedicated to the legal nature of insurance policies within the Serbian legal system.

D. *Insurance Policies as Debt Instruments*

202. Apart from the above functions, insurance policies normally have the characteristics of debt instruments. Policies are documents evidencing that the insurer (the issuer) is to perform the obligations listed in the policy under the condition that the insured event occurs. They in fact serve to the creditor as a proof on the existence of debt. Therefore, insurance policies, as all debt instruments, must be signed by their issuers (the insurer), that is, their agents. As all debt instruments can be divided into regular and qualified ones, the same applies to insurance policies. Without a special remark, a policy will have the character of only a regular debt instrument. Such a function grants the insurer the right to request its return upon termination of the insurance relationship.[349] The insurer is thus protected from potential further use of the policy as an eventual piece of evidence.[350] In case of policies as regular debt instruments, insurers may not postpone the fulfilment of their prestations until presentation of the policy if it evidently follows from other evidence that their obligation has become due.

203. As an exception, however, insurance policies may be qualified debt instruments. In case of policies as qualified debt instruments, insurers may postpone the fulfilment of their prestations until the policy or a decision on its amortization is presented to the insurer or until the insurer receives an adequate security from the insured party.[351] The insurer will not be deemed to be late with fulfilment until he/she is presented the policy or a decision on its amortization in case of the policy's loss.[352] However, such a situation needs to be agreed upon in advance (laid down in the policy). Should the insurer fulfil his/her obligation without the policy being presented to him/her, such a fulfilment usually does not have an exemptory function. This, however, does not mean that the insurer is not allowed to perform without the policy being submitted to him/her for inspection. The insurer may perform but is not obliged to do so. If the insurer makes the payment to an authorized person without inspecting the insurance policy, the insurer shall be exempted from his/her obligation.[353] The reason for this lies within the fact that insurance policies are not securities. The right indicated in the policy is not incorporated in it. Furthermore, the person receiving the payment is obliged to return the policy to the insurer. However, in case of payment pursuant to a policy having the character of a qualified debt instrument, the insurer is obliged to request its return so that it cannot be

349. Peter Schimikowski, *Versicherungs-vertragsrecht* (*Insurance Contract Law*) (München: Verlag C.H. Beck, 2004), 42.
350. *Ibid.*
351. *See* LMIN, Art. 935, para. 4.
352. Šulejić, *Pravo osiguranja* (*Insurance Law*), 196.
353. Veljko Tomašić, *Pravna priroda pomorske izvozne police* (*The Legal Nature of Marine Export Policies*) (Belgrade: Institut za uporedno pravo, 1961), 159.

transferred and used again in the capacity of a qualified debt instrument. Requesting the return of the policy is not only the insurer's right but also his/her obligation, for, on the contrary, the insurer is going to be obliged to pay damages caused by breaching the above duty (for instance, to the new bona fide policyholder). The interests of new creditors are thus protected in cases of assignment of claims stemming from insurance contracts. If only partial damages were incurred, a remark on the made payment is put on the policy. Once the policy is returned to the insurer a reversible presumption on the performed payment is created.[354]

204. Insurance policies as debt instruments (either regular or qualified) serve the interests of both contracting parties. They serve to the insurer as evidence on the authority of the request submitter. However, the insurance contractor is assured that, in the period of him/her being in possession of the policy, the insurer will not be exempted from his/her obligation by performance to a third, unauthorized party.

E. The Policy as Evidence on the Performance of Contractual Obligations or Evidence Necessary for the Realization of Rights from Other Legal Relationships

205. Insurance policies bear certain relevance not only from the viewpoint of insurance contracts but also from the aspect of other contractual relationships. Thus, insurance policies may serve as evidence on the performance of contractual obligations or evidence necessary for the realization of rights from other legal relationships. In sales contract with CIF clauses, for instance, the risk transfers from the seller to the buyer at the point of goods passing the ship's rail in the port of shipment.[355] This means the buyer bears the risk of loss or damage to the goods on the whole way of transport from the port of shipment to the port of destination. However, the seller has to procure marine insurance against the buyer's risk of loss or damage to the goods during the carriage. Once the seller (the insurance contractor) receives the policy from the insurer, by its presentation to the buyer (the insured party) he/she proves performance of one of his/her obligation under the sales contract. However, the insurance policy may serve as evidence necessary for the realization of rights from other legal relationships. Thus, for instance, the policy, along with other documents (certificates on the examination of goods, invoices, bills of lading, etc.), may serve as an inevitable document for substantiating one's rights from documentary letters of credit.[356]

---

354. Šulejić, *Pravo osiguranja* (*Insurance Law*), 196.
355. INCOTERMS 2000 (official rules for the interpretation of trade terms).
356. For details *see* Zoran Radović, 'Mesto osiguranja u dokumentarnom akreditivu' (The Place of Insurance within Documentary Letters of Credit), *Pravni život* 10 (2002), 1003–1011. And Stevan Šogorov, *Bankarsko pravo* (*Banking Law*) (Novi Sad: Poslovni biro, 2004), 218–224.

F. Insurance Policies as Security Devices

206. An insurance policy, more precisely, its pledging, may serve as a security device (for instance, in a loan agreement). A creditor fearing the early death of his/her debtor, by pledging the debtor's insurance policy with the creditor, the latter receives a security of performance from the debtor's insurance, should something happen to the former.[357] However, the right of pledging the policy before the occurrence of the insured event exists only in life insurance policies. The reason for this is that in life insurance the insured may effectively dispose of all rights stemming from the insurance contract even before the insured event occurs (the insurer may change the beneficiary, assign or transfer his rights or the beneficiary's rights, etc.). In case of pledging a life insurance policy the pledgee receives certain rights – the right to pay the premium, to request payment of the policy repurchase price if his/her claim secured by the policy is not settled upon maturity,[358] as well as to request payment of insurance compensations for the purpose of fulfilment of his/her secured claims. In other insurance contract types, it is not possible to pledge the policy before occurrence of the insured event. This is allowed after the insured event occurred, as with pledging all other matured claims.

G. The Legal Nature of Insurance Policies Within the Serbian Legal System

207. The right of compensation is not incorporated in the policy. It is based on the insurance contract and other facts connected with it, and not the policy itself.[359] However, a similar situation exists with other, so-called non-constitutive, causal securities (such as warehouse notes and bills of lading not appearing independently in legal transactions but always along with warehousing or marine carriage contracts). Therefore, the non-constitutive nature of rights is not per se a sufficient argument to differentiate insurance policies from such securities.[360] Due to the fact that the conditions of commerce made it inevitable that identification clauses are entered into insurance policies for the purpose of their easier circulation, because of their properties, in certain situations they are even closer to securities (particularly causal 'securities' – such as bills of lading or warehouse notes).[361]

208. Yet, in property insurance before an insured event comes about, there is no real – independent negotiability (transferability) of policies free from the necessity of fulfilling certain requirements falling outside of their scope. This is an important argument in favour of the opinion that insurance policies are not securities. In property insurance policies may not be transferred to any person, only to persons that

357. Šulejić, *Pravo osiguranja* (*Insurance Law*), 483.
358. *See* LO, Art. 954, para. 4.
359. For instance, if the policyholder acquires the right of ownership on the object of insurance and thus the insured interest as well.
360. Vladimir Marjanski, 'Funkcije polise osiguranja' (Insurance Policy Functions'), *Pravni život* 12 (2009), 888.
361. *Ibid.*

may also be insured parties. These are persons having at the moment of event occurrence a legally permitted material interest for the insurable risk not to occur on the object of insurance. Due to the above, property insurance policies may not be transferred independently, but only along with the object of insurance. The policyholder needs to prove the possession of the insured interest.[362] For this is a fact falling outside of the policy's scope, it is evident that insurance policies are not securities. After the occurrence of the insured event, there are no hindrances to the free transfer of the policy due to the fact that in such cases matured receivables are being transferred. However, because of the lack of incorporation of such receivables in the policy itself, such documents are not to be considered as securities. As opposed to property insurance, the transfer of life insurance policies is usually not limited by the necessity of fulfilling certain requirements falling outside of the policy's scope. A proof on the insured interest with the policyholder is not necessary; so it can be freely transferred even before the occurrence of the insured event. Yet, there are certain limitations in this regard as well. In case of life insurance in favour of third-party beneficiaries, beneficiaries may transfer their rights on the insured amount to third parties even before the insured event has occurred. However, the written consent of the insurance contractor is necessary in order to effectuate such a transaction (again a condition falling outside of the policy's scope). The name of the person to whom the right is transferred needs to be indicated in the written consent, and should the insurance relate to the life of another person, the same consent is necessary from that person as well.[363] Apart from the above, life insurance policies in Serbia may be made out to a specific person or to order.[364] They may be transferred exclusively by means of a full endorsement[365] containing an indication of the name of the beneficiary, the date of endorsing and the signature of the endorser.[366] However, regardless of the type of insurance contract and whether the policy is to be transferred by a simple handover (in case of bearer policies)[367] or by means of an endorsement (in case of policies transferable by order), whether they are transferable before or after the occurrence of the insured event, both transfer types have the effect of assignment. The right itself is not incorporated in the policy, so that all objections based on the insurance contract that the insurer (the policy issuer) might make towards the insurance contractor (objection of insurance premium non-payment, non-occurrence of the insured event, etc.) may also be expressed towards legitimate third-party policyholders. Finally, upon request of the contractor the policyholder must demonstrate the underlying facts of his/her creditor rights (the claims). With securities (e.g., warehouse notes, bills of lading), however, the issuer is responsible *ex scriptura* towards third-party legitimate holders of the security. The issuer (apart from the situation that the security holder acts in bad faith) may not make an objection that would have been substantiated towards the holder's legal successor that transferred the document to the new holder by means of a handover

362. For details on the insurance interest in damage insurance *see* Vladimir Marjanski, 'Interes u odštetnom osiguranju' (Interest within Damage Insurance), *Pravo i privreda* 5–8 (2006), 823–833.
363. *See* LO, Art. 962.
364. *See* LO, Art. 943, para. 2.
365. Endorsements are acts aimed at the transfer of securities transferable by order.
366. *See* LO, Art. 943, para. 3.
367. This is the case in transport insurance, for instance.

or an endorsement. The burden of proof regarding the opposite, as well as the bad faith of the security holder lies with the issuer. Due to the fact that insurance policies do not have such characteristics, this is another argument in favour of insurance policies not being securities in Serbian law. Furthermore, a life insurance contractor has the right to repurchase the policy.[368] If such a contractor requests payment of the policy repurchase value based on the above right, the rights of beneficiaries and all other policyholders to insurance compensations shall cease to exist. Similarly, an insurance contractor may, under certain exceptions, revoke the policy provision transferring the insurance benefit to a particular person. There are no such possibilities in case of securities. A legitimate holder of a security cannot be deprived of his/her rights from the security. Due to all of the above, we hold the view that insurance policies are not securities within the Serbian legal system. They are identification documents identifying the policyholder as the holder of certain claims towards the insurer. The contents of such claims are, however, determined by the effects of particular insurance contracts.

II. The Cover Note

209. Cover notes are documents issued when some elements necessary to draw up a policy are failing. The LO lays down that an insurance contract is concluded after the contracting parties have signed the insurance policy or the cover note.[369] Therefore, an insurance policy may be temporarily substituted by a cover note, which shall include the essential constituent elements of contract.[370] Cover notes may have various functions. First, they are certificates on the definitely concluded insurance contract (they may be subsequently substituted by insurance policies but the coverage is effective from the day following the date of cover note issuance). Second, cover notes may be temporary agreements between the insurance contractor and the insurer's agent until the final offer acceptance is received. If approved by the insurer, the issuance of a policy substitutes the cover note, and it shall be a final confirmation on contract conclusion. If the essential elements of the policy correspond to the cover note, it shall be deemed that the contract had been entered into at the moment of signing the cover note by the insurance contractor and the insurer's agent. Thus both material (insurance coverage) and technical (obligation of premium payment) aspects of the contract are effective. If the essential elements do not correspond, the policy shall be considered a new offer made by the policy issuer to the earlier offerer (the insurance contractor).

368. *See* LO, Art. 954.
369. *See* LO, Art. 901, para. 1.
370. *See* LO, Art. 902, para. 2.

§4. The Moment of Contract Conclusion and the Commencement of Its Effects

I. The Moment of Contract Conclusion

210. Special rules are applicable for the moment of insurance contract conclusion. If insurance contracts are entered into in a formal manner, it is deemed that an insurance contract is concluded after the contracting parties have signed the insurance policy or the cover note.[371] If the conditions for concluding a contract by the insurer's inactivity are met, that is, when the insurer's failure to respond to the insured party's offer is deemed as acceptance, the contract shall be considered as concluded at the moment of the offer reaching the insurer (acceptance theory).[372] The same applies in compulsory insurance. An offer made to the insurer may not be declined if the conclusion of such contracts falls within the scope of the insurer's regular business operations. Finally, if the terms of insurance provide for such a possibility, it is possible to enter into an insurance contract by premium payment.[373] Apart from the above cases typical for insurance contracts, according to the general rules of Serbian contract law, a contract shall be entered into at the moment when the offerer (the insurance contractor or the insurer) acknowledges the statement of the offeree accepting the offer (acceptance theory).[374]

II. The Commencement of the Insurance Contract's Effects

211. The commencement of a contract's effects needs to be differentiated from the moment of its conclusion. The issue of effects commencement is one of the most intricate dilemmas within contractual insurance law. Although in other contracts the moment of contract conclusion usually corresponds to the commencement of its effects, in insurance contracts this in most instances is not the case, which is one of the specificities of insurance contracts. In this respect it is necessary to differentiate between the moment of formal contract conclusion from its technical and material effects.

212. The technical commencement of effects is connected with the moment of the insurance contractor becoming bound to pay the insurance premium.[375] The material commencement of effects is connected with the start of insurance coverage (insurance protection). The start of insurance coverage primarily depends on the details of the contract itself. Statutory provisions are usually of a yielding character in this regard and are to be applied if the contract does not provide a regulation in this regard. The insurer's general terms and conditions (within the framework of

371. *See* LO, Art. 901, para. 1.
372. *See* LO, Art. 901, para. 4.
373. *See* LO, Art. 903.
374. *See* LO, Art. 31, para. 1 and Art. 39, para. 1.
375. Schimikowski, *Versicherungsvertragsrecht* (*Insurance Contract Law*), 60.

general and special terms of insurance) sometimes contain special rules on this subject.[376] Such provisions are normally very similar to those contained in laws. However, the commencement of insurance coverage is in insurance contracts often made dependent on the prior premium payment. Thus the insurance coverage starts to be effective at the moment of premium payment or at a particular later point in time. The insurance contractor, according to the 'principle of buy-off' buys the commencement of the insurance coverage's effects by means of paying the premium. If the premium is not paid until the occurrence of the insured event, the insurer is not going to be obliged to meet his/her basic contractual duty (compensation), even if the insured event did come about. Before premium payment, there is no valid insurance coverage, so that the contract's effects for the insurer are postponed.

213. If the start of insurance coverage is not contractually[377] regulated, the yielding statutory provisions shall be applicable. These provisions contain different solutions on the commencement of insurance coverage depending on the contract type. However, in all these contractual provisions the moment of contract conclusion is differentiated from the commencement of its material effects.[378] The underlying reasons for such a distinction are of a practical nature. Namely, it is possible that the insured event occurs on the day of contract conclusion. Due to this, certain difficulties may come about regarding the proof of the insured event's occurrence, which may at the same time be exploited by a contracting party acting in bad faith.[379] Such problems are solved by means of drawing a line and precisely establishing the commencement of insurance coverage. The general assumption of civil law on the correspondence of the moment of a contract's material effects with the moment of its conclusion are applicable only in rare instances when special regulation is not provided by contractual or yielding statutory provisions. If the periods of coverage are followed by one another, this issue does not have much practical relevance. If the insured event occurs on the very day of the new contract's conclusion, the policyholder is going to be covered based on the earlier insurance contract, the effect of which expires only at the end of that day.[380]

376. For instance, in livestock insurance contracts a specific waiting period is usually established lasting from contract conclusion to a particular moment (for instance twenty-one days from contract conclusion), after which the insurance coverage will start to be effective (from 0.00 hours of the day following the expiry of the waiting period). For detailed examples on various regulations of material coverage within general terms and conditions *see* Šulejić, *Pravo osiguranja* (*Insurance Law*), 207–208.
377. Contracts in their wider sense, the constituent parts of which are general terms and conditions.
378. *See* LO, Art. 913, 922, para. 1, LMIN, Art, 747, para. 1, Art. 776, para. 1, etc.
379. Šulejić, *Pravo osiguranja*, 206.
380. Jankovec, *Privredno pravo*, 586.

Chapter 4. Obligations of the Insured

214. Within Serbian insurance law, a difference is made between the insurance contractor, the insured, the insured party and the insurance beneficiary.

215. An insurance contractor is a person entering into an insurance contract on his/her own behalf incurring the obligation to pay the insurance premium to the insurer. An insurance contractor will at the same time have the capacity of an insured if the insurance contract is concluded in the contractor's name and on his/her behalf. In the course of the discussions on the obligations of the contracting parties the term insurance contractor shall be used, for it describes the contracting party entering into the insurance contract and incurring certain obligations towards the insurer.

216. An insured is a person, regardless of the fact whether he/she is the insurance contractor or not, having the rights from the insurance contract. The insurance rights in types of insurance where the principle of compensation is applied may pertain only to persons having material interest that the insured event does not take place at the moment of occurrence of damage.[381]

217. As opposed to the term 'insured', which is used both in property, as well as personal insurance, the term 'insured party' is only used within the insurance of persons. An insured party is the person whose certain personal categories (e.g., life, health, physical integrity) are insured by means of an insurance contract. The term 'insured party' is not exactly the same as the term 'insured' due to thc fact that such persons do not always enjoy rights from the insurance contract. An insured party may conclude a contract on the insurance of his/her personal assets (life, physical integrity, health) in his/her own name and on his/her own behalf if he/she is simultaneously the insured. Yet, it is possible that such persons in the capacity of insurance contractors denominate a beneficiary, which is usually the case of life insurance contracts for the event of death. In such instances the insured party does not have the capacity of an insured due to the fact that the rights from the insurance contract do not pertain to him/her, but to the insurance beneficiary. Finally, a situation may come about in practice where the insured party has the capacity neither of an insurance contractor nor of an insured. Namely, an insurance contract may be concluded against death or insurance of a third party, whereby this possibility is limited by the necessity of fulfilling certain conditions in order to exclude the possibility of speculations over personal assets.[382]

218. Insurance beneficiary is a term used within the field of personal insurance.[383] Insurance beneficiaries are persons, in favour of whom personal insurance contracts are entered into. This means that the insurance beneficiary will acquire certain rights after the occurrence of the insured event. Although they have certain

---

381. *See* LO, Art. 924, para. 2.
382. *See* LO, Arts 946–947.
383. *See* LO, Arts 957–965.

rights from the insurance contract, in order to implement them, in most personal insurance contracts, that is, those where the principle of compensation is not applicable (for instance, life insurance contracts), the existence of an insured event is not necessary.

§1. Description of Risk

219. Within Serbian insurance law, the duty of risk description is made of two obligations:

(1) the obligation to report to the insurer, at the conclusion of the contract, all circumstances which are material in assessing the risk, and which were known, or could not have been unknown;[384] and
(2) the obligation to notify the insurer on the changes of risk in the course of insurance coverage.[385]

The above two obligations differ according to the legal consequences of their non-fulfilment.

I. The Obligation to Report Circumstances Material for Risk Assessment

220. A person concluding the insurance shall be obliged to report to the insurer, at the conclusion of the contract, all circumstances which are material in assessing the risk, and which were known, or could not have been unknown, to him/her. By means of insurance contracts, certain security is provided against the consequences of various risks. Coverage of particular risks is sometimes impossible due to diverse reasons. Their coverage may transcend the capacities of particular insurers.[386] Furthermore, certain eventual insurance subjects (persons or goods) may not be covered by an insurance contract. Therefore it is inevitable that the insurance contractor, at the moment of entering into the contract, reports all circumstances relevant for risk assessment. Thus the insurer may provide coverage against the risk (in the extent suitable) or simply decline the offer to conclude the contract.

221. The information on circumstances relevant for risk assessment is usually contained in the insurance contractor's offer, which is normally drawn up by filling in the insurer's ready-made questionnaire. The questionnaire substantially narrows the number of facts necessary for reporting by the insured, but this does not exclude the insurance contractor's obligation (and the obligation of other persons in accordance with Article 910 LO) to report other facts, the importance of which is known to him/her, although they are not mentioned in the questionnaire.[387] The fact of

384. *See* LO, Art. 907.
385. *See* LO, Art. 914.
386. This problem is sometimes solvable by means of the so-called horizontal or vertical equalization of risks, that is, mutual insurance or reinsurance.
387. Jovanović, *Osiguranje u privredi* (*Commercial Insurance*), 84.

importance of factors that need to be reported depends on the circumstances of each particular case. These are circumstances existing at the moment of contract conclusion having an effect to the extent of risk and were known to the insurance contractor, but the insurer was not aware of them nor was he/she obliged to be aware of them at the point of contract conclusion.[388] It shall be deemed that the insurance contractor met his/her obligation if such circumstances were completely and correctly reported to the insurer. The legal consequences (sanctions) of failing to fulfil the above duty depend on the fact whether the insurance contractor (and other persons) acted in good or bad faith.[389]

222. First, if an insurance contractor makes an incorrect application or omits to supply necessary information unintentionally, the insurer may, at his/her own choice, within one month after becoming aware of the incorrectness or incompleteness of the application, state that he/she is terminating the contract, or propose an increase of the insurance premium, proportionally to the higher risk involved.[390] If the insurance contractor does not accept the insurer's offer on the premium increase, the insurance contract shall be terminated. When the insurer requests contract termination for the above reasons, the contract shall be terminated on the expiration of fourteen days from the day of the insurer's notifying the insurance contractor on the cancellation, while in the case of the insurer's proposal for insurance premium increase, the termination shall take effect on the ground of law, should the insurance contractor fail to accept the proposal within the fourteen-day period after being notified about it.[391] In case of termination, the insurer shall be obliged to restitute the part of insurance premium relating to the remaining share of the insurance period.[392] A special rule is applicable if the case covered by insurance takes place prior to establishing the incorrectness or incompleteness of the application, or after that but prior to the rescission, or prior to reaching an agreement on the premium increase. In such instances the compensation shall be reduced proportionally between the rate of the paid insurance premiums and the rate of insurance premiums which would have been payable according to the real risk.[393]

223. If, however, an insurance contractor acts in bad faith, that is, should a person concluding the insurance deliberately file an incorrect application, or intentionally suppress circumstances being of a nature which would induce the insurer, if he/she knew the real situation, not enter into the contract, the insurer shall be entitled to seek nullity of the contract. The insurer may also request from the court to annul the contract if the incorrectness of reporting is established after the occurrence of the insured event.[394] As opposed to the general rules applicable to contract annulment, in the above situation the insurer shall keep the collected insurance premiums, and, if premiums have not been paid, shall be entitled to claim payment of

388. Evident facts do not have to be subjects of notification.
389. *See* LO, Art. 909, para. 1.
390. *Ibid.*
391. *See* LO, Art. 909, para. 2.
392. *See* LO, Art. 909, para. 3.
393. *See* LO, Art. 909, para. 4.
394. Jankovec, *Privredno pravo* (*Commercial Law*), 571.

the premium for the insurance period within which he/she has requested the nullity of contract.[395] This is a type of sanction towards mala fide insurance contractors. An insurer who, at the moment of entering into contract, was aware, or could not have been unaware, of circumstances relevant for assessing the risk, which were incorrectly notified or suppressed by the insurance contractor, will not be able to invoke the incorrectness of the application or the fact of suppression.[396] The same applies if the insurer becomes aware of these circumstances in course of the insurance period, but fails to use his/her legal rights.[397] The insurer's right to request insurance contract annulment shall be terminated if within a three-month period from the day of his/her becoming aware of the incorrectness of the application or of suppressing the facts, he/she fails to notify the person concluding the insurance of his/her intention to use such a right.[398]

224. The general rules on the reporting duty of facts relevant for risk assessment and the consequences of failure to report apply accordingly in life insurance, but the specificities of this insurance type made it necessary to specially regulate the duty of reporting of important circumstances. In this insurance type, the age of the insured person is of particular relevance when entering into contracts. This circumstance might be important for delivering a decision on contract conclusion by the insurer or assessing the severity of risk. Therefore, apart from the general consequences of fraud or suppression of facts relevant for risk assessment, special rules apply in case of filing an incorrect report regarding age in life insurance contracts. A life insurance contract shall be void, and the insurer shall be obliged in any case to repay all received premiums, should at the moment of its conclusion the age of the insured person be incorrectly stated, while his/her real age exceeded the limit up to which the insurer, by his/her terms and tariffs, normally enters into life insurance transactions.[399] Should it be incorrectly reported that the insured person is of a lower age, but his/her real age does not exceed the limit up to which the insurer normally enters into life insurance transactions, the contract shall be valid, but the insured amount shall be reduced in proportion to the stipulated insurance premium and the insurance premium provided for the life insurance of a person of the age of the insured person.[400] Finally, should the insured person be of lower age than reported in the application to enter into contract, the insurance premium shall be reduced by a corresponding amount, while the insurer shall be obliged to repay the difference between the insurance premiums received and the premiums he/she is entitled to.[401]

395. *See* LO, Art. 908, para. 2.
396. *See* LO, Art. 911, para. 1.
397. *See* LO, Art. 911, para. 2.
398. *See* LO, Art. 908, para. 3.
399. *See* LO, Art. 944, para. 1.
400. *See* LO, Art. 944, para. 2.
401. *See* LO, Art. 944, para. 3.

II. The Obligation to Report Changes Within Circumstances Relevant for Risk Assessment

225. Risk is one of the most important elements for establishing the amount of premium. Therefore, it is evident that a certain proportion exists between the premium established in the course of contract conclusion and the severity of risk. If the circumstances relevant for risk assessment change, it is inevitable that the previously determined premium also needs to be modified because the amount of risk increased or decreased in the meantime. In such situations, it is necessary to determine the circumstances, the change of which needs to be reported by the insurance contractor. In property insurance, an insurance contractor shall be obliged to notify the insurer of every change in circumstances which may be relevant for assessing the risk, and in case of life insurance, only if the risk has increased because the insured party has changed his/her occupation.[402] It needs to be pointed out that the provisions concerning the consequences of incorrect application or of suppressing circumstances relevant for assessing the risk also apply in cases of insurance concluded on behalf and for the account of another, or to the benefit of a third party, should such persons be aware of the application's incorrectness or of suppressing the circumstances relevant for the assessment of risk.[403]

226. An insurance contractor is obliged to notify the insurer without delay of the increase in risk should the risk be increased by an act on his/her part,[404] and should the increase of risk take place without the contractor's participation, he/she shall be obliged to notify the insurer accordingly within fourteen days after becoming aware of the fact.[405] Therefore the manner of risk increase is exclusively relevant for the deadlines of performing the above obligations. However, the LMIN assigns the greatest importance to this circumstance. It contains the following solutions: 'a change in risk after the conclusion of an insurance contract that occurs independently from the insured's will has no effect on the importance of insurance and the parties' obligations'.[406] However, should as a result of the insured's activities or with his/her consent come to substantial risk increase, the insurer shall not be obliged to pay damages attributable to such changes in risk.[407]

227. In case of insurance contracts not falling within the scope of the LMIN's application, the legal consequences depend on the fact whether the insurance contractor performed his/her obligation, that is, whether he/she notified the insurer on the changed circumstances, as well as on the fact, whether the changed circumstances induced risk increase or reduction.

402. *See* LO, Art. 914, para. 1.
403. *See* LO, Art. 910.
404. A change in the insured person's profession is always deemed as his/her own act.
405. *See* LO, Art. 914, para. 2.
406. *See* LMIN, Art. 749, para. 1.
407. *See* LMIN, Art. 749, para. 2.

A. Legal Consequences in Case of Risk Increase

228. First, if insurance contractors (or parties having the same obligations) fulfil their obligation and notify the insurer on the change within the said circumstance, the legal consequences, that is, the insurer's rights are going to depend on the scope of increased risk. Should the increase in risk be of such scope that the insurer would not have concluded the contract if such situation had existed at the time of its conclusion, he/she shall be entitled to terminate the contract.[408] In such cases the contract shall be terminated from the moment when the insurer notifies the insurance contractor on the fact of repudiation. No notice period is prescribed for such termination. It only has a future (*ex nunc*) effect. A corresponding coverage shall cease to exist from the date of termination, while the insurance contractor is going to be entitled to request from the insurer to restitute the part of insurance premium relating to the remaining share of the insurance period.[409] If the increase in risk is of such scope that the insurer would have concluded the contract with an increased premium, he/she shall be entitled to propose a new rate for the insurance premium.[410] If the insurance contractor accepts the new premium rate, the increase shall be effective from the day of such acceptance. An insurance contractor is entitled, however, to decline such an increase. This is an essential element of contracts, for the amendment of which the consent of both parties is required. Therefore, if the insurance contractor declines the new rate of premium within a fourteen-day time limit after being notified on the proposal of the new rate, the contract shall be terminated on the ground of law.[411] But the contract shall remain valid, and the insurer shall no longer avail himself/herself of the right to propose a new rate of insurance premium to the contractor of insurance or to terminate the contract, if he/she fails to materialize such rights within a one-month time limit from the day of his/her becoming aware, by whatever means, of the increase in risk or if, even prior to the expiration of such time limit, he/she shows in some way his/her consent to the continuation of contract (by accepting payment of the premium, by paying the compensation for a case covered by insurance, which case has taken place after the increase of risk, and the like).[412]

229. If an insurance contractor (or another party having the same obligation)[413] fails to fulfil their obligation to notify the insurer on the changes in the described circumstances, the consequences of such non-fulfilment are going to be dependent on the scope of risk increase. First, if the insured event occurs before the insurer was notified on the risk increase, the compensation shall be reduced proportionately to the premiums already paid and those which would have to be paid according to the increased risk.[414] In such instances, the risk increase is such that it is still possible to determine the proportion between the rate of the paid insurance premiums

---

408. *See* LO, Art. 914, para. 3.
409. Analogous application of LO, Art. 909, para. 3.
410. *See* LO, Art. 914, para. 4.
411. *See* LO, Art. 914, para. 5.
412. *See* LO, Art. 914, para. 6.
413. *See* LO, Art. 910.
414. *See* LO, Art. 915.

and the rate of insurance premiums which would have been payable according to the increased risk. A parallel can be drawn between the above situation and the situation when the insurer is notified on the risk increase but the case covered by insurance takes place prior to contract termination or reaching an agreement with the insurance contractor regarding the insurance premium increase.[415] If, however, the risk increase is of such an extent that it is impossible to determine the proportion between the paid premium and the premium eventually payable for the increased risk, and the insurance contractor was aware or could not have been unaware of such circumstances, the insurer is not going to be obliged to pay any compensation. On the contrary, if the insurance contractor was unaware or could not have been aware of such a risk increase, he/she must not suffer any negative consequences. In such situations, it cannot be said that the insurance contractor did not meet his/her contractual obligations, so that the insurer shall be obliged to pay the compensation without any deductions.

B. Legal Consequences in Case of Risk Reduction

230. As opposed to the above, it can come to a reduction in risk due to changed circumstances. Should after entering into contract of insurance, a reduction of risk take place, the insurance contractor shall be entitled to demand a corresponding reduction of the insurance premium, counting from the day of his/her notifying the insurer of such risk reduction.[416] This is not, however, an obligation of the insurance contractor but his/her right. In such cases, the insurer may accept or decline the insurance contractor's request. If the insurer accepts such an offer, the premium shall be reduced from the moment when the insurance contractor notified the insured on the changed circumstances. The reduction has a future and not a retroactive effect. The insurer, however, is not obliged to accept the insurance contractor's request to reduce the premium. This is an essential contractual element, the change of which requires the consent of both parties. In such instances, the insurance contractor is entitled to terminate the contract.[417] In case of termination, the insurer shall be obliged to restitute the part of insurance premium relating to the remaining share of the insurance period. According to the LMIN, a different rule is applicable. Should, as a result of the insured's activities or with his/her consent, come to substantial risk improvement, the insurer shall not be obliged to return to the insured a proportional part of the premium, that is, to proportionally reduce the premium.[418]

415. *See* LO, Art. 915.
416. *See* LO, Art. 916, para. 1.
417. *See* LO, Art. 916, para. 2.
418. *See* LMIN, Art. 749, para. 2.

§2. PAYMENT OF PREMIUM

I. General Considerations

231. The premium is the insurance contractor's consideration consisting of the sum of money paid to the insurer as the price of insurance. The premium is simultaneously part of the insurer's total fund from which compensations are covered. Insurance premiums may be paid as single (one-time) or continuous (regular) premiums. Single premiums are paid in total for the whole period of insurance. If nothing to the contrary is agreed upon, premiums are payable in total for the whole period of insurance. If the premium is payable in a single payment, it shall be payable upon entering into the contract.[419] Regular premiums are paid successively over the period of insurance. In case of regular premiums, the first premium needs to be differentiated from all other premiums. Stipulating the obligation of a single premium is a substantially rarer occurrence in practice. Such provisions are present mostly in short-term insurance contracts.[420] In the majority of other insurance contracts a continuous payment of premiums within the contracted time limits is provided for. In insurance contracts for an indefinite period of time, a one-time premium payment is impossible due to the nature of such affairs where the contract period is unknown and thus the single premium indeterminable.[421]

232. The parties may assign a different degree of importance to the payment of the single or the first insurance premium. Namely, it is possible that the parties provide for a real character of insurance contracts. This means that a contract shall be deemed as concluded at the moment of premium payment.[422] If the contracting parties assign such a character to premium payment, the insurance contract will not be deemed concluded until the single premium or the first premium is paid. In the given case, the formal effects of contract will depend on the fact of premium payment.[423] Should, however, a potential insurance contractor not pay the premium, the insurer will not be entitled to request payment for the insurance contract that has not yet been entered into. It shall be deemed in such cases that in case of premium non-payment, the potential contractor withdrew from concluding the contract.

233. If no real form of contract has been provided for, the commencement of insurance coverage will normally depend on the payment of the single or first premium. The legal consequences of not paying the single or first premium depend primarily on the manner of determining the maturity of insurance premiums, but also on the fact whether the commencement of insurance coverage is conditioned on the payment of the single or first premium.[424]

419. *See* LO, Art. 912, para. 2.
420. For instance, baggage insurance contracts.
421. Marjanski, *Ugovor o osiguranju* (*Insurance Contract*), 209.
422. *See* LO, Art. 903.
423. *See supra* n. 227.
424. Marjanski, *Ugovor o osiguranju* (*Insurance Contract*), 209.

234. Should it be stipulated that the insurance premium is to be paid on entering into contract, the duty of the insurer to pay compensation or the amount specified by contract shall commence on the day following the day of payment of insurance premium.[425] Therefore, if the contracting parties opt for such a regulation regarding the payment maturity of the single or first premium, they simultaneously choose that the insurance coverage is dependent on payment. If the premium is to be paid as a lump sum, it is payable upon entering into the contract.[426] It follows from the previous two provisions that in case of single premium payments, the commencement of the contract's material effects (the insurance coverage) is conditioned on the payment of premium. Therefore, if the insurance contractor incurred the obligation to pay the premium upon entering into the contract (regardless of the fact whether this is a single or a first premium), the insurance coverage will not be effective until he/she meets such an obligation. This means that the insurer will not be obliged to pay compensation or the contracted amount in respect of insured events occurring after contract conclusion but before premium payment.[427] Conclusively, in such instances the contractor will not have a special interest to request the termination of the insurance contract. However, due to the fact that the obligation of premium payment is incurred at the moment of contract conclusion, the insurer will usually be entitled to judicially seek insurance payment from the contractor, but only for the future period of insurance.[428]

235. Should it, however, be stipulated that the insurance premium is to be paid after entering into contract, the duty of the insurer to pay the compensation or the amount specified by contract shall commence from the day determined in the contract as the day of commencement of insurance.[429] Such a provision regarding maturity is possible only in case of regular insurance premiums.[430] Thereby the commencement of insurance coverage may be made dependent on the payment of the first premium. If the commencement of insurance coverage is made dependent on the payment of the first premium payable at a certain moment after entering into the contract, in case of non-payment the same legal consequences shall be applicable as in the case if the premium had been payable upon entering into the contract. In both cases there is no valid insurance coverage before premium payment, so that the contract's effects for the insurer are postponed. The question of the insurance contractor's obligations regarding insurance payment arises at this point (technical effects of the contract). Although the insurance contractor's obligations stem from the concluded insurance contract, the view that they have a retroactive effect cannot be accepted. A claim for insurance premium payment for periods not covered would be contrary to the principle of causality in mutually binding contracts entered into for a consideration.[431] The part of the paid premium between contract

425. *See* LO, Art. 913, para. 1.
426. *See* LO, Art. 912, para. 2.
427. Slobodan Perović & Dragoljub Stojanović, *Komentar Zakona o obligacionim odnosima, knjiga II* (*Commentary to the Law on Obligations, Book II*) (Kragujevac: Kulturni centar, 1980), 807.
428. The insurer does not have this right only in life insurance contracts.
429. *See* LO, Art. 913, para. 2.
430. Single premiums are always payable upon entering into the contract.
431. Šulejić, *Pravo osiguranja* (*Insurance Law*), 209.

conclusion and the moment of payment would be without a consideration. Therefore, the request for premium payment can only be justified for a period where the insurer was responsible for covering the risk, that is, for the future.

236. If it is stipulated that the premium payment shall be due after contract conclusion, whereby the material effects of the contract are not made dependent on premium payment,[432] in case of non-fulfilment the following legal consequences shall be applicable. Should the insurance contractor fail to pay the premium that became due after entering into the insurance contract, no legal consequences shall apply automatically. There is going to be no suspension of insurance coverage (that commenced at an earlier point). Should the insurer want to avail himself/herself of the right to terminate the insurance contract due to premium non-payment, it is necessary to notify the insurance contractor by means of a registered letter on the consequences of non-fulfilment regarding premium payment. A subsequent time limit for premium payment needs to be left for the insurance contractor.[433] According to the LO such a time limit amounts to thirty days from the service of the insurer's registered notice to the insurance contractor. The subsequent time limit for insurance payment may not be shorter than thirty days from the premium becoming due. Therefore, even if the insurer's registered notice is served to the insurance contractor before the premium becomes due, the insurance contractor will have a window of thirty days from the maturity of the premium to perform his/her obligation.[434] The insurance coverage will be effective during this subsequent time limit for payment. This means that the insurer is going to be obliged to pay compensation should the insured event occur in the subject period. Apart from the possibility to claim premium payment becoming due after contract conclusion and the right to terminate the contract, an insurer is always entitled to claim default interests from the day of the premium becoming due. A debtor being late in the performance of a pecuniary obligation shall owe, in addition to the principal amount a default interest.[435] Apart from the right to claim default interest, under certain circumstances the insurer is entitled to compensation. If the insured event did come about, in the event of non-payment of the premium payable after contract conclusion, and the commencement of insurance coverage not being dependent on its payment, the insurer shall be obliged to pay compensation but may deduct the amount of the premium owed. Both claims are pecuniary and due.[436] Of course, irrespective of all of the above, an

432. The contract will have material effects from the date determined in the contract, irrespectively of the moment of premium payment.
433. This is in accordance with the general rules of contract termination in case of non-fulfilment. Should the creditor wish to terminate an agreement, the debtor needs to be afforded a reasonable subsequent time limit for performance (*see* LO, Art. 126, para. 2). The above time limit is precisely set: it amounts to a minimum of thirty days.
434. Perović, Stojanović, *Komentar Zakona o obligacionim odnosima, knjiga II* (*Commentary to the Law on Obligations, Book II*), 809.
435. *See* LO, Art. 277.
436. Perović, Stojanović, *Komentar Zakona o obligacionim odnosima, knjiga II* (*Commentary to the Law on Obligations, Book II*), 810.

insurer may file a claim before the competent court for the payment of due premiums.[437] A legal assumption shall apply in such instances that the insurer always wishes to keep the contract in force. If the insured event occurs and the commencement of coverage is not made dependent on insurance payment, the insurer shall be obliged to pay indemnification (compensation is again possible). Finally, the insurance contract shall be terminated within a year from the maturity if the insurer does not avail himself/herself of any of the above rights.[438] The contract shall terminate *ipso iure*, which means that no declaration or other action of the insurer is necessary to that effect.[439]

237. As opposed to the above general provisions regarding premium payment, special rules apply in insurance contracts regulated by the LMIN, as well as in life insurance contracts. In insurance contracts regulated by the LMIN premium, non-payment does not exempt an insurer from the obligations under the insurance contract and does not entitle him/her to terminate the insurance contract, unless otherwise provided.[440] Such a provision is of a yielding character but in practice it is rarely provided for to the contrary.[441] The specificities in life insurance contracts are even more emphasized.

II. Specificities of Premium Payment in Life Insurance Contracts

238. In life insurance contracts premium payment is an optional obligation of the insurance contractor. The insurer is not entitled to seek its payment before courts. Of course, if paid, the insurance contractor will have performed his/her obligation incurred by entering into the contract and may not seek its return. Such an obligation is optional for two reasons. Life insurance contracts are usually long-term legal transactions. Insurance contractors oblige themselves to pay the premium over a longer period of time. After a certain number of years passes, circumstances may be altered, and the contractor may decide that the life insurance contract once concluded is superfluous (due to lack of funds, descendants covered in another manner, etc.). It would be unfair, should the insurance contractor in such instances be judicially forced for premium payment. However, whole life insurance contracts have certain similarities with savings deposit contracts. A part of the paid premiums is separated for risk coverage, while the other part comprises the so-called mathematical reserve. Should the insurance contractor hold the view that there is no need for such savings, he/she cannot be forced to carry on with further payments.[442] The optional being of premium payment is a characteristic of all life

437. An exception is life insurance contracts.
438. *See* LO, Art. 913, para. 4.
439. Perović, Stojanović, *Komentar Zakona o obligacionim odnosima, knjiga II* (*Commentary to the Law on Obligations, Book II*), 810.
440. *See* LMIN, Art. 744, para. 4.
441. Šulejić, *Pravo osiguranja* (*Insurance Law*), 265.
442. Marjanski, *Ugovor o osiguranju* (*Insurance Contract*), 209.

insurance contracts. However, the consequences of premium non-payment are not the same in whole life insurance contracts and life insurance contracts concluded for a specific term.

A. *Legal Consequences of Premium Non-payment in Whole Life Insurance Contracts*

239. If at least three premium annuities[443] have been paid, the insurer will not be entitled to terminate the contract, but only to reduce the insured amount to the repurchase value of the policy. The insurer will have the above right only if the insurance contractor was invited by the insurer by means of registered mail to pay an insurance premium due within the time limit indicated in the insurer's letter, which time limit may not be shorter than one month,[444] under the condition, of course, that the contractor or another interested party failed to perform their obligations to the above effect. The insurer will in such cases not be entitled to terminate the contract due to the fact that a mathematical reserve has been created by premium payment in course of the period of three or more years. An important right of the insurance contractor stems from the formation of mathematical reserves: the right to claim the policy repurchase value (also claimable by a creditor with whom the policy is pledged). Therefore, in case of premium non-payment, the insured amount may be reduced up to the policy repurchase value after the premium becoming due.[445]

240. If however, the three annual premiums are not paid, no mathematical reserves are formed according to the LO. Due to the fact that no mathematical reserves are created, it is evident that no rights are going to follow from them (the right to claim the policy repurchase value). The insurer may in such instances terminate the contract if the time limit from the registered notice (not shorter than one month) calling upon the insurance contractor to perform his/her obligations regarding premium payment has passed.[446]

241. Should the insurer invite the insurance contractor for payment and if the insured event occurs prior to contract termination or the reduction of the insured amount, the insured amount shall be considered reduced, or the contract terminated – depending on the fact whether the insurance premiums were being paid for a minimum period of three years.[447] On the contrary, if the insurer does not invite the

443. Within the general terms of life insurance of Serbian insurance companies, this time limit usually amounts to two years. Such an exception from the LO's provisions is possible for it is in the insured's interest.
444. *See* LO, Art. 945, para. 2.
445. Up to the policy repurchase value taking into account that the insured amount may also be reduced to an amount higher than the policy repurchase value. Such a possibility is allowed for it is in the insured party's interest. The methods of calculation are not going to be discussed at this point.
446. *See* LO, Art. 945, para. 2.
447. *See* LO, Art. 945, para. 3.

insurance contractor to pay the due premium and the insured event occurs, the insurer shall be obliged to pay the insured amount with the right to deduct the amounts of premium owed.

B. Legal Consequences of Premium Non-payment in Life Insurance Contract Concluded for a Particular Term

242. No mathematical reserves are formed in this type of contract. Therefore the legal consequences of premium non-payment and the conditions of their creation are the same as with whole life insurance contracts where the three necessary premium annuities have not been paid.

§3. OBLIGATIONS IN THE CASE OF INSURANCE EVENT

243. Obligations incurred after the occurrence of the insured event are the duty to report the occurrence of the insured event and the duty of salvage – the obligation to remove and diminish the consequences of the insured event.

I. The Duty to Report the Occurrence of the Insured Event

244. The duty to report the occurrence of the insured event may be conceived in its narrower and wider sense. In its narrower sense, it comprises only the duty to report the occurrence of the insured event. This obligation is usually laid down in statutory provisions.[448] In its wider sense it comprises both the duty to report the occurrence of the insured event, as well as the duty to report a series of circumstances directly pertaining to the insured event (submission of documentation, information, evidence, etc.) The duty to report circumstances directly connected with the insured event stem from the particular insurance contract concluded, or, more precisely, the general terms and conditions representing its constituent part. It, however, along with the duty to report the occurrence of the insured event constitutes a single legal unit.[449] It needs to be especially pointed out that this is an obligation of the insured and not the insurance contractor (of course, only if these two parties are not the same). It shall be deemed that the insured performed his/her obligation within the provided time limit,[450] in a manner[451] and towards the person to be notified (the insurer or his/her agent, and sometimes the competent state too)[452] if the above persons are completely and correctly notified on the circumstances directly pertaining to the insured event.

448. *See* LO, Art. 917.
449. Šulejić, *Pravo osiguranja* (*Insurance Law*), 239.
450. Time limits are provided for by the law but may also be laid down in general terms and conditions. *See* LO, Art. 917, para. 1.
451. The form and contents are provided for by general terms and conditions and special forms on reporting drawn up by the insurer.
452. Usually in fire, explosion, theft or robbery insurance contracts, etc.

245. The legal consequences of non-fulfilment depend on the fact whether we are faced with non-reporting, untimely reporting or incomplete or incorrect reporting of circumstances directly connected with the insured event. Should the occurrence of the insured event not at all be notified to the insurer, the insurer's obligation will not become due. If the event covered by insurance takes place, the insurer shall be bound to pay the compensation or the amount specified by contract within the stipulated time limit which shall not exceed fourteen days, counting from the notification received by the insurer of the occurrence of the insured event.[453] Therefore the fulfilment of this obligation is important for the realization of the insured's rights. However, the insurer may receive the above information from the insured, but also from third parties or find it out by himself/herself. The manner of becoming aware of it is not important because the obligation needs to be fulfilled within a given time limit from becoming aware of the occurrence. Therefore, if the insurer becomes aware of the insured event but not from the insured, he/she must not invoke the fact that he/she had not been notified. The case of untimely reporting needs to be differentiated from non-reporting of insured event's occurrence. In case of untimely reporting, two situations need to be distinguished. First, if the insured reports the insured event's occurrence in an untimely manner along with satisfactory evidence that the insured event occurred, the insured must not be deprived of the right to claim compensation or the stipulated insured amount. Stipulating a forfeiture of rights would in such cases be void.[454] A potential sanction that may be employed in these instances would be the payment of damages caused by such actions to the insurer. Should the insured fail to fulfil this obligation within the designated time, he/she shall be obliged to compensate the insurer for loss sustained due to the above.[455] Second, if the insured reports in an untimely manner the insured event's occurrence, so that it is impossible to determine whether the insured event occurred at all, the insured will be deprived of his/her right to claim anything from the insurer. The burden of proof regarding the cause and extent of damages covered by insurance lies with the insured. Should the insured after a certain period of time upon the insured event's occurrence not be able to substantiate that damages were incurred due to the fact of untimely notification, he/she will not be able to claim compensation from insurance.[456]

II. The Duty to Take Measures Aimed at the Removal and Limitation of Damages (Salvage)

246. Should an insured event occur, an insured shall be obliged to take measures in his/her power to limit consequential damages.[457] Therefore the obligation of salvage, as described by the LO, comprises the measures aimed at preventing further adverse consequences and the mitigation of incurred damage. The fulfilment of

453. *See* LO, Art. 919.
454. *See* LO, Art. 918.
455. *See* LO, Art. 917, para. 2.
456. In this case untimely reporting is the cause of the inability to substantiate the occurrence of the insured event.
457. *See* LO, Art. 926, para. 1.

this obligation is assessed according to subjective criteria pertaining to the insured: 'the insured is obliged to take all measures within his power, but not all measures that might be in fact necessary in the given moment'.[458] A cooperation between the insurer and the insured is necessary in the course of taking such measures. General terms and conditions often provide for an obligation of the insured to respect the insurer's instructions. However, an insured is not obliged to request instructions from the insurer should the circumstances not allow such action due to the possibility of stalling for time. In any case, it is in the insured's interest to procure the insurer's consent regarding the measures to be taken due to the fact that this is going to be of importance when bearing the costs that might be triggered by such measures.[459] Should the insured fail to fulfil his/her obligation to prevent the occurrence of the insured event, or the obligation of salvage, the obligation of the insurer shall be reduced by an amount equal to the increase of damage due to such omission.[460] In order for such a sanction to come about the following conditions need to be met: (1) that damage was caused to the insurer by the insured's omission; (2) that the insured can be held liable for such omission (according to the LMIN[461] only intent and gross negligence will trigger the sanction); (3) that there is a causal relationship between the insured's default and the incurred damage.[462] Finally, it needs to be underscored that a duty of the insurer corresponds to the insured's obligation to reimburse the costs, expenditures and other losses that might be incurred as a consequence of taking such measures.

458. Šulejić, *Pravo osiguranja* (*Insurance Law*), 242.
459. *Ibid.*
460. *See* LO, Art. 926, para. 4.
461. *See* LMIN, Art. 762, para. 4.
462. Šulejić, *Pravo osiguranja* (*Insurance Law*), 238.

Chapter 5. Obligations of the Insurer

§1. Non-life Insurance

247. All insurance types where the object of insurance is not life as a personal category of the insured fall within the category of non-life insurance. In non-life insurance, the principle of compensation is applied as a rule.[463] This is a feature substantially differentiating it from life insurance. The principle of compensation means that an insured may not receive a payment higher than the losses incurred.

248. The basic obligation of the insurer upon the occurrence of the insured event in all insurance contract types consists of fulfilling an obligation pertaining to property. In non-life insurance, that is, in types of insurance where the principle of compensation is applicable, the fulfilment of the above obligation usually consists of the payment of indemnification. However, the insurer's obligation pertaining to property, although this is a much rarer occurrence, does not have to consist of only the payment of a particular sum of money. If provided for by the contract, an insurer may instead of pecuniary payment of compensation opt for procuring a new object replacing a destroyed one, or repairing the damaged object.[464] Additionally, in liability insurance, apart from the obligation of compensation payment to a third party incurring certain losses, a basic duty of the insurer is to bind himself/herself to offer legal protection to the insured against unjustified or exaggerated claims for damages.

249. Although the principle of compensation is applicable in non-life insurance, the compensation from insurance does not have the characteristics of indemnification in the sense of general rules of civil law. The insurer is not a tortfeasor, that is, a person responsible to repair damages, but rather a contracting party in an insurance relationship where the main obligation is to pay compensation after the insured event occurs or to perform another obligation pertaining to property (such as the replacement of a destroyed object or the reparation of a damaged one). Therefore, the relationship established by means of an insurance contract is to be assessed based on the rules regulating the underlying contract itself and not the general principles of tort. Accordingly, in non-life insurance the insurer is obliged to pay compensation from insurance, or to perform something else in accordance with the contract, and not to pay damages. The principle of compensation has as its sole purpose to prevent the insured from receiving a compensation higher than the actual losses incurred.

250. Certain rules follow from the principle of compensation. If the insured amount is not determined by the contract, the assumption shall apply that the upper

463. Exceptions to this rule are cases of insurance of the insured's physical integrity against accidents, where the principle of compensation is not applicable and the previously stipulated sum is to be paid in full or partially depending on the degree of the insured's incapacitation.

464. Perović, Stojanović, *Komentar Zakona o obligacionim odnosima, knjiga II* (*Commentary to the Law on Obligations, Book II*), 839.

limit of the insurer's obligation regarding compensation is the amount of loss actually incurred. If, however, an insured amount higher than the value of the insured interest (overinsurance) is provided for by the contract, the upper limit of the insurer's obligation would again be the incurred loss. This is due to the fact that the amount of compensation must not be higher than the losses actually incurred by the insured upon occurrence of the insured event.[465] In case of full insurance[466] and the occurrence of total loss, the amount of compensation and the amount of loss actually incurred are going to correspond. Apart from the above, the amount of loss actually incurred in case of underinsurance is one of the elements necessary for the establishment of the amount of compensation. The concepts of overinsurance, underinsurance, multiple and double insurance are connected with the principle of compensation applicable in non-life insurance. Therefore, these concepts are going to be presented below along with their potential legal consequences. However, before such a presentation, it has to be borne in mind that the rules of overinsurance, underinsurance, multiple and double insurance shall not be applicable in Serbia within the domain of personal insurance, regardless of the fact whether these fall into the category of life or non-life insurance, even in contracts where the principle of compensation is not applicable (e.g., in cases of covering the costs of treatment, reimbursement of lost daily salaries, in accident insurance of persons). In order to completely understand the principle of compensation, the concept of subrogation along with its underlying principles is going to be presented.

251. Finally, it needs to be pointed out that in insurance types where the principle of compensation is applicable, the person seeking compensation (the insured) must have an insurable interest. The interest in contracts where the principle of compensation is applicable consists of an economic relationship of the subject towards the object of insurance protected by a subjective right, which is going to be satisfied by means of the insurance relationship. In order for an interest to be insurable, it is necessary that the interest is material and legally permitted. An interest is going to be of a material (economic) nature if the holder of interest would suffer material damage should the insured event occur, that is, a damage appraisable in money. Therefore, it may stem from all legal relationships following from property law, contractual or tort law if the holder of interest would suffer damages by occurrence of the insured event. The existence of insurable interest is an essential element of the insured's legal capacity. Legally permitted are all interests not contrary to coercive provisions, the public order or the rules of business morals. Therefore, not all interests, even if material, are insurable. This, however, does not have to be a particular right based on statutory provisions. It can moreover be any interest not prohibited by law. An interest would be prohibited, e.g., if the objects of insurance would be goods the trade of which is prohibited, or the loss of profit stemming from illegal transactions, and so on.[467]

---

465. *See* LO, Art. 925, para. 2.
466. In such a situation, the amount of insurance and the value of the insured object correspond.
467. Drago Pavić, Osigurljiv interes (Insurable Interest), *Svijet osiguranja* 6 (2004), 40.

I. Over- and Underinsurance

A. Overinsurance

252. Within Serbian insurance law, the rules on overinsurance are applicable only in property insurance contracts. Overinsurance exists if the contracted amount of insurance is higher than the value of the insured interest. Overinsurance is often defined as the situation where the amount of insurance is higher than the value of the insurance object. Such a definition is, however, correct only in particular situations. There are insurance contracts where the value of the insurance object is lower than or equal to the contracted amount of insurance, and overinsurance is still being present. Namely, a contract on the insurance of particular objects may be concluded by non-owners having certain economic interests on the object (e.g., a mortgagee). Should such a person conclude an insurance contract with an amount of insurance higher than their insured interest (receivables secured by means of a mortgage on the insured object) a case of overinsurance would also exist.[468] The LO erroneously connects the concept of overinsurance exclusively to property insurance contracts, defining thereby the concept of overinsurance in relation to the value of the insured object, and not in relation to the insured interest. According to the LO, overinsurance exists if an amount of insurance higher than the real value of the insured object is stipulated.[469]

253. The purpose of property insurance contracts is to provide for indemnification in case of occurrence of the insured event. On the contrary, if overinsurance were permitted, such a contract may represent a source of the insured's enrichment due to the fact that by means of the insured event's occurrence the insured would acquire a compensation higher than the losses incurred. Nonetheless, property insurance may be contracted only by persons having an interest that the insured event does not take place, since such persons would suffer material losses on the contrary.[470] Although the principle of compensation does not allow the acquisition of payments higher than the incurred loss, laws usually contain provisions specially sanctioning the *mala fide* conclusion of property insurance contracts providing for overinsurance. Regarding legal consequences of overinsurance, the LO differentiates between situations where overinsurance exists at the moment of contract conclusion[471] from situations where overinsurance occurs after entering into the contract, that is, in the course of insurance coverage.[472]

254. In case of overinsurance, at the moment of contract conclusion the contracting parties may act in good faith (e.g., if the insured is not familiar with the real value of objects or interests) or they may act in bad faith (e.g., if the contract is concluded with the intention to acquire higher compensation than the amount of

468. Marjanski, *Ugovor o osiguranju* (*Insurance Contract*), 68.
469. *See* LO, Art. 932.
470. *See* LO, Art. 924.
471. *See* LO, Art. 932.
472. *See* LO, Art. 933.

loss incurred). Depending on the parties' good or bad faith, the law provides for various legal consequences. Should at conclusion of the contract one party deceive the other, stipulating an amount of insurance higher than the real value of the insured object, the other party shall be entitled to request nullity of contract.[473] Therefore, if the overinsurance results from the bad faith of one of the contracting parties we have a case of voidable contracts. Article 932 paragraph 1 LO does not expressly provide for the contracting party that might act fraudulently in the course of establishing the amount of insurance. In practice, however, it is virtually only the insured who would act in bad faith regarding the determination of the insured amount for the purpose of acquiring certain profits. However, the insurer as the bona fide party rarely avails himself/herself in practice of the right to seek nullity of the contract before the occurrence of the insured event due to overinsurance caused in bad faith.[474] Should, however, the stipulated amount of insurance be higher than the value of the insured object, and if both parties act in good faith, the contract shall remain valid and the amount of insurance shall be reduced to the real value of the insured object, while the premium shall be reduced proportionally.[475] In both cases an insurer acting in good faith (both in the case of the insured causing the overinsurance in good or bad faith) will have not only the right to keep the insurance premiums received, but he/she will also be entitled to a non-reduced premium for the current insurance period.[476] Such a provision is meant to stimulate the insurance contractor to act with the highest possible level of care regarding the establishment of the insured amount in course of contract conclusion. Departure from the statutory provisions is permitted only if it is to the obvious interest of the insurance contractor.[477] If both contracting parties acted in good faith, it is possible to provide for the reduction of the premium for the current insurance period. In such instances the insured amount and the premiums shall be reduced from the moment of seeking reduction.[478]

255. A situation is also possible that overinsurance occurs after entering into the insurance contract, that is, in course of insurance coverage. Should the insured amount be reduced in course of the insurance period, each contracting party shall be entitled to a corresponding reduction of the insurance amount and the premium, beginning from the day the first party submits to the other his/her request for reduction.[479] In the given situation, overinsurance occurs in the course of insurance coverage due to the reduction of the insured object's value. A consequence of such a

473. *See* LO, 932.
474. There are numerous reasons for that: the insured's bad faith is a subjective category hard to prove; it is in the insurer's interest not to lose the insured; an insured must never receive more than the actual loss incurred; the payment of higher premiums for a larger amount of insurance is usually a high enough punishment. For these reasons, general terms and conditions usually do not contain the insurer's right to seek the nullity of the contract due to overinsurance.
475. *See* LO, Art. 932, para. 2.
476. *See* LO, Art. 932, para. 3.
477. *See* LO, Art. 900, para. 2.
478. Such solutions are usually contained in general terms of property insurance.
479. *See* LO, Art. 933.

situation is a possible reduction of the amount of insurance and the premium starting from the day of submission of one party's request for reduction to the other. Overinsurance in such situations is caused by objective circumstances, so that the fact of good faith and honesty of the contracting parties is irrelevant. New circumstances came about not taken into account by the parties when entering into the insurance contract. Therefore, in such instances the same principle shall be applicable as if the insured object's value were lower at the moment of contract conclusion: the insured amount and the premiums shall be reduced.[480] This provision does not pertain to cases when the value of the insured object diminishes as a result of the insured event's occurrence.

B. Underinsurance

256. As opposed to overinsurance where the contracted amount of insurance exceeds the value of insured interest, underinsurance exists when the contracted amount of insurance is lower than its value. Similarly, as in overinsurance, the LO erroneously connects the possibility of underinsurance exclusively to property insurance contracts and defines the concept of underinsurance in relation to the value of the insured object, but not to the value of the insured interest. Should it be established that at the beginning of a relevant period of insurance, the value of the insured object was higher than the amount of insurance, the amount of compensation owed by the insurer shall be proportionally reduced, unless otherwise provided by contract.[481]

257. A consequence of underinsurance is the reduction of the compensation by application of the principle of proportionality[482] unless otherwise provided for by the contract. The principle of proportionality is employed for calculating the amount of insurance according to the following formula:

$$\text{Compensation} = \frac{\text{the amount of insurance x the incurred damage}}{\text{the value of the insured interest}}$$[483]

Therefore, as the amount of insurance is limited by the value of the insured interest, the compensation is also limited by the loss incurred, which in the bottom line, if total, will correspond to the value of insured interest.

---

480. Perović, Stojanović, *Komentar Zakona o obligacionim odnosima, knjiga II* (*Commentary to the Law on Obligations, Book II*), 860.
481. *See* LO, Art. 936, para. 1.
482. Peter Schimikowski, *die Skripte für Versicherungsvertragsrecht* (*Lecture Notes on Insurance Contract Law*) (Köln: Institut für Versicherungswesen, 2003), 79.
483. Within Serbian insurance law, this formula contains the insured object value instead of the insured interest value.

258. Due to the fact that in underinsurance the amount of insurance is lower than the insured interest, as well as that there is no danger of infringing upon the principle of compensation, the provisions on the application of the principle of proportionality are of a yielding nature. The parties are entitled to regulate their relationship in a manner different from the above rule. The insurer is even liable to pay the entire compensation up to the amount of insurance, if it is stipulated that the relationship between the value of the object and the amount of insurance shall have no relevance in determining the amount of compensation.[484] There are various exceptions to the principle of proportionality pertaining exclusively to property insurance contracts.[485]

II. Subrogation

A. *Introduction*

259. Subrogation is the replacement of a legal relationship's certain element by another in a manner that the identity and the legal regulation of the relationship remain unchanged. The subject of subrogation may be the parties (*personal subrogation*) and the object of a legal relationship (*real subrogation*).

B. *The Concept, the Importance and the Field of Application of Personal Subrogation in Insurance Contracts*

260. Personal subrogation in its wider sense comprises all changes within the parties of a legal relationship, on either side and regardless of the fact whether according to the law or to a contract. Types of contractual personal subrogation are the legal institutions of cession, transfer of contract, assumption of debt, and so on. Insurance contracts based on general rules applicable for all contracts may also provide for contractual personal subrogation.

261. In insurance contracts where the principle of compensation is applicable, apart from liability insurance contracts, a special rule of personal subrogation is established by law. Should the insured event occur by default of a third party (different from the insured), there are two legal bases for the compensation to be made to the injured insured party. These are the insurance contract (total or partial indemnification in the form of compensation, repair or replacement of the damaged object) and liability according to the general rules of civil law due to damages caused. The insured sustaining damages may choose between the above two legal bases for claiming compensation.[486] The insured is not obliged to claim compensation from

484. *See* LO, Art. 936, para. 2.

485. For details on exceptions regarding first risk, the insurance of objects to a new value and the insurance of objects to the contracted amount *see* Marjanski, *Ugovor o osiguranju* (*The Insurance Contract*), 80–82.

486. Of course, the nature of these compensation does differ.

the insurer. However, if compensation was claimed and received, the insured will not be entitled to demand compensation from the person responsible for the same loss. More precisely, he/she may employ both avenues up to the amount of actual loss incurred. On the contrary the principle of compensation would be infringed upon. However, should the insured first address the insurer and receive total compensation, failing the principle subrogation along with the simultaneous application of the principle of compensation, the person responsible for causing the damage would not suffer any consequences. Therefore, in insurance contracts where the principle of compensation is applicable, a special rule of personal subrogation is provided for by law. This rule reads as follows: 'upon payment of compensation from insurance, the insurer shall acquire, by law, all rights of the insured person against the person liable for damage on whatever ground, up to the total amount of compensation'.[487] In respect to the person liable the insurance contract represents a contract *inter alios acta.* The fact that the insured received compensation based on the insurance contract does not relieve the tortfeasor from liability. The legal status of the person liable cannot be made dependent on the fact whether the injured had been insured or not. Therefore the person liable for damage is obliged to repair it and, had the insured already been compensated by means of a payment from insurance, the tortfeasor shall be liable towards the insurer making the compensation to the insured.[488] Simultaneously, due to the principle of compensation, the insured must not accumulate compensations above the amount of the loss actually incurred. Consequently, the aim of subrogation is to respect the principle of compensation and have the actual tortfeasor ultimately repair the damages caused.

262. The statutory personal subrogation is not applicable in liability insurance contracts due to the fact that the insured himself/herself is responsible for the occurrence of the insured event. Accordingly, the insured is simultaneously the tortfeasor, so that he/she may not acquire two rights to compensation. The insured will receive only one right, to request compensation from the insurer based on the liability insurance contract. Furthermore, the application of subrogation is also excluded in insurance contracts where the principle of compensation is not applicable. The accumulation of both compensation from insurance and the repair of damages from the tortfeasor is not prohibited, so that by payment of compensation, the rights of the insured towards liable third parties (tortfeasors) are not transferred to the insurer. Due to the fact that in such contracts the principle of compensation is not applicable there are no limitations to the possibility of the insured to claim indemnification from the person liable as well.

C. Conditions of Statutory Personal Subrogation

263. Two conditions need to be cumulatively fulfilled in order to subrogate the insurer's rights to the insured's rights towards a third party liable for damages. First,

---

487. *See* LO, Art. 939, para. 1.
488. Perović, Stojanović, *Komentar Zakona o obligacionim odnosima, knjiga II* (*Commentary to the Law on Obligations, Book II*), 883.

it is necessary that the insurer paid compensation to the insured. The amount of compensation is irrelevant for the existence of subrogation, it is only important for the extent of rights acquired by the insurer towards the liable third party by means of subrogation. Second, the third party's liability is necessary for the occurrence of the insured event (the loss) on whatever base (tort or contractual responsibility).

264. Liable third parties are all persons different from the insured that may be held liable on whatever base for the occurrence of the insured event. However, as an exception to the transfer of the insured's rights to the insurer, such rights shall not pass to the insurer if the loss (insured event) was caused by a person in direct kinship with the insured,[489] or by a person for the actions of which the insured is responsible, or persons living in the same household with him/her, or persons employed by the insured, unless the above persons caused the damage by wilful misconduct.[490] However, should some of the persons specified in the preceding paragraph be insured against liability, the insurer may demand the redress of the amount paid to the insured person from his/her insurer.[491] As a general rule, if a liable third party is insured against liability, the insurer will be entitled to choose whether to claim redress from the person himself/herself or his/her insurer.

D. *Effects of Statutory Personal Subrogation*

265. If all the above requirements are met, the insurer's rights shall subrogate to the insurer's rights at the moment of insurance compensation payment, without a special form being necessary to that effect. The insurer shall not be obliged to inform the liable third party on the above circumstance. If, however, a liable third party voluntarily indemnifies the insured, such party will be exempted from his/her obligation, while the insured shall be obliged to return to the insurer the received compensation from insurance. If the insured had been fully indemnified by means of insurance compensation or in another manner (repair or replacement of the damaged object), his/her capacity to claim damages from the tortfeasor would cease to exist. The insured's creditors are not entitled to cease the insured's claims towards liable third parties. These, after all, are not his/her claims anymore. The insured's claims transfer to the insurer at the moment of compensation payment.[492]

266. The claim transferred to the insurer by means of subrogation is equal to the injured policyholder's claim towards a liable third party. This situation simultaneously has certain consequences in respect to the ability of the liable third party to file an objection of limitation, as well as an objection against the extent of the claim

489. An insurer will not have a claim towards persons in direct kinship with the insured due to the fact that an assumption exists to the effect that the insured himself/herself would not claim indemnification from such a person. The insured on the one hand would receive compensation from insurance and would be on the other hand responsible to fulfil the insurer's request in lieu of the person living in the same household with him/her.
490. *See* LO, Art. 939, para. 4.
491. *See* LO, Art. 939, para. 5.
492. Marjanski, *Ugovor o osiguranju* (*Insurance Contract*), 182–183.

for damages. All objections at the disposal of third parties towards the insured at the moment of compensation (moment of subrogation) may be made to the insurer too. Rights to raise objections towards the insured that came to existence at a later point, as well as those that lapsed before the given moment may not be made against the insurer. Apart from these objections, a liable third party is entitled to make personal complaints towards the insurer with no regard to the moment of the acquisition of such rights.[493] In respect to the insurer's limitation periods regarding claims towards liable third parties the following rule shall apply: 'The limitation period of the insurer's claim against the third party liable for the occurrence of the insured event, shall begin to run at the time otherwise applicable to the limitation period for the claims of the insured against such person, and shall be completed within the same time limit.'[494] The principle of identical claims shall be applicable in a situation when the insured event is caused by means of a criminal offence. The LO provides for a special statute of limitations in such instances. Should loss be caused by a criminal offence, and a longer unenforceability time limit be prescribed for the criminal prosecution, the claim for compensation against the person liable shall expire upon the expiration of the limitation period set forth in the statute of limitations of the criminal prosecution.[495] The extent of the insurer's claims towards liable third parties is limited twofold: by the amount of compensation from insurance paid to the insured and the amount owed to the insured by the third party. An insurer acquiring certain rights from statutory subrogation shall have the right to claim from liable third parties the amount paid to the insured based on insurance compensation but not more than the insured himself/herself would be entitled to claim from the liable third party, even if the insurance compensation had been higher than that amount. The insurer may, for instance, not claim from liable third parties the reimbursement of damage appraisal costs, and so on. This is because of the principle that liable third parties must not be put into situations more detrimental than those if the insured parties claimed indemnification directly from them. Similarly, the transfer of rights from the insured to the insurer must not be detrimental to the insured. Should the compensation received by the insured from the insurer be, on whatever ground, lower than the damage sustained (due to a franchise, underinsurance, etc.) the insured shall be entitled to reimbursement from the liable party's means for the remaining part of compensation, prior to the payment of the insurer's claim on the ground of rights which have been transferred to him/her.[496] The function of insurance is to defend the insured from the consequences of the occurred risk. Therefore the insured party's interests are privileged in comparison with the insurer's interests. It is true that the rights towards a liable third party

493. If the tortfeasor is simultaneously insured against liability for such damages with the same insurer, he/she may make an objection to set off the claim based on liability insurance with the insurer's claim based on subrogation because of the fact that the claims are connected, of the same nature and due. P. Šulejić, *Pravo osiguranja* (*Insurance Law*) (Belgrade: Pravni fakultet u Beogradu, 1992), 324.

494. *See* LO, Art. 380, para. 6.

495. *See* LO, Art. 377, para. 1.

496. *See* LO, Art. 939, para. 3.

are transferred to the insurer, but this is done for the purpose of excluding cumulation rather than of protecting the insurer's interests.[497] Should the insured not be entirely indemnified by means of insurance compensation, the insured in the capacity of an injured party must be afforded the possibility to recover the uncovered damages from the tortfeasor without the insurer making this harder for him/her by submitting a competitive claim against the tortfeasor. Therefore the insured shall be entitled to reimbursement from the liable party's means for the remaining part of compensation, prior to the payment of the insurer's claim on the ground of rights which have been transferred to him/her.

E. The Impossibility to Materialize the Rights Stemming from Personal Statutory Subrogation

267. The insurer's status towards a liable third party will depend on the insured's status (rights) towards the third party at the moment of subrogation, that is, of the transfer of rights. Thus, for instance, before the moment of subrogation (payment of insurance compensation) the insured may fully or partially cause the impossibility of the subrogation of rights stemming from compensation to the insurer. The insured may discharge a third party from an obligation, waive his/her right to compensation, fail to secure evidence after the occurrence of loss, miss the limitation period, and so on. Should the subrogation be made entirely or partially impossible through the fault of the insured, the insurer shall be released correspondingly from his/her obligation towards the insured.[498] If the insurer becomes aware of the impossibility of subrogation after the payment of compensation, he/she will be entitled to demand from the insured the full or partial amount of compensation corresponding to the impossibility to realize the rights of subrogation towards the liable third party.

F. Real Subrogation in Cases when the Insured Risk Occurs on a Pledged Object or an Item Subject to Other Property Rights

268. As opposed to personal subrogation representing a change within the parties to a legal relationship, real subrogation means a change within the object of the legal relationship where the identity and the regulation of the transaction remain unaltered. Apart from the already discussed notion of personal subrogation, a specificity of compensation payment in property insurance contracts is the possibility of real subrogation under certain conditions prescribed by law. Namely, a third party may have a security interest on the insured object (a pledge or a mortgage) or another right (e.g., a right of usufruct, easement) that may be brought into question in case of loss, destruction or damage to the particular object. In order to protect the holders of such rights the LO provides under particular circumstances for real subrogation. After the occurrence of an insured event, a security right and other rights existing previously in relation to the insured object shall have as their subject the

---

497. The insurer's interest is expressed by the received insurance premium.
498. *See* LO, Art. 939, para. 2.

compensation owed, both in the case of insuring one's own objects, and in the case of insuring another person's objects because of a duty to keep and restitute them, so that the insurer shall not be able to pay compensation to the insured without the consent of the holder of such rights.[499] Therefore, security and other rights previously existing on the insured object shall have as their subject the full or partial amount of the compensation owed.[500] As a result of the above, a prohibition has been established in that the insurer must not pay compensation to the insured without the prior consent of the holders of such rights. This means in principle that in case of insurance compensation payment without the consent of the above persons, the insurer shall not be relieved from his/her obligations. The holders of such rights would still be entitled to claim payment directly from the insurer, unless the insurer was unaware, or could not have been aware, of such rights.[501] Therefore the assumption for realizing such a right is the insurer's awareness of the existence of the rights of third parties on the insured object. The insurer must be adequately informed that third-party rights exist on the insured object. If, however the insurer was unaware of such rights, he/she may pay the compensation to the insured and thus relieve himself/herself from the pertaining obligations from the insurance contract. Furthermore, apart from the fact that compensation may not be paid without their consent to the insured, these persons may directly demand that the insurer satisfies their claims within the limits of the amount of insurance, and according to the statutory order of payment.[502] Against the above persons the insurer may raise only objections originating prior to the occurrence of the insured event.[503] Direct claims of the holders of rights, however, are indeed limited. As regards their extent they are limited by the contracted amount of insurance (if provided for, of course) and the value of the third party's interest (e.g., by the amount of claims towards the insured). Therefore the claim's upper limit is the amount of insurance but only if the interest of the third party is higher than or equal to the amount of insurance. On the contrary, if the value of such interests is lower, the upper limit of compensation payable to the holder of a security right is going to be the actual value of their interest. Second, if there is a conflict of claims of such third parties, the possibility of realizing their interests is limited by the insurer's obligation to respect the statutory order pertaining to the payment of claims[504] (e.g., in case of a mortgage, the person first entered into the land register).

269. Finally, apart from real statutory subrogation pertaining to the holders of particular rights on the insured object, it may be stipulated by insurance contracts that regular creditors of the insured shall have certain rights towards the insurer, the claims of which are not secured by security interests on the insured object. Such provisions are usually entered into insurance contracts by means of clauses on the assignment of the right of recovery (*vinculation*). This would, e.g., be the case if

499. *See* LO, Art. 938, para. 1.
500. Whether full or partial compensation is going to be made depends on the value of the entitled person's interests.
501. *See* LO, Art. 938, para. 3.
502. *See* LO, Art. 938, para. 2.
503. *See* LO, Art. 921, para. 2.
504. *See* LO, Art. 938, para. 2.

the purchaser in a credit purchase agreement would incur the obligation to enter into an insurance contract of the goods purchased on credit. Thus would the credit purchaser assign the whole or part of the compensation from insurance, under fulfilment of certain conditions, to the seller (e.g., if the insured [purchaser] does not meet his/her obligation towards the seller [creditor] and the insured event [damage destruction, loss] occurs on the insured object). However, such a case would represent a conditional assignment of a future uncertain claim, not a real subrogation.

III. Multiple and Double Insurance

A. *Multiple Insurance*

270. Should an object be insured with two or more insurers against the same risk, for the same interest and for the same period of time, so that the sum of the insured amounts does not exceed the value of such objects (multiple insurance), each insurer shall be responsible for complete performance of obligations stemming from the contract entered into.[505] Therefore, for the existence of multiple insurance the following requirements need to be met: (1) that the same object is insured with two or more insurers against the same risk; (2) that the same object of insurance is insured with two or more insurers for the same interest; (3) that the same object of insurance is insured with two or more insurers within the same period of time;[506] (4) that the sum of the insured amounts does not exceed the value of the insured interest. Multiple insurance is permitted taking into account the fact that the value of insured interest does not exceed the sum of the insured amounts. The principle of compensation is thus not infringed upon. Consequently, an insured, should the insured event occur, will be entitled to demand compensation from all insurers with whom the same object had been insured, in accordance with the particular insurance contract entered into with the respective insurer. An insurance contractor will in such a state of affairs, be liable for the performance of his/her obligations towards each of the insurers. One of the specific obligations of the insurance contractor that may come about both in multiple and double insurance is the duty to report that an insurance contract with the same object against the same risk and for the same interest has been entered into with one or more other insurers. The LO, however, provides for such an obligation only upon occurrence of the insured event.[507] The notification needs to contain the names and addresses of the other insurers, as well as the insured amounts of each particular insurance contract. The above duty of the insurance contractor is indeed important due to the fact that the consequences of multiple and double insurance are substantially different. Yet the LO did not provide for consequences for an insurance contractor not meeting such obligations. The loss of rights from insurance in such situations is obviously out of question. An

505. *See* LO, Art. 934, para. 1.
506. It is possible that time periods only partially overlap.
507. *See* LO, Art. 934, para. 3.

insurance contractor not fulfilling his/her obligation (either in double or in multiple insurance) is obliged to indemnify the insurers,[508] of course if damages were caused by such an omission.

B. Double Insurance

271. Double insurance exists if the same object is insured with two or more insurers against the same risk for the same interest within the same period of time, whereby the sum of insured amounts exceeds the value of insured interest. In case of double insurance an insurer is entitled to request compensation from each individual insurer in compliance with the contract entered into with that person, but never above the amount of loss incurred. Everything laid down in respect of multiple insurance pertaining to the conditions of its conclusion applies accordingly in double insurance. The elementary difference is that in double insurance the sum of insured amounts from two or more concluded contracts exceeds the value of insured interest. Therefore the legal institute of double insurance is resembling to overinsurance, so that their legal consequences are similar to a certain degree.

272. Double insurance may come about as a result of entering into more insurance contracts simultaneously, subsequently or if, due to depreciation of the insured object in course of insurance coverage, multiple insurance becomes double insurance. Similarly, as in overinsurance, double insurance may be caused by the insurance contractor in good or bad faith. The LO provides for different solutions depending on that circumstance.

273. If the insurance contractor acted in good faith, all contracts remain in force but will not have full legal effect due to the fact that the principle of compensation would on the contrary be infringed upon. The insured shall be entitled to demand from each insurer the compensation according to the contract entered into, but no more, in total, than the amount of damage incurred.[509] The insurer's liability towards the insured remains in the full contracted amount. Only thereafter, in the course of mutual relationships, will it come to the proportional distribution of the burden of compensation. Therefore, due to the possibility of unequal burdening of particular insurers because of the entitlement of the insured to demand full compensation from one insurer while requesting less or nothing from others, the LO provides for the possibility of a reimbursement procedure where each insurer shall bear the part of compensation in proportion between the insured amount he/she is obliged to pay and the sum of insured amounts, so that the insurer paying more shall be entitled to demand from other insurers reimbursement of the surplus paid.[510] It is necessary to emphasize at this point that despite the fact that the insured may

---

508. Perović, Stojanović, *Komentar Zakona o obligacionim odnosima, knjiga II* (*Commentary to the Law on Obligations, Book II*), 863.
509. *See* LO, Art. 934, para. 2.
510. *See* LO, Art. 934, para. 4.

address each of the insurers to pay compensation, there is no joint and several liability between the insurers, due to the fact that each of them is liable up to the amount of their respective contractual obligation. Similarly, if some of the insurers are unable to perform, the remaining insurers shall be liable for payment of the respective insurer's obligation proportionally to their respective parts.[511] As regards the insurance contractor's obligations, they remained unaltered towards each of the insurers, irrespectively of the fact whether such an insurer made full compensation or a compensation proportional to the obligations of the other insurers. An insurance contractor is accordingly obliged to pay the full amount of premium to every insurer for the periods of insurance that are currently running.[512] Similarly, as in multiple insurance, after the occurrence of the insured event, an insurance contractor shall be bound to notify each insurer of the risk and to communicate the names and addresses of the remaining insurers, together with information on the amounts of insurance provided in particular contracts concluded with them.[513] The good faith of insurance contractors is however hardly going to exist if it came to double insurance by means of simultaneously entering into multiple insurance contracts. Therefore, the LO grants a specific right to bona fide insurance contractors only if it came to double insurance as a result of subsequent conclusion of insurance contracts. If an insurance contractor enters into an insurance contract being unaware of the fact that a relationship of double insurance is thus created, irrespectively of the fact whether the previous insurance had been concluded by him/her or someone else, he/she will be entitled to request, within a period of a month from becoming aware of such an insurance, the proportional reduction of the insured amount, as well as the reduction of the subsequent insurance premiums, but the insurer will be entitled to keep the premiums received and demand the premium for the current insurance period.[514]

274. If in the event of double insurance, the insurance contractor fails to act in good faith, each insurer may request nullity of contract, keep the premiums received and demand the non-reduced premium for the current insurance period.[515] Similarly, as in overinsurance, in case of causing double insurance in bad faith by the insurance contractor, each insurer may request the nullity of contract. An insurer winning the case will be entitled to keep the received premiums and to request a non-reduced premium for the current insurance period. The law has no provisions regarding the responsibility of risk coverage. Yet, according to the general rules on contract nullity, such an obligation has a future (*ex nunc*) effect rather than an effect from the commencement of the relationship (*ex tunc*), that is, from contract conclusion.

275. Finally, double insurance may come about also as a consequence of the insured object's depreciation in the course of insurance coverage. If the double

511. *See* LO, Art. 934, para. 6.
512. *See* LO, Art. 934, para. 2.
513. *See* LO, Art. 934, para. 3.
514. *See* LO, Art. 934, para. 9.
515. *Ibid.*

insurance takes place due to the reduction of value of the insured object in the course of the insurance period, the insurance contractor shall be entitled to a corresponding reduction in the insurance amount and of the premiums, from the day his/her request for reduction reaches the insurer.[516]

§2. Life Insurance

276. Life insurance contracts are contracts having the life of a person as their object. Life insurance has a number of special characteristics in comparison with other insurance types, so that views are often expressed that the basic division of insurance is into life and non-life insurance Such a division is, for instance, contained in the LI.[517] However, life insurance contracts fall into the wider category of personal insurance contracts so that they bear certain resemblance to them.[518] Basic forms of life insurance are insurance against death (for a particular term or for the insured's whole life), survivorship insurance for a certain period of time (e.g., up to a certain age or to an event – marriage, childbirth) or mixed insurance covering both of the above risks (death and survivorship of a person of a certain age). Besides life insurance, insurance against accident consequences is often concluded as supplementary insurance covering, apart from the risk of death, cases of disability or the imperilment of the insured's health.[519]

277. As opposed to property insurance contracts and contracts where the principle of compensation is generally applicable, in life insurance contracts the insurer's obligation is comprised of paying a previously established sum of money. This means that in case that the insured event occurs, the previously contracted amount shall be payable instead of compensation according to the loss incurred. Therefore, the insured amount represents an essential contractual element in life insurance. Such a position of life insurance stems from the belief that human life has the highest possible value indeterminable in money. Similarly, the value of one's parents, children, spouse, other close relatives is incalculable. Their mutual relationship has above all a sentimental (a subjective) and not an economic value. Therefore, in an

516. *See* LO, Art. 934, para. 8.
517. *See* LI, Arts 8–10.
518. Apart from life insurance contracts, agreements on insurance against consequences of an accident fall into the category of personal insurance contracts.
519. It is interesting that accident insurance contracts, although personal insurance contracts, may sometimes have a compensatory character, which is a basic feature of property insurance. For example, insurance of health treatment expenses is of a compensatory character, due to the fact that the amount of indemnification is calculated according to the value of expenses. Within the above limits the principles of indemnification (as in property insurance) apply for accident insurance. However, if the accident insurance contract provides for a fixed daily payment for hospital treatment or the temporary incapacitation for work, such payments will not have the characteristics of compensatory insurance, due to the fact that the amount of payment is determined in advance rather than according to actual expenses. Due to the fact that elements of compensatory insurance are not dominant within accident insurance and it is, after all, connected with human lives, it is justified to classify such insurance types, along with life insurance contracts, into the category of personal insurance.

economic sense, such a value may not be insured as is the case with the real value of property.[520] Whereas the purpose of property insurance is to compensate in a pecuniary manner an incurred material loss, life insurance does not have a compensatory character. This circumstance renders life insurance specific in comparison with property insurance contracts. The criterion of establishing the insured amount in property insurance, if contracted at all,[521] is the value of insured interest. However, the above value in life insurance is established by means of a mutual agreement when entering into the contract, which is to be obligatorily stated in the insurance policy. The amount of eventual damages is not taken into account as a criterion for determining the above value. The amount of insurance is payable by the insurer upon occurrence of the stipulated circumstances (death, survivorship). The issue of potential damages incurred is absolutely irrelevant.[522] Therefore the principle of compensation is not applicable in life insurance contracts, nor the rules connected with the implementation of that principle. As opposed to types of insurance where the principle of compensation is applicable, in life insurance the insurer will not have the right of subrogation upon payment of the contracted amount, that is, the insurer will not be entitled to seek reimbursement from the person liable for the occurrence of the insured event. Furthermore, an insured may receive compensation from more insurers due to the fact that the rule on double insurance is neither applicable. Apart from the above, an insured may accumulate the compensation from the insurer and the party liable for the loss incurred (the prohibition to accumulate compensations is not applicable). The rules pertaining to the relationship of the insured amount and the value of the insured interest, that is, the provisions regulating over- and underinsurance, shall not apply in life insurance. Finally, within Serbian insurance law, in life insurance contracts insurable interest is not a requirement for the effectiveness of the contract and the right of the parties (the insured or the insurance beneficiary) to seek payment of the insured amount from the insurer. No material interest on the side of the insurance contractor is requested for the insurance of third parties, even if there is some kind of a subjective relationship between them (kinship, for instance). The only limitation pertaining to the insurance of a third party's life is regarding the fact that the validity of contract shall depend on his/her written consent to the contract conclusion and to the insured amount.[523] Certain limitations apply furthermore for insurance against the death of a third-party minor.[524] Finally, a distinctiveness of life insurance is the fact that it shall be effective even if the occurrence of the insured event is certain (e.g., death in case of contracts concluded for the insured's whole life), but it is unknown when it will occur.

---

520. Pavić, *Ugovorno pravo osiguranja–Komentar zakonskih odredaba* (*Contractual Insurance Law – Commentary to the Statutory Provisions*), 335.
521. In insurance types where the principle of compensation is applicable the insured amount is not an essential contractual element.
522. Pavić, *Ugovorno pravo osiguranja–Komentar zakonskih odredaba* (*Contractual Insurance Law – Commentary to the Statutory Provisions*), 336.
523. *See* LO, Art. 946, para. 3.
524. *See* LO, Art. 947.

Chapter 6. Insurance and Third Parties

278. In insurance contracts, as in all other bilateral legal transactions, there are two contracting parties. The parties to an insurance contract are the insurer and the insurance contractor. Apart from the contractors themselves, certain third parties may also have certain interests in the concluded insurance contract. These are the insured (if different from the insurance contractor), the insured person, insurance beneficiaries, holders of property rights on the insured object, acquirers of the insured object, third-party claimants in liability insurance contracts, creditors of the insurance contractor, creditors with whom the policy is pledged and persons suffering damage in the course of preventing the occurrence of the insured event. Due to the fact that the legal status of the insured, the insured person and the insurance beneficiary had been explained above, the status of other third parties possibly having certain interests in the insurance contract is going to be discussed in the present section.

279. It is possible that apart from the owner a third party has a security interest in the insured object (a pledge or a mortgage) or another right (e.g., a right of usufruct, easement) that may be brought into question in case of loss, destruction or damage to the particular object. In order to protect the holders of such rights the LO provides under particular circumstances for real subrogation. After the occurrence of an insured event, a security right and other rights existing previously in relation to the insured object shall have as their subject the compensation owed, both in the case of insuring one's own objects, and in the case of insuring another person's objects because of a duty to keep and restitute them, so that the insurer shall not be able to pay compensation to the insured without the consent of the holder of such rights.[525] Therefore, security and other rights previously existing on the insured object shall have as their subject the full or partial amount of the compensation owed.[526] As a result of the above, a prohibition has been established in that the insurer must not pay compensation to the insured without the prior consent of the holders of such rights. This means in principle that in case of insurance compensation payment without the consent of the above persons, the insurer shall not be relieved from his/her obligations. The holders of such rights would still be entitled to claim payment directly from the insurer, unless the insurer was unaware, or could not have been aware, of such rights.[527] Therefore the assumption for realizing such a right is the insurer's awareness of the existence of the rights of third parties on the insured object. The insurer must be adequately informed that third-party rights exist on the insured object. If, however the insurer was unaware of such rights, he/she may pay the compensation to the insured and thus relieve himself/herself from the pertaining obligations from the insurance contract. Furthermore, apart from the fact that compensation may not be paid without their consent to the insured, these persons may directly demand that the insurer satisfies their claims within the limits of

525. *See* LO, Art. 938, para. 1.
526. Whether full or partial compensation is going to be made depends on the value of the entitled person's interests.
527. *See* LO, Art. 938, para. 3.

the amount of insurance, and according to the statutory order of payment.[528] Against the above persons, the insurer may raise only objections originating prior to the occurrence of the insured event.[529] Direct claims of the holders of rights, however, are indeed limited. As regards their extent, they are limited by the contracted amount of insurance (if provided for, of course) and the value of the third party's interest (e.g., by the amount of claims towards the insured). Therefore the claim's upper limit is the amount of insurance but only if the interest of the third party is higher than or equal to the amount of insurance. On the contrary, if the value of such interests is lower, the upper limit of compensation payable to the holder of a security right is going to be the actual value of their interest. Second, if there is a conflict of claims of such third parties, the possibility of realizing their interests is limited by the insurer's obligation to respect the statutory order pertaining to the payment of claims[530] (e.g., in case of a mortgage, the person first entered into the land register).

280. As the acquirer of the insured object, that is, a person acquiring the right of ownership from the insured, may also be a subject of the insurance relationship. A rule exists in this respect in that by acquisition of the insured object, the insurance contract is also transferred to the new owner. In such a case, the rights and duties of the insurance contractor shall pass to the acquirer (the new owner) *ex lege*, unless otherwise provided by contract.[531] The insurer and the acquirer of the insured object may withdraw from the insurance, honouring a fifteen-day notice period, on the condition that their notice is submitted within thirty days of becoming aware of the transfer.[532] The insurance contract shall not be terminated should the insurance policy be issued as a bearer policy or a policy transferable by order.[533] Such a solution is, however, justified only in case of contracts that may not be terminated by the insurer. By issuing such a policy, the insurer consented for its transfer to a third party, so that he/she should not be entitled to exploit such transfers for contract termination. In case of the acquirer, however, we hold the view that he/she should be afforded the right to terminate the contract due to the fact that at the moment of entering into the insurance contract he/she was not obliged to be aware of its conclusion. The policy following the object is transferred to him/her only upon acquiring ownership on the insured object. Yet, if the insurance contractor entered into the contract in his/her own name but on behalf of another undetermined person,[534] the first acquirer of the insured object (i.e., on whose behalf the contract has been entered into) will have the status of the original insured not deriving rights towards the insurer from the insured's earlier right. Therefore, the application of Article 937 LO and the possibility of contract termination are not justified in the above situation.

528. *See* LO, Art. 938, para. 2.
529. *See* LO, Art. 921, para. 2.
530. *See* LO, Art. 938, para. 2.
531. *See* LO, Art. 937, para. 2.
532. *See* LO, Art. 937, para. 5.
533. *See* LO, Art. 937, para. 6.
534. Such a modality of contract conclusion is provided for by LO, Art. 905.

281. Third-party claimants may in some situations have certain interests from the insurance contract. A third-party claimant is each person incurring losses caused by the actions and/or omissions of persons insured against liability (or persons that had the obligation to enter into such contracts but failed to do so).[535] By occurrence of the insured event, third-party claimants acquire *ex lege* the right to compensation from the insurer, the insured of which caused certain damage to them. The rights of third-party claimants, the legal nature of direct claims for compensation towards the insurer, as well as the possible objections that the insurer may raise against them are going to be discussed in detail within the section pertaining to liability insurance contracts.

282. Regular creditors are creditors, the claims of which are not secured in any manner (not having security interests in the insured object, or the policy not being pledged with them). Such creditors may in certain situations have interests from the insurance contract because, under particular conditions, they may claim reimbursement of the premiums paid by their debtors. Regular creditors are not in direct contact with the insurance, but if the requirements for refuting certain transactions of their debtors to their detriment are met, they may request from the insurer the reimbursement of premiums paid above the amount exceeding the possibility to satisfy the creditor's claim.[536]

283. An insurance policy, more precisely its pledging, may serve as a security device in loan agreements. Therefore, creditors, with whom the policy is pledged may have certain interests from the concluded insurance contracts. However, the right of pledging the policy before the occurrence of the insured event exists only in life insurance policies. The reason for this is that in life insurance the insured may effectively dispose of all rights stemming from the insurance contract even before the insured event occurs (the insurer may change the beneficiary, assign or transfer his/her rights or the beneficiary's rights, etc.). Life insurance policies may be issued as policies transferable by order or registered policies. If issued as policies transferable by order, policies may be pledged by full endorsement, while in case of registered policies, pledging may occur by means of assignment. In order for the pledging to be effective towards the insurer, apart from the prescribed form, it is necessary to notify the insurer that the policy has been pledged with a specific creditor.[537] These are the conditions necessary for the pledgee to receive certain rights pertaining to him/her in such a capacity (the right to pay the premium, the right to request payment of the policy repurchase price if his/her claim secured by the policy is not settled upon maturity, as well as the right to request payment of insurance compensations for the purpose of fulfilment of his/her secured claims). In other insurance contract types it is not possible to pledge the policy before occurrence of the insured event. This is allowed after the insured event occurred, as with pledging all other matured claims.

535. Jankovec, Miladinović, *Pravo osiguranja* (*Insurance Law*), 16.
536. *See* the provisions of the LO on refuting the debtors legal acts (Arts 280–285), as well as LO, Art. 961, para. 2 regulating the insurance contractor's creditors in life insurance contracts.
537. *See* LO, Art. 956, para. 2.

284. Persons incurring damage while trying to prevent the occurrence of the insured event or in the course of salvage may also have certain interests from insurance. Although such persons fall completely outside of the relationship established between the insurer and the insurance contractor, in judicial practice cases exist where the court obliged the contractor to indemnify such persons regarding their losses incurred while preventing the occurrence of the insured event or in the course of salvage.[538]

538. In a case involving a person participating in a fire-fight, in the course of which his/her health and clothes were damaged, the court afforded him/her damages because greater damage was prevented by means of his/her actions. Professional institutions are not entitled to indemnification when preventing the insured event to occur or in the course of salvage (e.g., fire brigades).

Chapter 7. Termination of the Insurance Contract

285. Insurance contracts may terminate in different manners: by means of performance, expiry of their term, cancellation, nullity, rescission, due to the insolvency of the contracting parties, due to termination of the object of insurance or other objects,[539] due to the occurrence of an event different from the insured event or out of other reasons provided for by the insurance contract.

§1. Termination by Means of Performance

286. The aim of the contract is fulfilled by means of performance. In insurance contracts an essential precondition for the creation and performance of the basic obligation of the insurer is the occurrence of the insured event. However, for the termination of the insurance relationship by means of the insurer's performance, it is necessary that the insured event causes certain consequences.[540] The heterogeneous being of insurance contracts determines the material difference between such consequences. In life insurance contracts, these are death or surviving a particular moment (age, marriage, birth of a child, etc.).[541] In insurance contracts of persons against consequences of an accident, these are also death or total disability (100% disability). In property insurance, these are the instances of total destruction of the insured object, objects in respect of the use of which a liability insurance contract has been concluded or objects insured against incidental damages by means of liability insurance. In all of the enumerated situations, it is impossible that the insured event occurs, so that it is not necessary that the insurance contract remains in force.[542] However, the occurrence of such an insured event is only a condition of the insurer's performance. Only upon the insurer's performance will it come to the termination of rights and obligations established prior to that moment. In all other instances (e.g., partial destruction of the insured object or partial disability) the occurrence of the insured event is not sufficient to trigger performance having as its effect the termination of the insurance relationship. In such cases the contract is going to remain in force with the same or altered effects (e.g., reduction of the amount of insurance).

§2. Termination by Means of the Contractual Term's Expiry

287. If a specific period of duration is provided for by the contract, the insurance relationship normally ends upon expiry of such a term. Expiry of the term leads to the automatic termination of the contract's effects. No notices of the contracting

539. Objects in respect of the use of which a liability insurance contract has been concluded or objects insured against incidental damages by means of liability insurance.
540. Marjanski, *Ugovor o osiguranju* (*Insurance Contract*), 226.
541. *Ibid.*
542. *Ibid.*

parties are necessary to that effect. The moment of expiry may be precisely determined or only determinable. If precisely determined, the insurance relationship ceases to exist at the end of the last day of the time limit stipulated.[543] If the term of contract is only determinable, it shall be deemed that the contract expires upon the occurrence of a particular event, or by commencement or performance of a certain action. Stipulation of determinable terms is typical in transport insurance contracts.[544] Upon the contractual term's expiry an insurance contract will have no effects for the future (*ex nunc*). Its existing effects will remain in force. New obligations may not be created, but the already existing ones need to be performed due to the fact they are effective until the period of limitation expires.

288. However, so-called prolongation clauses may be entered into contracts representing an exception to the above rule. According to such clauses the effects of an insurance contract will continue to be in force unless a contracting party cancels the contract before expiry of the stipulated term. The contract shall be effective under the same conditions. This is practically a prolongation of effects of a contract concluded for a definite period of time rather than a new contract. In accordance with the above, it is not necessary to issue a new policy, nor to repeatedly hand over the general terms and conditions. The clause needs to provide for the period, in which the contract is going to remain effective. Despite the fact that in certain legal systems the prolongation of the term of contract by means of prolongation clauses is excluded by coercive provisions, the LO does not have a corresponding rule. According to general terms and conditions on property insurance of Serbian insurers, if a policy contains only the beginning of the insurance period while prolonging the insurance on an annual basis, the insurance shall be prolonged each year unless a contracting party cancels the contract within the provided time limit (three months before the end of the current year).[545]

§3. Termination by Means of Cancellation

289. Insurance contracts are continuous legal transactions that, if concluded for an indefinite period of time, may be terminated by means of cancellation, as all other continuous contracts. All contracting parties are entitled to cancel the contract concluded for an indefinite period of time within the given notice period (provided for by the law, the contract or business practices), at any time apart from instances of hardship, by means of a unilateral notice to the other party. The notice period must be equal in respect of both parties. In insurance contracts, the notice period depends on the type of contract, as well as on the modalities of contracting. Should an insurance period be not provided by contract, each party shall be entitled to cancel the contract on the day of maturity of the insurance premium, after notifying the other party accordingly in writing, three months before the maturity of the premium

543. *See* LO, Art. 922, para. 1.
544. For details *see* Šulejić, *Pravo osiguranja* (*Insurance Law*), 220.
545. Šulejić P., *Pravo osiguranja* (*Insurance Law*), 180.

at the latest.[546] In such long-term insurance relationships, it is usually stipulated that the insurance contractor is obliged to pay the premium annually on the day corresponding to the day of contract conclusion. Accordingly, the contract may also be cancelled on that day. Apart from the above, within Serbian insurance law a contract may be cancelled even if concluded for a definite period of time if this period is longer than five years. In such cases the parties shall be entitled to notify the other party by a letter of their intent to cancel the contract, honouring a six-month notice period. The right of the parties to cancel the contract in the above manner may not be excluded by the contract.[547] Cancellation has a future effect, that is, the already established rights and obligations are going to remain in force. This, among others, means that the obligation to pay the premium is going to be effective for the whole period of the year when cancelling the agreement. If, however, the parties especially stipulate that the contract shall terminate at an earlier point (before expiry of the current year of insurance), such an obligation is going to be effective only up to the day determined as the date of contract termination. Naturally, the insurer shall also be obliged to bear the consequences of the insured event's potential occurrence up to the expiry of the above time limits. Therefore, within Serbian insurance law the effects of insurance contracts may be terminated by means of cancellation in case of contracts concluded for an indefinite period of time or contracts concluded for a period longer than five years. The above rule is not applicable in life insurance contracts due to the fact that an insurance contractor may withdraw from the contract at any time, regardless of the contractual term.

§4. Termination by Means of Nullity

290. Insurance contracts may terminate by means of nullity. Within this category contracts may cease to exist by a declaratory establishment of nullity if reasons of absolute nullity exist or by means of its annulment in instances of relative nullity (voidable contracts). The nullity of contract may be established, or the contract may be annulled if the cause of its termination existed at the moment of contract conclusion. Similarly, as in other agreements, insurance contracts may be either absolutely null (e.g., in case of a subject that is prohibited or against the morals or if their consideration is prohibited) or relatively null (in case of deficiencies of will due to mistake, threat, unlawful compulsion or fraud). Otherwise, nullity may pertain either to the whole contract or to its particular provisions.[548] Naturally, a contract shall cease to exist by means of the establishment of nullity or voidance only if the nullity of the entire contract is established. Therefore, the nullity of a particular contractual provision will not have as a consequence the nullity of the whole

546. *See* LO, Art. 922, para. 3.
547. *See* LO, Art. 922, para. 4.
548. For instance, null shall be provisions of an insurance contract regulating the termination of rights to a compensation or the insured amount, should the insured after the occurrence of the insured event not perform some of the statutory or contractual obligations. Similarly, null shall be provisions in an insurance policy regulating the insurer's responsibility if the contractor, the insured or the insurance beneficiary causes the insured event on purpose or by means of fraudulent misrepresentation. *See* LO, Art. 918, para. 920 and Art. 929, para. 2.

contract if the contract may survive without the null provisions not representing the condition, nor the decisive underlying reason of contract conclusion.[549]

291. Should the general interest be infringed upon by means of an insurance contract (the coercive statutory provisions or the public order), such a contract shall be absolutely null. Apart from general causes rendering a contract absolutely null, the absolute nullity of insurance contracts may be established in a relatively large number of cases typical to such legal transactions. The large number of such situations is also determined by the great variety of insurance contract types. An insurance contract shall be absolutely null in the following situations specific to such agreements:

- If there is no uncertainty as to the occurrence of the insured event (if, at the moment of contract conclusion, the insured event already occurred or already started to occur, or if its occurrence was evident, or if the possibility of occurrence ceased to exist by then).[550]
- If it is stipulated that the insurance will cover a certain period preceding the contract conclusion (retroactive insurance), the contract shall be null only if, at the moment of its conclusion, the interested party was aware that the case covered by insurance had already taken place, or that the possibility of its taking place had already ceased to exist.[551] For a contract to be absolutely null in case of retroactive marine insurance, it is not sufficient that an interested party was aware of the fact that an insured event occurred, but it is necessary to be aware of the amount of loss incurred.[552]
- If upon conclusion of life insurance contracts, the age of the insured has been erroneously reported while his/her real age exceeded the limit up to which the insurer, by his/her terms and tariffs, normally enters into life insurance transactions;[553]– if the insurance pertains to the death of a third party, the validity of contract shall depend on his/her written consent, indicated on the face of the insurance policy, or in a separate letter at the moment of signing the insurance policy, with an indication of the insured amount.[554]
- If the insurance contract pertains to the death of a third party younger than fourteen, or to a person completely deprived of business capacity.[555]

Should the insurance contract infringe upon individual interests of the contracting parties, it may be voided due to relative nullity. Relative nullity leading to contract annulment usually exists as a form of sanction for *mala fide* actions of contracting parties in course of performing their obligations at the moment of contract conclusion. An insurance contract shall be voidable in the following situations specific to such agreements:

549. *See* LO, Art. 105, para. 2.
550. *See* LO, Art. 898, para. 2.
551. *See* LO, Art. 898, para. 3.
552. *See* LMIN, Art. 751.
553. *See* LO, Art. 944.
554. *See* LO, Art. 946, para. 3.
555. *See* LO, Art. 947, para. 1.

- in case of deliberate non-performance of the obligation to report circumstances relevant for risk assessment at the moment of contract conclusion (if the insurance contractor deliberately files an incorrect application, or intentionally suppresses circumstances being of a nature which would induce the insurer, if he/she knew the real situation, not to enter into contract, the insurer shall be entitled to seek nullity of contract;[556]
- in case of causing overinsurance in bad faith (should at conclusion of the contract one party deceive the other, stipulating an amount of insurance higher than the real value of the insured object, the other party shall be entitled to request nullity of contract);[557]
- in case of causing double insurance in bad faith (if in the event of double insurance the insurance contractor fails to act in good faith, each insurer may request nullity of contract, keep the premiums received and demand the non-reduced premium for the current insurance period).[558]

292. Should the nullity of a particular contract be established or if it is voided, it shall be deemed that such a contract never existed. Therefore, the establishment of nullity (in absolute nullity) or voidance (in relative nullity) will lead to identical consequences. One of such consequences will be the obligation of both contracting parties to return everything received based on the contract. Therefore, if nullity is a consequence of a contracting party's bad faith, the opposing contracting party, if acting in good faith, will be entitled to seek damages. Therefore, in case of insurance, the insurer will be entitled to keep the paid premiums (or, if the premium had not been paid, seek its payment for the insurance period in which he/she became aware of the cause of nullity) if a null contract has been concluded by default of a *mala fide* insurance contractor (and/or insured). As in certain cases, it is possible to depart from coercive statutory provisions in the interest of the insured,[559] by means of general terms and conditions it is sometimes laid down that the presence of a reason for voidance shall not have as a consequence contract nullity as provided for by law, but rather the potential rescission of contract with an *ex nunc* effect (regarding, for instance, the payment of premiums).

§5. Termination by Means of Rescission

293. Effectively concluded contracts are terminated by means of rescission. Upon contract termination its effects also cease to exist. A contract may be rescinded in compromise or unilaterally. As contracts are entered into according to the autonomous will of contracting parties, they may also cease to exist according to their

556. *See* LO, Art. 908, para. 1.
557. *See* LO, Art. 932, para. 1. Art. 741 LMIN does not provide for contract nullity in case of causing overinsurance in bad faith but sets out that in case of damage liquidation the contracted, that is, the real value of the insured object is going to be taken into account.
558. *See* LO, Art. 934, para. 9. Art. 743, para. 1 LMIN does not provide for contract nullity in case of causing double insurance in bad faith but sets out that the total compensation received must not exceed the amount of damage coverable by insurance.
559. *See* LO, Art. 900, para. 2.

agreement. However, contracts may be unilaterally rescinded only in cases provided for by the law or the contract. The most important reasons for unilateral rescission are non-performance of contractual obligations or changed circumstances. However, as certain property insurance contracts have specific characteristics, a reason for rescission may also be the transfer of ownership on the insured object, in connection to the use of which a liability insurance has been concluded. General rules of civil law on rescission due to non-performance are applicable to insurance contracts but only if no special rules are laid down regarding particular cases of rescission or if such rules are insufficient.

294. The nature of insurance contracts is such that only the obligations of one contracting party – the insurance contractor (and/or the insured) are unconditional. Therefore, it is usually only one contracting party (the insurer) invoking the provisions on rescission due to the other party's non-performance. Obligations, the non-performance of which may cause contract rescission are the duty to report circumstances relevant for risk assessment, the duty to report changed circumstances in the course of insurance coverage and the duty of premium payment. Regarding contract rescission due to non-performance of the listed obligations please refer to the discussions from the section entitled 'Obligations of the Insured'.

295. In property insurance contracts, one of the reasons for contract rescission may be the transfer of ownership on the insured object. According to the LO, both the insurer and the acquirer have the right to seek contract rescission due to such change of ownership. The insurer and the acquirer of the insured object may withdraw from the insurance, honouring a fifteen-day notice period, on the condition that their notice is submitted within thirty days of becoming aware of the transfer.[560] The insurance contract shall not be terminated should the insurance policy be issued as a bearer policy or a policy transferable by order.[561]

§6. Insurance Contract Termination Due to the Initiation of Insolvency Proceedings

296. One of the methods of winding up business companies is insolvency. Whereas insurers in insurance contracts are always insurance companies (joint stock insurance companies) insureds may be both natural persons and legal entities (commercial companies or other legal entities). Accordingly, within Serbian law insolvency is a method of winding up legal entities. The initiation of insolvency proceedings against contracting parties having the status of legal entities may have certain effects on the insurance contract. Regarding the effects of the initiation of insolvency proceedings to insurance contracts, two legally relevant situations may come about depending on the fact whether the insolvency proceedings are initiated against the insurer or the insurance contractor (in most cases the insured).

560. *See* LO, Art. 937, para. 5.
561. *See* LO, Art. 937, para. 6.

297. In the case of the insurer's bankruptcy, the insurance contract shall be terminated upon the expiry of thirty days from the institution of bankruptcy proceedings.[562] This is a special rule not affording the bankruptcy estate manager representing the bankruptcy creditor's (the insurer's) interests to terminate the insurance contract within the first thirty days from the institution of bankruptcy proceedings. Therefore, if the insured event takes place within a time limit of thirty days from the initiation of bankruptcy proceedings, the insured shall be entitled to a compensation from insurance. The insurance contractor (often the insured) will also owe the payment of premiums for the subject period. Should the premium be paid in advance for the whole period of insurance, the insurance contractor will be entitled to seek reimbursement of the part of premium pertaining to periods not covered by insurance.[563] This rule is in accordance with the principle of insurance premium divisibility and the synallagmatic nature of insurance contracts.[564] The insured's claims are subject to a treatment equal to the claims of other creditors, rather than being privileged. The insured does not have a status of a bankruptcy estate creditor due to the fact that his/her claim, although created after the initiation of bankruptcy proceedings, is not a consequence of actions taken in the course of the bankruptcy proceedings aimed at the gathering, preservation and realization of the bankruptcy debtor's assets.[565]

298. In contracts on compulsory insurance within the transport sector, a special rule applies. In case of initiating bankruptcy proceedings against the insurance company, the concluded compulsory insurance contracts remain in force up to the point of their expiry.[566]

299. In the case of the insurance contractor's bankruptcy, the insurance shall continue, but each party shall be entitled to rescind the insurance contract within a three-month time limit from the institution of bankruptcy proceedings, in which case the contractor's insolvent assets shall be increased by the part of the paid insurance premium corresponding to the remaining time of insurance.[567] Therefore, the insurance contract shall remain in force in case of bankruptcy proceedings against the insurance contractor without the contracting parties rescinding the contract within a time limit of three months. It continues to be effective between the bankruptcy estate and the insurer. Should the insured event occur, the bankruptcy estate shall become the insurer's creditor regarding the payment of compensation or indemnification. However, not all claims based on the insurance contract concluded by the insurance contractor may become the bankruptcy estate's claims. If the insurance contractor (against whom bankruptcy proceedings have been subsequently

562. *See* LO, Art. 923, para. 2.
563. Slobodan Perović, *Komentar Zakona o obligacionim odnosima* (*Commentary of the Law on Obligations*) (Belgrade: Savremena administracija, 1995), 1502.
564. *See supra* n. 149.
565. Zoran Arsić, 'Dejstva otvaranja stečajnog postupka na dvostrano obavezne ugovore' (Effects of the Initiation of Bankruptcy Proceedings to Mutually Binding Contracts), *Glasnik advokatske komore, Vojvodine* 2 (1982): 9.
566. *See* the Act on Compulsory Insurance within the Transport Sector, Art. 4, para. 2.
567. *See* LO, Art. 923, para. 1.

instituted) concluded an insurance contract to the benefit of a third party, the eventual claim shall pertain to the insurance beneficiary (the third party) instead of the insurance contractor, that is, the bankruptcy estate. If one of the contracting parties rescinds the contract within three months from the initiation of bankruptcy proceedings, the part of paid premiums corresponding to the remaining period of insurance shall become a part of the bankruptcy estate.

300. In compulsory insurance contracts, there is a special rule as to the settlement of claims in case of bankruptcy proceedings. The insured, the insurance beneficiary or a third-party claimant may in case of the insurer's bankruptcy demand insurance compensation from the guarantee fund specially formed to that effect.[568]

301. Finally, an insurance contractor (or an insured) may cease to exist by means of death if the insurance contractor is a natural person. However, in the event of the insurance contractor's (or insured's) death, the insurance contract usually does not terminate. This is because of the fact that insurance contracts are concluded *intuitu rei* rather than *intuitu personae.* In property insurance contracts where an economic asset is the object of insurance, in the event of the insurance contractor's (or insured's) death the contract shall remain effective with his/her heirs. Upon inheritance of the economic asset representing the object of insurance, the heirs acquire an interest in the inherited object of insurance, so that there are no hindrances for the contract to remain in force. In personal insurance contracts, the contract shall terminate by means of the insured's death not because a contractual party or another participant in the insurance relationship ceases to exist but rather because of the termination of the insured object due to the materialization of the insured event (e.g., in life insurance contracts against death) or due to circumstances not representing the insured object (e.g., in life insurance contracts for survivorship, where the insured does not accomplish a certain age).[569]

§7. Termination of an Insurance Contract Due to Loss of the Insured Object or Other Objects Due to Occurrences Different from Insurance

302. An insurance contract may terminate if the insured object or person completely cease to exist due to causes different from the materialization of risks covered by insurance. In case of property insurance one or more things may be objects of insurance. Should an insured object be lost in course of the insurance period, due to an event not provided for in the insurance policy, the contract shall cease to be valid for the future, while the insurer shall be obliged to restitute to the insurance contractor a part of the insurance premium proportionate to the remaining period.[570] In such cases, the object of insurance ceases to exist. Naturally it cannot be exposed

568. *See* the Act on Compulsory Insurance within the Transport Sector, Art 17, paras 2–3, Arts 74–77.
569. Of course, under the presumption that a mixed insurance contract is not concluded simultaneously.
570. *See* LO, Art. 928, para. 1.

to risk anymore, so that it is certain that the insured event is not going to occur, and the insurer is not going to incur the obligations to bear the consequences of its occurrence. The conditions for application of the principle of premium divisibility are thus fulfilled (the period of insurance coverage is running, while the insured object stopped being exposed to the risk as a consequence of an event different from the insured event), so that the contract shall automatically be annulled with a future effect.[571] In accordance with the above, the premiums for the previous periods shall be due towards the insurer because of the assumption that the insurer was uncertain as to the obligation of bearing the consequences of the insured event's occurrence. The insurer shall be obliged to return the premiums pertaining to future periods of insurance coverage (under the condition, of course, that premiums were paid in advance). Should the insured object be only damaged, the principle of divisibility shall not be applicable due to the fact that the insurer's obligation is not diminished in compliance with Article 925 paragraph 6 LO. If, however, it is impossible to repair the object, it may come to a modification of the insured amount and the premium due to overinsurance. Should one of several objects encompassed by one contract be lost due to an event not provided for in the insurance policy, the insurance shall remain valid regarding the remaining objects, but necessary amendments shall be introduced because of the reduction of the object of insurance.[572] The amendments may be carried out in form of lowering the insured amount and the premium for the next period. The same rules are accordingly applicable to liability insurance contracts in relation to the use of precisely defined objects if such objects are lost within the insurance period due to events not provided for by the policy.[573] For instance, if a car, the use of which has been insured against liability is lost, it is evident that the owner is prevented from being responsible for damages due to using that particular car in the future. Insurance coverage is thus rendered unnecessary for the future. The insurance contract's effects automatically cease to exist.[574] In case of personal insurance contracts, a total loss of the insured object will occur in the event of death or total disability. If such events are caused by events different from the insured event, the contract's effects shall cease to exist (e.g., death before a certain moment in survivorship life insurance, or total disability due to circumstances different from materialization of the insured risk).

§8. Other Causes of Insurance Contract Termination

303. Apart from the above causes of termination regulated by the law, it is possible to provide for other reasons for terminating the contract's effects by means of insurance contracts (or by general terms and conditions representing their constituent parts). Of course, these reasons must not be contrary to coercive provisions, the public order or the business morals. A couple of most common situations provided

571. Borislav Blagojević, Vrleta Krulj, *Komentar Zakona o obligacionim odnosima, knjiga II* (*Commentary to the Law on Obligations, Book II*) (Belgrade: Savremena administracija, 1980), 500.
572. *See* LO, Art. 928, para. 2.
573. *See* LO, Art. 928, para. 1.
574. Perović, Stojanović, *Komentar Zakona o obligacionim odnosima, knjiga II* (*Commentary to the Law on Obligations, Book II*), 852.

for by general terms and conditions of Serbian insurers shall be discussed as examples. An insurance contract against accident consequences shall be terminated if the insured becomes mentally ill or if the year passes in which the insured accomplishes the age of 70, as well as if in contracts lasting longer than one year the insurer proposes an increase to the premium and informs the insured on that fact, while the insured declines such an offer.[575]

575. Marjanski, *Ugovor o osiguranju* (*Insurance Contract*), 245.

Part III. Property and Liability Insurance

Chapter 1. Fire Insurance

304. Fire insurance is one of the oldest insurance types. Within the domain of property insurance the risk of fire falls into the category of usual risks covered by insurance.[576] Fire as an insured risk comprises fires breaking out outside of a certain furnace or fires leaving such places which are capable of spreading on their own.[577] Fire insurance is possible both in civil[578] and in industrial insurance. All types of property, both movable and immovable may be covered by fire insurance. In all cases only the object listed in the policy shall be deemed to be covered.

305. The compensation in case of destruction or loss of the object is determined according to the insured object's value at the moment of the insured event's occurrence less the value of remainders. The compensation in case of damage shall be established in the amount of the price of reparation according to the price of materials and labour at the moment of the insured event's occurrence less the amount of estimated depreciation and the value of remainders, unless otherwise stipulated. Higher costs of repair incurred due to modifications, betterment or perfection of the damaged object in the course of repairs shall be borne by the insured.

306. Apart from compensation, the insured is to reimburse the costs incurred by collapse, movement and provision of help due to the occurrence of the insured event, as well as cleaning costs and the costs of preventing detrimental consequences.

307. Besides insurance against the risk of fire, it is a common practice to simultaneously insure the object of insurance against other risks by means of the same insurance contract (policy) – for instance, against lightning, explosion, thunderstorms, hail, aircraft crashes, and so on. In all cases, the insured risk must be listed in the policy. The same terms of insurance are applicable to other risks covered besides fire under the condition of setting out their details in the pertaining terms of

576. For instance if the CIF INCOTERMS clause does not expressly provide for the risks that are to be covered by the seller in course of the carriage, it shall be deemed that one of such risks is fire.
577. For example, the insurance of objects in construction, the insurance of objects being installed, the insurance of warehoused goods, the insurance of companies fall into the category of industrial insurance.
578. For instance, household insurance, the insurance of items exhibited on fairs, the insurance of glass against breakage, fall into the category of civil insurance.

insurance. Regarding circumstances not regulated within the special terms of insurance against fire, the general provisions pertaining to property insurance contained in general terms of property insurance and other sources of insurance law (the LO, for instance) shall be applicable in accordance with the rules on the hierarchy of their application.

Chapter 2. Loss of Benefits Insurance

308. Usually only actual losses incurred on the insured object, that is, on the insured movable or real property are covered by means of property insurance contracts. However, if specially provided for by the contract (the policy), it is possible that lost business profits and certain business costs incurred as a result of the suspension of business operations or production due to the destruction, damage or loss of the insured objects, that is, the basic means of production are also covered by insurance. A distinctive feature of such an insurance is that the insured may only be a legal entity active within a particular field of commerce (production, for instance), based on which profits are generated. Furthermore, this type of insurance may only be concluded as additional insurance, which means that previously or simultaneously an insurance of basic and non-pecuniary current assets against the same risks (e.g., fire and other perils) needs to be concluded.

309. Objects of such an additional insurance may be: business profits and certain business expenses. Business profits are considered only profits derived from the business revenues from registered commercial activities. The amount of lost business profits is usually established according to the data from the previous business year. Profits not in a causal relationship with the insured activity generated independently from such activities, such as financial profits, non-business and irregular profits and revalorization profits shall not be considered as business profits Only determined fixed costs that need to be borne by the insured and which are incurred irrespectively of the fact whether the commercial activity is performed or not shall be deemed as costs. Costs directly connected with the performance of commercial activities (costs of raw and regular materials, costs of gas and spent sources of energy, etc.) may not be objects of the insurance.

310. Damages caused by the suspension of commercial operations are the amounts of business profits that the insured was not able to generate in course of the suspension, as well as the uncovered amount of insured costs incurred in such a period. The insurer is obliged to pay compensation for damages incurred from the suspension of activities within the contracted period in duration of minimum three but up to twelve months (the guarantee period) from the point of the insured event's occurrence. A guarantee period of up to twenty-four months may also be stipulated by a special provision on the condition that a special premium is also paid to that effect. It is accustomed that so-called excluded risks are also stipulated.[579] For instance, an insurer is not obliged to compensate damages increased due to irregular circumstances occurring in duration of the suspension, or because of consequences of legal entities with which the insured has certain business relations, and so on.

311. Regarding circumstances not regulated by special terms of insurance against the risk of employment termination (loss of profit), the special terms of

579. *See supra* n. 181.

insurance against fire and other risks shall be applicable, as well as the general provisions pertaining to property insurance contained in general terms of property insurance and other sources of insurance law (the LO, for instance), in accordance with the rules on the hierarchy of their application.

Chapter 3. Marine Insurance

312. The following is to be understood under the term Marine Insurance: legal transactions pertaining to the insurance of ships, goods carried on vessels, the responsibility of ship-owners and other interests exposed to marine risks or risks connected with navigation at sea (freight insurance, insurance of costs pertaining to ship equipment, general average insurance, etc.)[580] Although pertaining statutory regulation providing for relationships of marine insurance dating from the period of the FRY does exist, due to the geographical location of the Republic of Serbia not having an exit to sea, after the dissolution of the state community of Serbia and Montenegro marine insurance lost on its relevance. However, relationships within the domain of navigation insurance, which is a wider concept than marine insurance, are regulated in the Republic of Serbia in a unique manner[581] irrespectively of the fact whether the insurance pertains to marine or internal navigation (rivers, lakes, canals, etc.). Due to the variety and importance of internal navigation in the Republic of Serbia, the above regulations have practical relevance within navigation insurance in internal waters. Due to the unique regulation of marine insurance and internal navigation insurance, the term navigation insurance shall be used instead of marine insurance hereinafter.

313. Navigation insurance contracts in the Republic of Serbia may, according to the classification of the LMIN, be divided into a couple of major categories: ship insurance contracts,[582] insurance contracts of goods carried on ships,[583] freight insurance contracts,[584] insurance contracts against the ship-owner's liability[585] and other insurance contracts not falling into the above categories (insurance against the costs of insurance, etc.). Ship insurance contracts cover the hull, machinery, installations and outfit, ordinary stores of fuel, lubricants and other materials, as well as reserves of food and drink necessary for the crew. Extraordinary stores of fuel, lubricants and other materials, reserves of food and drink above the crew's ordinary necessities and also outfitting expenses and insurance costs are covered by a ship insurance only if expressly stipulated.[586] The following categories are covered by means of contracts on the insurance of goods carried on ships: the value of goods at the port of shipment, the costs of insurance, freight, customs duties and other expenses relating to the carriage and delivery of the goods as well as expected profit, whereby it is not necessary to expressly stipulate coverage for such expenses or expected profits covered by the same insurance contract.[587] By means of freight

580. Pavić, *Ugovorno pravo osiguranja – Komentar zakonskih odredaba* (*Contractual Insurance Law – Commentary to the Statutory Provisions*), 385.
581. *See* LMIN, Arts 728–791.
582. *See* LMIN, Arts 769–774.
583. *See* LMIN, Arts 775–782.
584. *See* LMIN, Arts 783–786.
585. *See* LMIN, Arts 787–789.
586. *See* LMIN, Art. 769, para. 1.
587. *See* LMIN, Art. 769, para. 2.

insurance contracts the gross amount of freight is covered, unless otherwise provided.[588] Insurance contracts against the ship-owner's liability for losses caused to third parties[589] cover the indemnity for such amounts as the insured is bound to pay to third parties in connection with his/her liabilities covered by the insurance and also the expenses necessary for the ascertainment of his/her obligation.[590]

314. Apart from the above statutory classification of navigation insurance contracts they may also be categorized according to different criteria. According to one, they may be divided into special and general contracts. Special contracts provide for the insurance of particular ships or precisely determined shipments carried on particular destinations. General contracts provide for the insurance of more ships or a greater number of shipments carried simultaneously which are listed only generally within the contract. Second, according to the criterion of their duration, navigation insurance contracts may be divided into contracts entered into for a particular term and contracts with an undetermined duration. The duration of the insurance relationship or the insured voyage represent essential contractual elements that need to be listed within the policy. Ship insurance contracts are usually contracts for a particular term, while contracts on the insurance of goods in carriage are normally entered into for a particular voyage.

315. Navigation insurance contracts differ from other property insurance contracts due to a few specificities. First, as already mentioned, they are regulated by means of a special law. The provisions of the LMIN are applicable in their respect rather than the provisions of Chapter XXVII LO. Second, the provisions regulating relationships within the domain of navigation insurance are in the great majority of a yielding character as opposed to other types of property insurance where the provisions are of a coercive or semi-coercive nature. The reason for this is the fact that the economical inequality of contracting parties within the domain of navigation insurance is not as expressed as in other types of property insurance; so there is no need to protect the interests of the party not participating in drawing up the policy and the terms of insurance by means of coercive provisions. Autonomous sources of law have particular relevance in the capacity of legal instruments regulating contractual relationships. Business practices within navigation insurance are characterized by a great number of standardized insurance conditions, contractual clauses and terms. Third, navigation insurance contracts are informal agreements. An insurer is obliged to issue a formal and signed policy only if this is requested by the insurance contractor.[591] Fourth, the possibility to conclude a valid insurance contract with retroactive effects is greater in navigation insurance. By means of such contracting,

588. *See* LMIN, Art. 775.
589. Third parties are persons that are not signatories of the insurance contract.
590. *See* LMIN, Art. 787, para. 1.
591. *See* LMIN, Art. 735, para. 1.

under certain circumstances, risks that materialized in the period preceding the contract conclusion may also be covered (so-called putative risks). Fifth, legal institutes such as general average and abandonment[592] applicable in navigation insurance without their express stipulation, are inapplicable without expressly providing for them in other branches of insurance. Sixth, there are special provisions regarding limitation periods of claims stemming from navigation insurance contracts differing from the general statutes of limitation applicable in property insurance contracts. Thus, for instance, claims stemming from navigation insurance contracts shall expire within a time limit of five years, while those from other property insurance contracts shall expire within a time limit of three years.[593]

592. *See* LMIN, Art. 753, para. 3, Arts 759 and 781. Abandonment is an institute typical for property insurance. Insureds are enabled to transfer ownership on the insured object to the insurer upon its damage with the provision that the insurer pays full compensation according to the insurance contract (as if the object had been destroyed). An insured may have interest for the application of such a provision especially in situations where the damaged object may not anymore be used for all of its purposes and if the costs of its reparation or delivery are particularly high. An insurer, however, will be interested to apply such a provision if the insured already received and spent the compensation and the lost (stolen) object is subsequently found. As opposed to navigation insurance where the application of abandonment is assumed, in order to apply such an institute in other types of insurance contracts, it is necessary to provide for such a possibility expressly.

593. For details *see* LMIN, Art. 767 and LO, Art. 380.

Chapter 4. Liability Insurance

316. Liability insurance contracts are agreements where one party (the insurer) incurs the obligation to: (1) provide legal protection to the insured for his/her defence against unjustified or excessive claims for indemnification from third-party claimants; (2) compensate the costs of measures taken with the insurer's consent aimed at protection of unjustified or excessive claims of third parties; (3) reimburse the costs of reasonable measures of the insured taken without the insurer's consent (if the insured was unable to procure such a consent); and (4) reimburse the amounts payable by the insured towards third-party claimants in relation with their civil law liability covered by insurance, as well as the costs necessary for the establishment of the value of such obligations, while the other contracting party is obliged to pay the insurance premium.

317. Liability insurance contracts may be classified according to risk types, that is, the type of liability covered by insurance. In this regard there are practically four types of liability contracts. Contracts on the insurance against liability for damages caused to third parties by means of dangerous objects fall into the first group. These are insurance contracts of motor vehicle owners[594] against liability for damages caused to third parties, insurance contracts of aircraft owners against liability for damages caused to third parties and insurance contracts of boat owners against liability for damages caused to third parties. Within Serbian law, the above contracts fall into the category of compulsory insurance. The most important among them due to their practical relevance are insurance contracts of motor vehicle owners against liability for damages caused to third parties. The second group comprises liability contracts of various persons against damages caused to third parties in the course of carrying out professional activities. These are, for instance, insurance contracts against liability of physicians, solicitors/barristers, project-engineers, and so on. The third group comprises liability contracts of commercial entities against damages caused to third parties in the course of carrying out their business operations. The fourth group comprises general liability contracts against damages caused by activities falling outside of the scope of professional and business operations.

318. Liability insurance contracts have a compensatory character. This means that the principle of compensation is applicable to them. The object of insurance is the insured's property as a whole (Latin: *patrimonium*), that is, possible future debts because of liability. The insured is protected against claims directed towards his/her property as a whole, rather than against particular losses to his/her property or personality. He/she may be called upon to pay indemnification for losses suffered by

594. The category of motor vehicle owners shall be deemed to comprise users and all other persons to the name of which a vehicle is registered according to the pertaining statutory provisions. By means of the owner's insurance against liability caused to third parties all damages caused by the vehicle to third parties are covered regardless of the fact of who drove the vehicle at the moment of causing damage. *See* the Act on Compulsory Insurance within the Transport Sector, Art. 2, paras 2–3.

third parties as a consequence of the insured event. Therefore the insured (the tortfeasor) is by means of liability insurance contracts relieved from adverse consequences of his/her civil law liability (both contractual and non-contractual). Liability insurance contracts, however, may not provide for coverage of criminal, misdemeanour, disciplinary or liability based on commercial offences. Insurance against such liability types would be contrary to the public order. Similarly, as in all other property insurances, the person claiming indemnification (the insured or the third-party claimant) must have an insurable interest, that is, a legally permitted proprietary interest for the insured event not to occur. Furthermore, third-party claimants, as in all other types of property insurance may not cumulate insurance compensation with indemnification. Due to all of the above, liability insurance contracts fall into the wider category of property insurance contracts.

319. However, liability insurance contracts do have certain specificities in comparison with other property insurance contracts. As opposed to contracts on the insurance of particular objects, the value of insured interest is indeterminable in liability insurance contracts against damages caused on an unidentifiable object. Property as the object of insurance does not imply a limit of perils to which the object may be exposed due to the fact that the amount of the possible future debt is unknown. Very important consequences follow from the above fact. In such liability insurance contracts, certain principles otherwise applicable within the insurance of particular objects are not going to be employed. The amount of premium is determined by the frequency of the insured risk, rather than by the value of the insured object, so that the principle of proportionality typical for underinsurance, e.g., shall not be applicable in cases of liability insurance.[595] If liability insurance is not dependent on the occurrence of damages on a particular object, the principles pertaining to the transfer of the insurance contract in case of the insured object's abalienation shall not be applicable. The amount of insurance that may be stipulated in these contracts is the upper limit of the insurer's obligation, but it may also serve as a presumption of the amount of future losses caused. Furthermore, regardless of the fact whether we are faced with a case of liability insurance contracts against damages on a previously determined or undetermined object, liability insurance contracts differ from regular property insurance contracts regarding other features too. Apart from the insurer's basic obligation to pay insurance compensation (which is present in all other types of property insurance), the insurer is obliged to provide legal aid to the insured within his/her defence against unjustified or excessive third-party claims.

320. By means of liability insurance contracts injured parties are simultaneously afforded certainty regarding their indemnification for damages that could have remained unrepaired due to the tortfeasor's insolvency. Due to the fact that in such

595. However, this is not the case in all types of liability insurance. There are types of liability insurance against damages caused on particularly listed items where the insured shall be relieved from the proprietary consequences of civil law liability that may come about by means of a loss or damage to a particularly determined object (for instance, contracts on the carrier's liability insurance against potential damages to the carried goods), so that the value of the insured interest is in such cases determinable.

instances the insurance compensation is received by the third-party claimant rather than the insured, there is a necessity for the legal protection of the insured party's interests. The most important form of such protection is the right to address the insurer directly (by means of a direct claim) for compensation although the two are not in a contractual relationship. In case of liability insurance the person sustaining damage may request the compensation for loss sustained due to an event falling within the sphere of liability of the insured directly from the insurer, but only up to the amount of the insurer's obligation (the amount of insurance, if stipulated).[596] The person sustaining damage shall have, from the day of the insured event's occurrence, his/her own right to compensation from the insurance, so that any subsequent change in the insured's rights against the insurer shall have no effect on the right of an injured to compensation.[597] The right to a direct claim represents a statutorily regulated relationship of indemnification, the contents of which may or may not be influenced by the insurance contract depending on the fact whether we are faced with compulsory or voluntary liability insurance (for instance, the insurance contract will not have any effect to the direct claim in compulsory liability insurance where a contract has not at all been concluded in spite of the obligation to enter into such an agreement). Liability insurance contracts often have an influence on the contents of injured party's rights. First, liability insurance contracts may be important in regard to the amount of insurance coverage due to the fact that the insurer is responsible up to his/her obligation determined by the insured amount. Thereby it needs to be taken into account that the insured amount in compulsory insurance must not be lower than the statutorily provided amounts of insurance. An insurer shall only be obliged to bear the procedural costs in the lawsuit pertaining to the insured's liability. Second, if a compulsory liability insurance contract has not been entered into, the party sustaining damage is going to be entitled to claim indemnification from the Guarantee Fund seated in the territory where the damage has been caused. If, however, damage is caused by a person covered by means of compulsory insurance, the party sustaining damages may seek indemnification directly only from the insurance company with which the insured is in a contractual relationship.

596. *See* LO, Art. 941, para. 1.
597. *See* LO, Art. 941, para. 2.

Chapter 5. Legal Aid Insurance

321. Legal aid insurance is a type of insurance having as its subject the costs incurred in the course of legal assistance to the insured. Legal aid costs comprise solicitor's/barrister's fees, as well as fees of court and other procedures. Legal aid insurance is a type of property insurance classified by the LI into the wider group of non-life insurance.[598] Therefore, the provisions of the LO on property insurance are applicable in its respect.

322. Legal aid insurance as a special type of insurance is not common in Serbia, so that it is quite undeveloped.[599] However, the risk of legal aid insurance is often an ancillary risk in several liability insurance types which is a consequence of the fact that the defence of unjustified and excessive claims within liability insurance is a very important obligation of the insurer. Therefore, legal aid insurance is in the offers of Serbian insurance companies often combined with the professional liability insurance of physicians.

598. *See* LI, Art. 10.
599. According to the data at hand, only one insurance company has in its offer this type of insurance.

Chapter 6. Aviation and Space Insurance

323. The branch of transport insurance providing for the insurance of airplanes (for the transport of passengers and goods) and other aircraft (helicopters, agricultural aviation, sport aviation, paragliders, motor gliders, balloons, etc.), their equipment, goods and other transported movables, the owners and users of airplanes against liability for damages caused to passengers and third parties, as well as other interests (freight, insurance costs, expected profits, security interest and other legal and material benefits) exposed to risks within air transport or connected with it, is to be understood under the concept of aviation insurance.[600] Contracts on the insurance of aircraft and other objects within air transport may be entered into for a particular term or specially determined flight.[601] The basic features of such insurance contracts are similar to those of other branches of transport insurance. Space insurance is absent from practice in the Republic of Serbia.

324. Aviation transport insurance is regulated by means of the Law on Contracts and Property Relations in Air Transport (1998). In Chapter IV of the above Law (Articles 124–131) in the section entitled 'The Insurance Contract within Air Transport' certain specific issues regarding this type of insurance are regulated. The Law provides for possible objects of insurance,[602] the term of insurance,[603] damages excluded from insurance,[604] the application of other enactments.[605] In issues not specially regulated by the above Law the provisions of the LMIN shall be applicable accordingly.[606] The LO's provisions on the insurance contract (Chapter XXVII) are not applicable to aviation insurance contracts. The statutory provisions on aviation insurance are mostly of a yielding character, so that contracts (along with general and special terms of insurance) are the major sources of law for regulating insurance relationships within air transport.

325. Aviation insurance is normally of a voluntary nature in the Republic of Serbia. As an exception the law provides for certain situations when such insurance is compulsory. Two types of compulsory contractual insurance are provided for within the field of aviation insurance.[607] These are accident insurance of passengers within public air transport and liability insurance of aircraft owners against damages caused to third parties and passengers.[608]

600. Pavić, *Ugovorno pravo osiguranja – Komentar zakonskih odredaba* (*Contractual Insurance Law – Commentary to the Statutory Provisions*), 631.
601. *See* the Law on Contracts and Property Relations in Air Transport, Art. 126, para. 1.
602. *See* the Law on Contracts and Property Relations in Air Transport, Art. 124.
603. *See* the Law on Contracts and Property Relations in Air Transport, Art. 126, para. 1.
604. *See* the Law on Contracts and Property Relations in Air Transport, Art. 127.
605. *See* the Law on Contracts and Property Relations in Air Transport, Art. 131.
606. *Ibid.*
607. The term compulsory contractual insurance is employed to denominate a situation where the law provides for the obligation of particular subjects to conclude a compulsory contractual insurance where the conditions of insurance are partially provided for by the law.
608. *See* the Act on Compulsory Insurance within the Transport Sector, Art. 2.

Chapter 7. Theft and Embezzlement Insurance

326. Insurance against the risk of theft falls into the category of property insurance due to the fact that the insured is covered against the risk of theft of various objects in his/her ownership. Therefore all rules on property insurance within the Serbian legal system are applicable to this type of insurance. Within the special terms of insurance of Serbian insurance companies, this type of insurance is usually described as burglary and robbery insurance. A burglary is a theft where a person (the thief) breaks into the premises where the insured objects are located by means of entering by force through the doors or windows, attic, walls, floors or by opening the premises by means of false keys or their duplicates acquired in an illegal manner. Robbery is the taking of the insured object by threat of jeopardizing the insured's life or health. Risks covered by this type of insurance are burglary and robbery, the attempts of burglary and robbery, as well as acts of vandalism in course of committing these crimes.

327. Objects of this type of insurance may be all movables (furniture, appliances, reserves, small inventory, equipment), money and other payment vehicles, valuables situated in a certain object, money and all valuables in the course of transport on the condition that the insured or members of his/her household are their owners, as well as objects belonging to employees or third parties received for repair, sale, leased and pledged objects, objects handed over for safe custody, if such situations are specially stipulated.

328. Should the property be insured for an amount corresponding to its total value, in the event of theft or destruction, the total value is going to be compensated, while in case of damage to the object the value of work and materials necessary for its repair. Should the property be insured for an amount lower than its total value, the provisions pertaining to underinsurance shall be applicable.[609] It is common, however, in this insurance type to stipulate insurance against the so-called first risk. In such instances, under the condition of paying premiums lower than in case of insurance amounts corresponding to the total value of insured property, the incurred damages will be compensated fully, while the coverage limit (the insurance amount) shall be reduced in the course of insurance duration by the compensated amount. Apart from the above, as in other types of property insurance, the costs incurred as a result of measures aimed at preventing and diminishing the damage are also covered by the insurance.

329. Regarding circumstances not regulated within the special terms of insurance against the risks of burglary and robbery, the general provisions pertaining to property insurance contained in general terms of property insurance and other sources of insurance law (the LO, for instance) shall be applicable in accordance with the rules on the hierarchy of their application.

---

609. *See* nn. 272–274.

330. Embezzlement insurance is a type of insurance against losses through the dishonesty of individuals entrusted with money or other property, who violate the trust. Despite the fact that all the legal conditions for providing such insurance services do exist, this type of insurance is not present within practice. At the time being, Serbian insurance companies do not have such an insurance type in their offers.

Chapter 8. Agricultural and Livestock Insurance

331. Agricultural insurance is an indeed important branch of insurance. It comprises the insurance of agricultural crops and fruits, that is, plant production, as well as livestock insurance. Agricultural insurance is on a relatively low level in Serbia, which is a consequence of the economic status of agriculture.

332. According to the general rules of agricultural insurance delivered by Serbian insurance companies, the objects of such insurance may be the following: crops (including stubble crops, sub-crops and inter-crops), fruits, field grass, medicinal herbs, decorative plants, orchards and vineyards, willow, reed, and so on. For the insurance of crops and fruit, it is important to precisely determine the object of insurance (for instance, in grain crops, the grain itself is insured, while the stalk only if it is expressly provided for, while in tobacco the leaves are insured unless grown for seeds, and these shall be insured only if expressly stipulated so).

333. Basic risks covered by this type of insurance are: hail, fire, lightning, while the crops or fruits are not harvested or picked. If, however, additional insurance with special terms is stipulated and the underlying additional premium paid accordingly, additional risks may also be covered by insurance: such as floods, spring frost, thunderstorms, and so on. In agricultural insurance, the limits of particular occurrences (frost, for instance) important for risk materialization are precisely determined by means of general insurance terms, as well as the period in which they may occur. Thus, e.g., in agricultural insurance against frost the risks of late spring and early autumn frosts are covered, but not winter frosts, which represent a common occurrence.

334. Crops and fruits are insured for an amount established by the insured (the insured amount) but up to the expected real value of yield in the given year, unless otherwise provided. The expected value of yields and the expected free market value of the given year upon harvesting, the guaranteed price if so stipulated or the price agreed upon with the production organizer shall serve as the base of calculating the value of crops and fruits. Furthermore, it is common to provide for an insurance franchise,[610] so that losses incurred below a certain percentage (e.g., 5%) are not compensated.

335. The other group of agricultural insurance is livestock insurance. According to the general terms and conditions of Serbian insurance companies pertaining to livestock insurance, animals may be objects of insurance only if of a certain age (e.g., within the insurance of ungulates – horses, donkeys, mules, it is possible to insure an animal aged between 10 days and 18 years, etc.). Sick animals or animals believed to be sick, degenerate animals, blind animals, and so on may not be covered by insurance. Furthermore, coverage is provided only while the animals are located at the places listed in the policy. Apart from the above, animals shall be

610. Franchise is part of the losses incurred upon occurrence of the insured event, which shall be borne by the insured in spite of entering into an insurance contract.

deemed to be covered by insurance while being located on the insured's estate (in the course of grazing), during participation on fairs, as well as in the course of transport to the place of grazing, the fair, and so on.

336. Risk covered by insurance are death of the insured animal caused by disease or accident, emergency slaughtering, as well as costs of treatment if expressly stipulated. Additional risks may be covered by insurance in accordance with the special conditions on livestock insurance. Furthermore, insurance terms especially provide for risks excluded from insurance.

337. Crops and fruits insurance, as well as livestock insurance fall into the category of property insurance, so that regarding circumstances not regulated within the general and special terms of insurance, the general provisions pertaining to property insurance contained in general terms of property insurance and other sources of insurance law (the LO, for instance) shall be applicable in accordance with the rules on the hierarchy of their application.

Chapter 9. Catastrophe Insurance

§1. General

338. Catastrophe risks within insurance law comprise events leading to great devastations and destructions as a result of disasters. In the Republic of Serbia insurance against various types of catastrophe risks caused by nature or by the human factor, is a common occurrence. Basic risks caused by natural or human factors and covered by means of property insurance are the following: fire, lightning, thunderstorms, hail, explosions, crashing one's own motor vehicle or movable machinery into an insured construction, as well as aircraft crashes. Supplementary types of risks caused by natural or human factors, which may be covered by insurance in case of express stipulation and the payment of additional premiums are: floods, torrents, landslides, earthfall, soil subsidence, avalanches, leakages, leakage of glowing melted materials, self-ignition of reserves, crash of unknown vehicles into an insured construction, breakage of exposed items and their stands.

§2. Nuclear Risks

339. At the time being, there are no nuclear power plants in Serbia, so that there is no practical necessity of insurance against such risks. Hence, this insurance type would gain importance only upon building such power plants. It is interesting, however, that due to the application of certain enactments dating from the former Socialist Federal Republic of Yugoslavia, the liability insurance of inland nuclear power plant owners still represents a compulsory insurance despite the fact that such a provision is not applied out of the above practical reasons.

§3. Natural Catastrophes

340. As already pointed out, insurance against various natural disasters is a common practice in the Republic of Serbia. The only difference is that certain risks caused by natural catastrophes are within the category of so-called basic risks. Basic risks are risks that are always covered by means of property insurance. According to the general terms and conditions on property insurance of Serbian insurance companies, the following risks are categorized as risks caused by natural catastrophes: lightning, hail, thunderstorms, fire (both natural and manmade). Additional risks are risks covered only if expressly stipulated and if supplementary premiums were paid for them. According to the general terms and conditions on property insurance of Serbian insurance companies, the following risks are categorized as supplementary risks caused by natural catastrophes: floods, torrents, landslides, earthfall, soil subsidence and avalanches.

Chapter 10. Credit Insurance

341. Credit insurance falls into the wider category of claims insurance. In order for a claim to become the object of insurance, it is necessary that a legal relationship exists at the time of contract conclusion, that is, a claim stemming from such relationship is due or may become due. There are two types of credit insurance in practice: insurance against the risk of losing the entitlement to certain claims and insurance against the risk of the inability to collect outstanding claims.

342. Insurance against the risk of losing the entitlement to certain claims exists if the objects of insurance are freight or a fee for the provision of certain services. If, for instance, it comes to the loss of goods due to force majeure in course of carriage, the carrier shall not be liable for damages incurred on the goods, nor shall he/she be entitled to claim the amount of freight from the opposing contracting party. Accordingly, the entitlement to a claim that would exist had the legal transaction been completed, would be lost. Therefore, the amount of freight shall be covered by means of compensation from insurance.

343. Insurance against the risk of the inability to collect outstanding claims is typical for insurance contracts of receivables based on loan contracts. Credit insurance contracts are those where the creditor (in the capacity of an insurance contractor or a person on whose behalf the contract has been entered into) is entitled to a compensation from insurance if the insured event occurs, that is, when the receivables are not collected from the debtor as a consequence of certain risks. Within Serbian insurance law, there are two basic types of insurance contracts: *del credere* credit insurance contracts and guarantee credit insurance. *Del credere* credit insurance is where the creditor enters into a contract on the insurance of his/her receivables from the credit agreement. In such an insurance contract, the creditor will simultaneously be the insurance contractor and the insured. This means that only the creditor is in a contractual relationship with the insurer. Hence the credit beneficiary as the debtor is not in a contractual relationship with the insurer. However, should as a consequence of the impossibility to collect receivables the insurer pays compensation to the creditor, the insured (the creditor) shall, by means of assignment, transfer all rights towards the credit beneficiary based on the credit contract to the insurer. Guarantee credit insurance is a type of insurance where the credit beneficiary (the debtor) enters into a credit insurance contract in his/her own name but on behalf of the creditor. The credit beneficiary (the debtor) is in a contractual relationship with the insurer. This means that he/she is obliged to pay the insurance premiums. However, as the contract is entered into on behalf of the creditor, should the creditor not succeed in collecting his/her receivables from the credit beneficiary, the insurer shall pay compensation from insurance to the creditor due to the credit insurance contract that was entered into on his/her behalf. Similarly, as in other types of property insurance, there has to be a legally permitted material interest for the insured event not to occur, failing which material losses would be incurred. This interest is manifested here as the impossibility to collect the claims (the principal debt along with the pertaining interests) stemming from the concluded credit contract. Guarantee credit insurance is normally concluded as a precondition to approving credits to a bank's customers. This type of insurance is one of the possible security vehicles of returning the received loan. Should as a consequence of the impossibility to collect receivables the insurer pays compensation to the creditor, the insured (the creditor) shall, by means of assignment, transfer all rights towards the credit beneficiary based on the credit contract to the insurer. Within the practice of credit insurance in Serbia the most commonly concluded contracts are on the insurance of retail consumer credits, insurance of permitted current account overdrafts, housing loan insurance, insurance of small enterprise credits and the insurance of credits based on leasing contracts.

344. Due to the fact that credit insurance contracts fall into the category of the insurance of claims, the provisions of Chapter XXVII LO shall not be applicable in their respect.[611] Credit insurance contracts are mainly regulated by means of autonomous sources of law (general terms and conditions, etc.) However, taking into account that particular receivables bear larger social importance, special laws have been passed within the domain of insurance of particular receivables. These are primarily credits based on export transactions of domestic commercial entities. Credit insurance stemming from export transactions offers coverage in case of non-payment by foreign customers for delivered goods or rendered services. Credit insurance is a constituent part of the export financing procedure. In order to increase or maintain the existing level of business operations, commercial entities are forced to sell goods at longer repayment periods. Thus numerous exporters incur losses due to untimely payment or the insolvency of their customers. Different instruments of risk protection have been developed in the practice. The conclusion of contracts on the insurance of export credits turned out to be one of the best mechanisms of such protection. However, as such risks often transcend the capacities of domestic insurance companies, an agency specialized for the insurance of export credits against commercial[612] and non-commercial[613] risks of domestic commercial entities has been established by means of the Law on the Export Credit and Insurance Agency of the Republic of Serbia. Apart from the above, the National Housing Loan Insurance Corporation has been established in Serbia by means of the Act on the National Housing Loan Insurance Corporation, which is a specialized legal entity for credit insurance based on approved housing loans. The corporation provides insurance of approved housing loans if the real estates are secured by means of a mortgage in favour of banks. The creditor (the bank) shall be entitled to compensation from insurance only if its claims may not be collected from the debtor. If the conditions for compensation are met, it shall be paid in instalments corresponding to the loan repayment schedule.

---

611. *See* LO, Art. 899, para. 2.
612. Commercial risks are for instance the non-payment of a matured debt upon written notification, insolvency, bankruptcy, cessation of the debtor's assets, the debtor's impossibility to perform the contractual obligations due to circumstances within the debtor's fault.
613. Non-commercial risks are various direct and indirect political risks (e.g., payment moratorium).

Chapter 11. Technical Insurance

345. The concept of technical insurance comprises in the Republic of Serbia a whole spectrum of various insurance types. In its narrower sense technical insurance means the combined insurance of movable technical apparatus. In the wider sense, apart from the insurance of movable technical apparatus, this type of insurance also comprises the insurance of computers, processors and similar appliances, the insurance of objects under construction, objects in the process of installation, the property insurance of electrical companies, underground mine property insurance, property insurance of railway companies, insurance of film companies and warranty insurance.[614] All of these insurances are types of property insurance. Furthermore, the above insurances are regulated by means of special terms of insurance,[615] while in the absence of such, that is, in parts not regulated by means of special rules, the general insurance terms of Serbian insurance companies are applicable, such as: General Terms of Property Insurance, Special Terms of Insurance against Fire and other Hazards, Special Terms of Insurance Against Machine Breakage and other Hazards and Special Terms of Burglary and Robbery Insurance. Their application depends on the legal loophole within the special terms of insurance governing the particular insurance type, as well as on the object of insurance and the type of risks that materialize on the object of insurance in the particular case at hand.

346. In all of the described insurance types, the special rules precisely provide for the object of insurance, the parts excluded from insurance (usually consumable or exploitable materials), as well as items normally not covered by insurance, the coverage of which may be expressly provided for under the condition of additional premium payment. All of the listed insurance types provide the insured party with coverage against various risks. These risks are usually divided into three groups within special terms of insurance. The first group consists of fire, lightning, explosion, thunderstorms, hail, floods, torrents, landslides, and so on. The second group of risks consists of production accidents comprising unforeseeable and sudden events in connection with the usage of insured objects (e.g., errors in construction, in materials, falling apart due to centrifugal power) Risks such as loss or damage of the insured objects due to burglary or theft or their attempts fall into the third category of risks. Due to the fact that such diverse risks are usually covered by the same policy, the term combined insurance has been introduced in practice (for instance, combined insurance of movable technical apparatus). Furthermore, it is not uncommon to provide within the special terms for risks not covered by insurance, as well as the place and time of the coverage being effective (for instance,

---

614. By means of such insurance the insured (a producer of particular items) issuing a warranty for proper functioning, provides for an insurance coverage for the case of damages caused to the owner by the object's malfunction.

615. The following special insurance terms are common within the domain of technical insurance: Special Insurance Terms of Movable Technical Apparatus, Special Insurance Terms of Computers, Processors and Similar Appliances, Special Insurance Terms of Objects under Construction, Special Insurance Terms of Objects in the Process of Installation, Special Property Insurance Terms of Electrical Companies, Special Terms of Property Insurance in Underground Mines, Special Insurance Terms of Film Companies, etc.

until the items are at the insured's premises, in the course of carriage to the place of use but nut during utilization itself) As in other insurance types, the insurer is obliged, apart from paying compensation from insurance, to reimburse the costs of preventing or diminishing the losses caused by the insured event's occurrence, as well as the costs of repairing the consequences of the insured event (e.g., cleaning the area stricken by fire) Finally, another specificity of this type of insurance (e.g., production line insurance in various companies) is that the insurer's experts often examine the object of insurance prior to entering into the contract.

Chapter 12. Miscellaneous Insurance

347. 'Directors and Officers Insurance' (commonly referred to as D&O) protects the insured directors and officers from suits against them alleging negligence in their corporate capacity. The policy will also reimburse the corporation for amounts paid to defend insured directors or officers from such suits or to reimburse them pursuant to an established corporate policy. The policy will typically exclude coverage for claims alleging fraud, dishonesty or wilful violation of law. In contrast to standard liability policies, the coverage limit for D&O insurance typically includes defence costs.

348. 'Errors and omissions' (known as 'E&O') or professional liability coverage is business risk insurance for professionals such as doctors or lawyers. The coverage protects the policyholder for mistakes made in the course of its business. These policies are almost always written in the claims-made format, providing coverage for claims first made during the policy period. In addition, they will typically contain a retroactive date which bars claims arising out of underlying occurrences that took place prior to a specific date. As noted above, one unique feature of these policies is a provision that the insurer may not settle a claim without the consent of the insured, which was inserted to protect the policyholder's professional reputation.

349. A property insurance policy will indemnify the insured for tangible damages it suffered as the result of a covered peril, but it will not reimburse it for any lost profits it sustained as a result. To cover loss of profits, the insured must also obtain 'business interruption' or 'use and occupancy' protection.

350. A business interruption policy is usually written in conjunction with a property policy, and it applies only where there has been an actual suspension of the business as a result of direct physical loss of or damage to insured property from a covered peril. Business interruption insurance is a time-element insurance, which means that it provides coverage only for a specific period of time. The business interruption time measure is hypothetical; the time which would be required with the exercise of due diligence to physically repair the damage or restore the property. The measure of loss can be either 'valued' as a stipulated sum per day or 'open'. If it is open, the insured is entitled to recover its net profits, fixed expenses and extra expenses incurred in reducing the loss.

Part IV. Motor Vehicle Insurance

351. This group of insurance comprises in the Republic of Serbia the owner's or user's liability insurance against damages caused to third parties and the insurance of vehicles against damage and theft, also known as 'casco' insurance. Insurance companies will in case of motor vehicle liability insurance normally pay compensation of medical costs comprising costs of medical treatment and other ancillary costs triggered by treatment, so that their coverage is not regulated by means of special insurance types. Furthermore, for the purpose of protecting the interests of passengers in public transport as well as third-party claimants, in cases when damage is caused by uninsured or unknown vehicles, the Serbian Act on Compulsory Insurance within the Transport Sector provides for a Guarantee Fund, which is a legal entity paying compensation to passengers in public transport and third-party claimants in cases when damage is caused by uninsured or unknown vehicles,[616] as well as for damages that are due for indemnification by a bankrupt insurance company.

616. The following are deemed as transportation vehicles: motor vehicles, aircrafts, boats and other means of transport. The term 'transportation vehicle' provided for by the Act on Compulsory Insurance within the Transport Sector shall mean vehicles as defined by the law regulating the relevant type of traffic, provided that the term 'motor vehicle' shall also comprise trailers.

Chapter 1. Liability Insurance

352. Liability insurance contracts of motor vehicle owners and/or users against damages caused to third parties represent a type of compulsory insurance. Compulsory liability insurance of motor vehicle owners and/or users against damages caused to third parties is regulated by means of statutory provisions, as well as by means of contracts entered into by the insurer and the insured. The legislator's intervention in this case is of utmost importance due to the fact that the framework of the relationship between the insurer, the insured and the party suffering damages is thus established. However, despite the fact of being compulsory, this is a type of contractual insurance, meaning in fact that legal relationships are created by means of entering into contracts rather than automatically, based on the law itself, that is, by fulfilling certain preconditions laid down by statutory provisions (by entering into particular relationship or having certain features).[617] A compulsory liability contract must be concluded before a vehicle is permitted to enter the traffic. Furthermore, the conclusion of such a contract represents a precondition of motor vehicle registration.[618] The basic source of law for this insurance type is the Act on Compulsory Insurance within the Transport Sector (2009). The provisions contained in the above Act are mostly of a coercive nature. Therefore, the subject of contractual regulation is the relationship stemming from insurance (the relationship between the insurer and the insured, as well as the legal position of injured parties), unless provided for by the law.[619] Particular contracts are thus an important supplement to the coercive statutory provisions. Under the term 'contracts' the insurer's general terms and conditions representing a constituent part of insurance contracts are to be understood. As regards matters not regulated by the Act on Compulsory Insurance within the Transport Sector or contractual provisions, the rules of Chapter XXVII LO pertaining to property insurance, especially the provisions on liability insurance (Articles 940–941 LO) shall be applicable.

353. Persons operating motor vehicles (hereinafter 'driver') are obliged to have in the course of such operation an insurance policy[620] or other confirmation of a concluded insurance contract, as well as a European Accident Report[621] and are obliged to present such documents upon request of authorized officials.[622] Should

617. Šulejić, *Pravo osiguranja* (*Insurance Law*), 421.
618. *See* the Act on Compulsory Insurance within the Transport Sector, Art. 20.
619. Šulejić, *Pravo osiguranja* (*Insurance Law*), 421.
620. Such insurance policies are uniform on the territory of the Republic of Serbia. The contents of the policy form and the record keeping of concluded policies are provided for by the NBS. *See* the Act on Compulsory Insurance within the Transport Sector, Art. 19.
621. In case of a traffic accident, the participants are obliged to fill in, sign and exchange the European Accident Report pursuant to the law governing road traffic safety. An orderly filled in European Accident Report may be used by the party sustaining damages and the insured as a compensation claim from motor vehicle liability insurance. *See* the Act on Compulsory Insurance within the Transport Sector, Art. 31, para. 1.
622. In case that a vehicle is operated by a person other than the vehicle's owner, the owner shall be obliged to enable the driver to dispose of the insurance policy or another proof on the concluded insurance contract in the course of their operation of the owner's vehicle. *See* the Law on Compulsory Insurance within the Transport Sector, Art. 8.

the motor vehicle be operated by a driver other than the owner, the owner shall be obliged to provide the driver with the insurance policy during the usage of the vehicle, or some other type of evidence on the concluded insurance contract, and the owner should also dispose of the European Accident Report.[623] Conclusively, the motor vehicle owner is the party obliged to enter into a compulsory insurance contract. The insurer's obligation to accept the contract conclusion (if active within the particular field of insurance and under the conditions of such insurance operations) corresponds to the above obligation of the motor vehicle owner. Within Serbian insurance law, only the vehicles of the Serbian Army are exempted from the obligation to dispose of a concluded compulsory insurance contract.[624]

354. Persons covered by compulsory insurance are motor vehicle owners, as well as persons driving the subject motor vehicle. Motor vehicle owners are persons entitled to use the vehicle in their own interest, as well as to dispose of it. Due to the fact that their liability for damages caused to third parties is covered by insurance, such liability shall be equally covered in instances of objective liability, as well as when liability exists regarding fault not only for their own actions but also for actions of other persons (e.g., in the capacity of parents, employers, legal entities). Persons entrusted with the use or supervision of the vehicles are persons authorized by the owner to use the vehicle or persons that incurred the obligation to supervise the vehicle (e.g., a door-keeper). Terms of insurance cover the liability of the person in possession of the motor vehicle, that is, the persons entrusted with the use or supervision of the vehicle. Motor vehicle third-party liability insurance shall include damages caused by motor vehicles used and/or driven by unauthorized persons.[625] However, the liability of unauthorized persons is not covered by insurance. The Insurance Company which has paid compensation to the claimant for damages caused by unauthorized vehicle users shall be entitled to subrogate against the person liable for damage up to the amount of paid damages, the interests paid on such a compensation, as well as procedural costs.[626]

355. An insured person shall forfeit their insurance rights in the following instances: (1) if the driver[627] did not use the vehicle for its intended purpose; (2) if the driver did not possess a valid driver's licence for the appropriate type or category, except during driving lessons when a driving candidate was operating the motor vehicle and abiding by all regulations regulating such lessons; (3) If the driver's licence was taken away, or the vehicle removed from the traffic, or the driver has been forbidden to operate the vehicle by means of an interim measure, or the driver may not use the foreign driver's licence in the territory of Republic of Serbia; (4) if the driver has operated the vehicle under the influence of alcohol above

623. Regarding pecuniary fines *see* the Act on Compulsory Insurance within the Transport Sector, Art. 100.
624. *See* the Act on Compulsory Insurance within the Transport Sector, Art. 11.
625. *See* the Act on Compulsory Insurance within the Transport Sector, Art. 30, para. 1.
626. *See* the Act on Compulsory Insurance within the Transport Sector, Art. 30, para. 2.
627. All persons sitting behind the wheel influencing the vehicle's movement shall be considered as drivers. However, the concept of a driver is not limited to the above function. It is much wider, and it is construed in practice according the circumstances of the particular case at hand.

the regulated limit, narcotics and illegal medicines or other psychoactive substances; (5) if the driver has caused the damage intentionally; (6) if the damage occurred because the vehicle was significantly technically defective, and the driver was aware of this circumstance; (7) if the driver left the location of the accident without providing his/her personal data and insurance data.[628] Deprivation of insurance rights does not influence the right of the claimant to compensation.[629] The insurance company which has paid compensation to the claimant for damages shall be entitled to subrogate against the person liable for damage up to the amount of paid damages, the interests paid on such a compensation, as well as procedural costs.[630]

356. Compulsory insurance is concluded against the liability for damages caused to third parties. An injured party is a person entitled to seek indemnification pursuant to the Act on Compulsory Insurance within the Transport Sector. According to Article 21 of the Compulsory Traffic Insurance Act persons not entitled to seek damages are: (1) owners of motor vehicles the use of which caused them damage, for damaged objects; (2) drivers of motor vehicles the use of which caused them damage; (3) persons entering into the vehicle at their own free will and the vehicle being the one use of which caused damage to the particular person, such persons being aware that the vehicle had been illegally taken away; (4) persons affected by damage: (a) caused by motor vehicles used during officially approved automobile and go-kart racing or parts of competitions on closed race-tracks, aimed at developing maximum speed, as well as during the tests (trainings) for such races; (b) due to the impact of nuclear energy during the transport of nuclear materials; (c) caused by military operations, military manoeuvres, riots, or acts of terrorism provided that any cause and effect relationship exists between such actions and the damage occurred.

357. The minimum amounts of insurance to be contracted by compulsory liability insurance of motor vehicle owners and/or users for damages caused to third parties are provided for by means of coercive statutory provisions. The minimum amounts of insurance to be contracted by compulsory liability insurance of motor vehicle owners and/or users for damages caused to third parties are provided for by the Government upon the proposal of the NBS, while such amounts may not be lower than:

(1) for damage to persons, caused by a single event of damage, regardless of the number of damaged persons: EUR 1,000,000;
(2) for damage to objects, caused by a single event of damage regardless of the number of damaged persons: EUR 200,000.[631]

---

628. *See* the Act on Compulsory Insurance within the Transport Sector, Art. 29, para. 1.
629. *See* the Act on Compulsory Insurance within the Transport Sector, Art. 29, para. 2.
630. *See* the Act on Compulsory Insurance within the Transport Sector, Art. 29, para. 3.
631. *See* the Act on Compulsory Insurance within the Transport Sector, Art. 22, para. 1.

358. Other minimum amounts of insurance to be contracted by motor vehicle liability insurance shall be established by the Government of the Republic of Serbia upon the proposal of the NBS.[632] The Government regulates the manner and criteria for the assessment of material damage, and the manner and criteria for the assessment of non-material damage, depending on the gravity of bodily injury or damaged health, and/or depending on the degree of partial disability for work, as well as the persons entitled to compensation and maximum compensation for pain and suffering due to death or serious disability of another person.[633] In cases where there is more than one claimant, and the total compensation of damages exceeds the above amounts, the rights to which the claimants are entitled against the insurance company shall be proportionally reduced to the above amounts. The amount payable by the insurance company under the compulsory insurance shall be limited to the sum insured applicable at the day the insured event occurred unless a higher amount has been provided for by the insurance contract.[634] The amount of insurance shall mean the maximum amount payable by the insurance company against a single event of damage.[635]

359. If a claimant submits a compensation claim to the insurance company, the insurance company shall not be afforded the right to raise objections based on the law or contract, which are otherwise permitted towards the insured due to violation of law or contract.[636] The Insurance Company paying compensation to the claimant shall be entitled to subrogate against the person liable for damages up to the amount of paid compensation, the interest on such paid compensation, and the procedural costs, unless the obligation of the insurance company has not taken effect according to the terms of the motor third-party liability insurance contract.[637] The Act on Compulsory Insurance within the Transport Sector provides for the procedure of indemnification, whereby it is different depending on the fact whether we are faced with great or small damage.[638] Claims for damages lower than EUR 1,000 in its RSD counter-value substantiated by evidence demonstrating the obligation of the insurance company shall be considered as small damage.

360. Motor vehicle third-party liability insurance concluded in the Republic of Serbia shall cover damages occurring within the territory of EU Member States and the territory of International Insurance Card System Member States or in the territory of the states whose national insurance bureau is a signatory of a multilateral agreement, without payment of additional insurance premiums.[639] A liable insurance company shall cover damages occurring in the territory of the EU Member States and the territory of International Insurance Card System Member States or in

632. *See* the Act on Compulsory Insurance within the Transport Sector, Art. 22, para. 2.
633. *See* the Act on Compulsory Insurance within the Transport Sector, Art. 26, para. 2.
634. *See* the Act on Compulsory Insurance within the Transport Sector, Art. 7, para. 1.
635. *See* the Act on Compulsory Insurance within the Transport Sector, Art. 7, para. 2.
636. *See* the Act on Compulsory Insurance within the Transport Sector, Art. 28, para. 1.
637. *See* the Act on Compulsory Insurance within the Transport Sector, Art. 28, para. 2.
638. *See* the Act on Compulsory Insurance within the Transport Sector, Arts 23–27.
639. *See* the Act on Compulsory Insurance within the Transport Sector, Art. 33.

the territory of the states whose national insurance bureau is a signatory of a multilateral agreement, up to the amount established by the regulations on motor vehicle third-party liability insurance of the state where the damage occurred. If the lowest insured sum of the given state is lower than the amount referred to in Article 22 of the Act on Compulsory Insurance within the Transport Sector, the damage shall be covered up to the amount referred to in that article.[640] Should the liable insurance company fail to indemnify, the compensation shall be paid by the Association of Serbian Insurers. A specialized bureau is established under the auspices of the Association of Serbian Insurers for the purpose of indemnification – the Claims Compensation Bureau.[641]

361. In case of damages caused by motor vehicles with foreign licence plates, the system of international card insurance (the green card system)[642] and the border insurance system are simultaneously employed within the Republic of Serbia.[643] Persons entering the Republic of Serbia by foreign motor vehicles must possess an international third-party liability insurance valid for the territory of the Republic of Serbia providing for coverage against damages at least up to the amounts prescribed in Article 22 of the Act on Compulsory Insurance within the Transport Sector (the green card system). International documents capable of substantiating the existence of insurance shall be documents recognized by the Association of Serbian Insurers in accordance with the pertaining international conventions. The document's validity is examined by the organ competent for internal affairs at the border crossing, as well as in the course of traffic controls.[644] The requirement regarding the possession of an international insurance document pertains to motor vehicles carried from abroad by means of a transport vehicle (tow trucks, for instance), unless such vehicles are not meant to be employed in traffic. Persons sustaining damage caused by foreign motor vehicles in the territory of the Republic of Serbia disposing of valid international documents on motor vehicle third-party liability insurance or other evidence on insurance, shall submit their damage claims to the insurance company that obtained authorization of the Association of Serbian Insurers for performing activities pursuant to international agreements on the insurance of motor vehicle owners for damages arising from the use of motor vehicles in the country or abroad.[645] Should the insurance company, to which compensation claims have been submitted, fail to pay compensation within sixty days from the receipt of claims, the claimant shall be entitled to submit such compensation claims to the Association of Serbian Insurers.[646] Should the Association fail to pay compensation within thirty days upon the claim's receipt, the claimant may sue the Association of Serbian Insurers or the insurance company and accordingly inform the NBS about these circumstances.[647] It needs to be pointed out that in case of causing damage by

640. *See* the Act on Compulsory Insurance within the Transport Sector, Art. 34, para. 1.
641. *See* the Act on Compulsory Insurance within the Transport Sector, Arts 53–57.
642. For details *see* Šulejić, *Pravo osiguranja* (*Insurance Law*), 460–462.
643. For details *see* Šulejić, *Pravo osiguranja* (*Insurance Law*), 462–463.
644. *See* the Act on Compulsory Insurance within the Transport Sector, Art. 38, para. 1.
645. *Ibid.*
646. *See* the Act on Compulsory Insurance within the Transport Sector, Art. 39, para. 2.
647. *Ibid.*

means of foreign motor vehicles, the rights of third-party claimants to seek compensation directly from the foreign tortfeasor and/or his/her foreign liability insurer remain absolutely protected. In such cases, the rules on private international law shall be applicable. In order for a claimant to seek damages directly from a foreign insurer, it is necessary that such entitlement is recognized according to the law of the country where the damage occurred, as well as that the right to submit a direct claim is recognized in the country of the foreign insurer.[648] Persons not having a valid international document are obliged to enter into a motor vehicle liability insurance contract with a domestic insurance company at the border (the system of border insurance). Compensation for damages caused by foreign motor vehicles, provided that the owners of such vehicles have concluded a motor vehicle liability insurance contract with a local insurance company, shall be paid by such an insurance company according to the provisions of the Act on Compulsory Insurance within the Transport Sector applicable to insurances contracted by owners of local registration motor vehicles.[649]

362. The Act on Compulsory Insurance within the Transport Sector contains detailed provisions on the realization of this type of insurance.[650] As regards matters not regulated by the Act on Compulsory Insurance within the Transport Sector or contractual provisions, the rules of Chapter XXVII LO pertaining to property insurance, especially the provisions on liability insurance (Articles 940–941 LO), shall be applicable.

648. Šulejić, *Pravo osiguranja* (*Insurance Law*), 464.
649. *See* the Act on Compulsory Insurance within the Transport Sector, Art. 40.
650. *See* the Act on Compulsory Insurance within the Transport Sector, Arts 45–59.

Chapter 2. Medical Payments

363. Insurance companies will, in case of motor vehicle liability insurance, normally pay compensation for medical costs comprising costs of medical treatment and other ancillary costs triggered by such treatment, as well as funeral expenses of the party sustaining damage. Due to the fact that such expenses may occur as a consequence of damage caused to persons, the minimal amounts set out in Article 22 of the Act on Compulsory Insurance within the Transport Sector pertaining to damage to persons shall be accordingly applicable. The minimal insurance sum pertaining to a single event of damage, regardless of the number of damaged persons, amounts to EUR 1,000,000. In cases where there is more than one claimant, and the total compensation of damages exceeds the above amount, the rights to which the claimants are entitled against the insurance company shall be proportionally reduced to the above amount.

364. The reimbursement of medical expenses caused by a traffic accident in the Republic of Serbia, in accordance with the pertaining statutory social security provisions, may be covered by compulsory social security. Legal entities involved in health, disability and retirement insurance may, on account of payments made for their beneficiaries, express recourse claims from insurance companies on the basis of motor vehicle third-party liability insurance in the amount of real damage, up to the amount of the highest liability of the company in cases where such claims may be made towards the persons liable for damage, according to existing regulations.[651] The real damages are the costs of medical treatment and other costs caused by medical treatment, as well as proportionate amounts of the claimant's and/or his/her family member's pension established as a capitalized amount according to the remaining period of insurance and according to the number of years the person would need to be entitled to retirement pension.[652]

651. *See* the Act on Compulsory Insurance within the Transport Sector, Art. 35, para. 1.
652. *See* the Act on Compulsory Insurance within the Transport Sector, Art. 35, para. 2.

Chapter 3. Uninsured and Underinsured Motorist Coverage

365. Regardless of the fact that the Act on Compulsory Insurance within the Transport Sector provides for the motor vehicle owner's obligation to enter into an insurance contract prior to its use, in practice we are not seldom faced with situations where vehicles are used without a concluded liability insurance contract out of various reasons. Furthermore, situations do exist in practice when third parties sustain damages without being able to identify the damage-causing vehicle's owner, either due to the fact that such are trying to conceal their identities or for other reasons.[653] For the purpose of protecting the economic interests of passengers and third-party claimants in public transport, in instances when damage is caused by uninsured or unknown vehicles the Act on Compulsory Insurance within the Transport Sector provides for the establishment of a Guarantee Fund with the capacity of a legal entity. The Guarantee Fund pays compensation to passengers and third-party claimants in public transport in instances when damage is caused by uninsured on unknown vehicles, as well as indemnification representing the obligation of an insurance company against which bankruptcy proceedings have been initiated.

366. In the event that damages are caused by an uninsured transportation vehicle, indemnification shall be paid in the amounts and according to the conditions that would have been applicable, had a compulsory liability insurance contract been concluded. This means that a party sustaining damages has the right of a direct claim towards the Guarantee Fund, while the Guarantee Fund is not going to be entitled to raise objections that would not be permitted for insurance companies had an insurance contract been concluded. Upon compensation payment, a recourse claim may be submitted against the uninsured motor vehicle owner (for the amount of paid compensation, the interests and the procedural costs).

367. The situation is somewhat complicated in instances when damage is caused by unknown vehicles because of the problems regarding the demonstration of the unknown driver's liability. Although the identity of the driver causing damage is unknown, in order for an injured party to receive compensation from the Guarantee Fund, it is necessary that civil law liability on the part of the unknown driver is established in respect to the damage caused. Yet, certain difficulties may come about regarding the substantiation of such allegations (for instance, in case of hit-and-run accidents caused by unknown vehicles at night without the presence of witnesses). The fact that damage was caused by a vehicle the owner and licence plate numbers of which are unknown, may be substantiated by all means of evidence (witnesses, for instance).[654] It is irrelevant whether the accident was caused by a motor vehicle of unknown foreign or Serbian licence plates. Damages due to death, injury or affected health caused by unidentified motor vehicles, aircraft, boats or other means of transportation shall be compensated up to the amount to which the liabilities of

---

653. I. Jankovec & Z. Miladinović, *Pravo osiguranja* (*Insurance Law*) (Niš, 2006), 371.
654. It shall not be deemed that damage is caused by an unknown vehicle if uncertainties exist only regarding the circumstances as to what insurance company the owner has a concluded liability contract with or in the event that the owner's identity is known but not his/her place of residence.

the insurance company are limited in respect of any damage caused by using such means of transportation on the day of accident occurrence.[655] In case of damage caused by an unknown motor vehicle, the Guarantee Fund shall indemnify the damages on goods in case it has compensated a party in the accident for grave bodily injury requiring hospitalization with a 10% franchise, providing that it cannot be more than EUR 500 in its RSD counter-value on the day of the loss event.[656] Such a restrictive rule in case of damage to goods has been set up due to the fact that instances of fraud on parts of vehicle owners acting in bad faith were common in practice, where such persons represented that damage was caused by unknown vehicles although this was not the case.[657] Should it be determined, after settlement of compensation, that a motor vehicle, aircraft, or boat has caused damage, the recourse claim shall be addressed to the insurance company providing the compulsory insurance coverage, in an amount equal to the compensation paid, plus interests from the payment of compensation and procedural expenses.[658]

368. In the event that a compulsory insurance contract was concluded with an insurance company in respect of which bankruptcy proceedings have been initiated, compensation of damages caused by motor vehicles, aircraft, boats or other means of transportation, shall be provided by the Guarantee Fund.[659] The rights of the claimant in respect of the bankruptcy estate shall be transferred to the Guarantee Fund that paid the insurance amount and/or compensation. The Guarantee Fund is entitled to report such claims until the completion of bankruptcy proceedings.[660]

369. Situations where the insured amount is lower than the damage sustained by a third-party claimant may come about in practice. The insurer shall in such cases be liable up to the amount of the stipulated sum of insurance,[661] and not up to the amount of damage caused (underinsured motorist coverage). The amount of insurance shall mean the maximum amount payable by the insurance company against a single event of damage regardless of the number of persons sustaining damage.[662] In cases where there is more than one claimant, and the total compensation of damages exceeds the amounts provided for, the rights to which the claimants are entitled against the insurance company shall be proportionally reduced to the amount of insurance. Should the insurer pay full compensation corresponding to the amount of insurance, indemnification for the remaining uncovered part of damage may be sought only from the tortfeasor.

655. *See* the Act on Compulsory Insurance within the Transport Sector, Art. 92, para. 1.
656. *See* the Act on Compulsory Insurance within the Transport Sector, Art. 92, para. 2.
657. Šulejić, *Pravo osiguranja* (*Insurance Law*), 459.
658. *See* the Act on Compulsory Insurance within the Transport Sector, Art. 92, para. 3.
659. *See* the Act on Compulsory Insurance within the Transport Sector, Art. 93, para 1.
660. *See* the Act on Compulsory Insurance within the Transport Sector, Art. 93, para. 2.
661. The minimum amount of insurance is set out in coercive statutory provisions (*see* the Act on Compulsory Insurance within the Transport Sector, Arts 22 and 26).
662. *See* the Act on Compulsory Insurance within the Transport Sector, Art. 22.

Chapter 4. Physical Automobile Damage

370. Objects of this insurance type may be all types of road and railroad vehicles, machinery and their accessories (e.g., tools, spare parts, fire extinguishers).[663] Special terms of insurance precisely define the motor vehicle accessories suitable for insurance. Special and additional equipment[664] may also be insured if such coverage is expressly stipulated under the condition of additional premium payment. Coverage shall not be provided for damages incurred on parts of the vehicle spatially separated from it at the moment of accident. As opposed to third-party liability insurance, the insurance of motor vehicles is voluntary, and it is denominated within the offer of Serbian insurers as 'casco' insurance.

371. Within the offers of Serbian insurers, there are three types of automobile insurance depending on the objects and risks covered. These are total, partial and supplementary casco insurance. Total casco insurance provides coverage for damage and loss of the insured vehicle, as well as its constituent parts as a consequence of the following risks: traffic accidents, sudden outer thermal or chemical influence, fall or hit by objects, fire, lightning, explosion, thunderstorm, hail, aircraft crashes, manifestations or demonstrations, earthquakes, wilful misconduct or vandalism of third parties, floods, and so on.[665] Accordingly, vehicles are insured against various risks triggered by natural or human factors. Therefore, this type of insurance may be entitled as combined vehicle insurance. Only the risk of theft from the group of so-called common risks is not comprised in this type of insurance. The risk of theft may, however, be expressly stipulated within the framework of supplementary insurance against payment of additional premiums. Supplementary casco insurance is concluded along with total casco insurance and provides coverage against theft and misappropriation by persons entrusted with the vehicle (e.g., in cases of leasing, rent-a-car). Apart from the above, supplementary casco insurance may cover the luggage in buses, advertisements and other graphical designs on the vehicle, and so on. Partial casco insurance provides coverage of the windows on the motor vehicle against breakage or damage caused by any of the risks covered by total casco insurance. Partial insurance is usually concluded on the condition of additional premium payment along with the compulsory insurance of motor vehicle owners against liability for damages caused to third parties, and it is valid until the expiry of the compulsory insurance contract. Partial casco insurance is normally

663. Within special terms of insurance, it is precisely laid down which equipment shall be covered by insurance.
664. It is deemed that special equipment comprises subsequently built-in equipment, the coverage of which needs to be expressly provided for by the policy. Additional equipment is furthermore serially manufactured equipment built into the vehicle upon the purchaser's request upon payment of additional prices.
665. The extent of each risk is defined within the special terms of casco insurance.

contracted for the amount of the first risk,[666] which becomes partially exhausted by means of each payment of compensation up to the amount of insurance.

372. Within the domain of casco insurance, it is accustomed to provide for an insurance franchise, that is, for a rule that the insured himself/herself bears a certain portion of the damage. The franchise may be stipulated: in an absolute amount determined in Dinars, when the insured covers all damages on the insured object up to a certain amount, while the insurer will be obliged to cover all damages above the stipulated amount but up to the amount of insurance, and/or in a relative percentage amount when the insured participates in the compensation up to a certain percentage, while the insurer compensates damages above the given amount but up to the contracted amount of insurance.

373. Motor vehicle insurance is a type of property insurance, so that regarding circumstances not regulated within special terms of insurance, the general provisions pertaining to property insurance contained in general terms of property insurance and other sources of insurance law (general terms of property insurance, LO, for instance) shall be applicable in accordance with the rules on the hierarchy of their application.

---

666. The conclusion of first risk insurances is the most frequent exception to the application of the principle of proportionality. It stems from the efforts to exclude the negative effects of the above principle. There are two modalities of concluding first risk insurance contracts: property insurance contracts against *absolute* and *relative* first risk.

In absolute first risk property insurance contracts, a situation will come about where the insured amount is lower than the value of the insured interest (as in all other cases of underinsurance). The insured amount in first risk property insurance contracts is usually an expected damage. Certain insured risks are usually insufficient to cause the destruction of the whole insured abject or the loss of all insured objects, so that it is beneficial to conclude insurance only against sustainable damages, that is, damages lower than the value of the insured object. One of the most important consequences of first risk insurance is the exclusion of the principle of proportionality. This means that all compensations lower than the amount of the first risk are paid in total amounts, while those equal to or exceeding the amount of first risk shall be paid up to that amount.

In relative first risk property insurance contracts, the situation is somewhat different. The insured amount is in this case also lower than the value of the insured interest. The principle of proportionality is for instance not applicable if the insured amount is lower for less than 10% of the insured object's value at the moment of the insured event's occurrence. However, should the insured amount be lower for 10% or more of the insured object's value (underinsurance), the principle of proportionality shall be applicable due to the fact that the compensation from insurance shall be paid proportionally to the insured amount and the value of the insured object.

In first risk property insurance contracts, the insurance contractor is going to pay a somewhat higher premium than the one otherwise due for the same insurance amount (in case of the application of the principle of proportionality) but not as high as in insurance contracts for the object's full value.

Part V. Insurance of the Person

Chapter 1. Workers' Compensation

374. The insurance of workers against work accidents or professional illnesses partly falls into the category of compulsory public social health insurance of the Republic of Serbia,[667] but this domain is covered also by voluntary health insurance,[668] as well as private accident insurance.[669]

375. Compulsory health insurance comprises insurance against illness and injuries sustained outside of the workplace, as well as insurance against workplace injuries and professional illnesses. The rights from the domain of compulsory health insurance comprise the entitlement to health protection (irrespectively of the fact whether we are faced with a workplace accident, an occupational illness or accidents outside of the workplace and regular illnesses), the right to compensation in case of temporary occupational disability of the employee (compensation paid to employees) and the right to a reimbursement of travel expenses incurred in connection with health protection. The health insurance rights are conditioned on the payment of due health insurance contributions. State health insurance is compulsory meaning that the necessary funds are provided by means of obligatory compensation payment by employees and employers, as well as other persons obliged to pay contributions in accordance with the Compulsory Social Security Contributions Act,[670] which simultaneously represents a condition for exercising the rights from compulsory health insurance. Compulsory health insurance is concluded and administered by the Republic Health Insurance Institute, as well as its branch offices.

667. *See* the Health Insurance Law, Art. 9.
668. *See infra* nn. 382–387, within the Ch. 3. Private Health Insurance.
669. All persons, including employees not younger than 15 and not older than 75 may be insured against accidents. *See infra* Nos within the Ch. 2. Bodily insurance.
670. OJ RS, 84/2004, 61/2005, 62/2006, 5/2009, 52/2011, 101/2011, 7/2012, 8/2013,47/2013, 108/2013,6/2014, 57/2014, 68/2014, 5/2015, 112/2015, 5/2016, 7/2017, 113/2017, 7/2018, 95/2018, 4/2019, 86/2019, 5/2020, 153/2020, 6/2021, 44/2021, 118/2021 and 10/2022).

Chapter 2. Bodily Insurance

376. Bodily insurance is a type of insurance where the insurer is obliged to pay the insured or the beneficiary the amount of insurance should in the course of insurance come to the covered accident, death or disability of the insured (or the insured person), as well as to repair damages caused by necessary medical treatment, as well as lost salaries should the accident's consequence by a temporary inability to work or health impairment of the above persons.[671] Accidents are defined in general terms of insurance as all sudden events independent from the insured's will, which by means of affecting the insured's body normally from external sources have as a consequence death, total or partial disability, temporary inability to work or health impairment requiring medical assistance. Therefore, in order for an event to be considered an accident from the viewpoint of insurance, it needs to meet the following requirements: to affect the insured person's body, to be sudden and abrupt, to be external in respect to the insured person, to be independent from the insured person's will and that a causal relationship between the external influence and the consequences to the insured's body exists.

377. Within the Serbian legal system persons not younger than 15 years[672] and not older than 75 years may be insured against accident consequences under the condition that their general labour capacity is not thereby diminished. Persons with diminished labour capacity may also be insured upon payment of higher premiums, except in the case of collective insurance when no additional premiums are paid. Mentally ill persons may not be covered by this type of insurance. The above limitations are not applicable to compulsory accident insurance in public transport. In this insurance type, it is only relevant whether the person in question is a passenger or not according to Article 15 of the Act on Compulsory Insurance within the Transport Sector.

378. In case of death or disability, the insurer's obligation will be to pay the previously stipulated insurance amount (in total or a certain percentage). In such situations, bodily insurance against accident consequences does not have a character of indemnification, due to the fact that its purpose is to pay the previously determined stipulated sum of money irrespective of the damages incurred, rather than indemnification. Accordingly, if it comes to the insured's (or insured person's) death as a consequence of an accident, the insurer shall be obliged to pay the stipulated insurance amount, that is, the total amount. Due to the fact that disability, that is, the permanent (life-long) loss of labour capacity may be total or partial (1%–99%), the amount payable by the insurer is going to be dependent on this fact. In case of total disability, the insurer shall pay the insurance amount in total, while in case of partial disability, a proportional amount corresponding to the percentage of disability shall be payable. Insurance compensation in case of disability is previously determined in the insurance policy and varies depending on the amount of insurance and

671. Šulejić, *Pravo osiguranja* (*Insurance Law*), 495.

672. Exceptionally persons younger than 15 may be insured within the framework of collective insurance.

the level of disability, regardless of the actual damages incurred. Compensation in case of death or disability may be accumulated with treatment costs and lost salaries provided it is stipulated that the insurance shall cover these amounts too.

379. In case of temporary inability to work or health impairment requiring medical assistance, the insurer's obligation will comprise compensation of lost salaries and the reimbursement of medical costs incurred as a consequence of the accident covered by insurance. In such cases, the insurance will have a compensatory nature due to the fact that the insurer is obliged to reimburse the above costs up to the amount of insurance (if contracted),[673] but always up to the actual amount of damages. Therefore the rules of property insurance stemming from the principle of compensation (the prohibition to accumulate insurance compensation and indemnification from the tortfeasor, the rule of subrogation,[674] etc.) shall be applicable within this field of bodily insurance. The compensation of lost daily wages in case of temporary inability to work shall be payable from the first day of medical treatment up to the last day of temporary inability to work and/or up to the death or the establishment of disability, but not longer than 200 days. As regards medical cost reimbursement, in case of health impairment requiring medical assistance, the insurer shall be obliged to reimburse medical treatment costs up to the period of one year counting from the accident. The insurer's obligation to compensate the daily lost wages and the medical treatment costs needs to be expressly provided for along with additional premium payment (either separately from or together with the basic bodily insurance).

380. As regards the risks excluded from this type of insurance, their majority is provided for by general terms of bodily insurance (e.g., accidents caused by earthquakes, by premeditated crimes, under the insured's influence of alcohol, suicide or attempted suicide). However, certain exclusions are provided by the LO too. These are wilful accident causing[675] and war manoeuvres.[676]

381. In all of the instances of bodily insurance, apart from the death of the insured (or the insured person), it is usually the insurance beneficiary that suffers disability, temporary inability to work or the necessity of medical treatment due to health impairment. Should the insured wish to provide for another person as the beneficiary, such circumstance needs to be expressly stipulated. In case of the insured's death the beneficiary may be a person denominated in the insurance policy as such. If, however, the beneficiary is not determined by the contract, the provisions pertaining to insurance beneficiaries shall be applicable taking into account the order of inheritance provided for by the inheritance law of the Republic of Serbia.

---

673. Due to the fact that this is a type of compensatory insurance, it follows from the transaction's nature that the insurance amount is not an essential contractual element.
674. *See supra* nn. 246–250.
675. *See* LO, Art. 951.
676. *See* LO, Art. 952.

382. Bodily insurance is concluded voluntarily, apart from accident insurance of passengers in public transport, which is compulsory. Owners of vehicles used for the public transport of passengers shall be required to enter into contracts providing accident insurance for passengers in public transport.[677] This specific type of insurance contract against accident consequences is regulated by the Act on Compulsory Insurance within the Transport Sector. Regarding issues not regulated by the Act on Compulsory Insurance within the Transport Sector or by contractual provisions (including special and general terms of insurance) the provisions of Chapter XXVII LO are applicable. The concept of passengers,[678] as well as the minimum amount of insurance suitable for compulsory insurance of passengers in public transport[679] is provided for by the Act on Compulsory Insurance within the Transport Sector. A passenger affected by accident, or a beneficiary specified by the terms of insurance in case of such passenger's death, shall be entitled to request direct payment to be made under the insurance contract by the insurance company the insurance has been concluded with.[680] In cases where an accident occurs, whereas the insurance has not been contracted by the owner of the means of transportation, or such owner has contracted the insurance with an insurance company in respect of which bankruptcy proceedings were initiated, the above persons may request the payment of the insured sum from the Guarantee Fund.[681] The persons entitled to the amount of insurance are passengers or insurance beneficiaries regardless of the fact whether such persons also have the right to indemnification based on the transporter's liability.[682]

677. *See* the Act on Compulsory Insurance within the Transport Sector, Art. 14.
678. *See* the Act on Compulsory Insurance within the Transport Sector, Art. 15.
679. *See* the Act on Compulsory Insurance within the Transport Sector, Art. 16.
680. *See* the Act on Compulsory Insurance within the Transport Sector, Art. 17, para. 1.
681. *See* the Act on Compulsory Insurance within the Transport Sector, Art. 17, para. 2.
682. *Ibid.*

Chapter 3. Private Health Insurance

383. Voluntary private health insurance is insurance against the risk of medical treatment costs (participation[683] in accordance with the Health Insurance Law) of persons not covered by compulsory health insurance according to the above Law, that is, persons not within the system of compulsory health insurance, as well as persons wishing to provide for wider coverage, higher standards or other types of health insurance rights.[684] Voluntary health insurance policies are within the offers of insurance companies engaged in non-life insurance in the Republic of Serbia.[685] Only exceptionally may companies active within the field of life insurance provide services of insurance against so-called ancillary accidents and voluntary health insurance in parts covering treatment costs, but exclusively under the condition that such insurances pertain to persons already having a concluded life insurance contract.[686]

384. The domain of voluntary health insurance in the Republic of Serbia is in principle regulated by means of the Health Insurance Law,[687] while its details are provided for by general voluntary health insurance terms of particular insurance companies, as well as by the pertaining special insurance terms of insurers regarding certain types of voluntary health insurance (e.g., special voluntary health insurance terms against risks of severe illnesses or surgical interventions, special terms of passenger health insurance).

385. There are various types of voluntary health insurance contracts (policies). According to the type of health protection covered by insurance there are supplementary, additional, as well as private health insurances. Supplementary health insurance is insurance that covers the costs of health care that arise when the insured person supplements the rights from the compulsory health insurance in terms of content, scope and standards.[688] Additional health insurance is insurance that covers the share in the costs of health care, i.e., covers the costs of health services, medicines, medical devices, or cash benefits that are not covered by the rights from the compulsory health insurance.[689] Private health insurance is health insurance of persons not covered by compulsory health insurance or persons not within the system of compulsory health insurance for coverage of costs, the contents, extent and standard of which are to be stipulated by the chosen insurance company.[690] Therefore, by means of private health insurance in accordance with the provisions of the Health Insurance Law, all natural persons may be covered regardless of the fact whether they are insured according to the provisions on compulsory health insurance or not.

683. *See* the Health Insurance Law, Arts 134–135.
684. *See* the Health Insurance Law, Art. 6.
685. *Ibid.*
686. *See* LI, Art. 25, para. 1.
687. OJ RS, 25/2019.
688. *See* the Health Insurance Law, Art. 174, para. 1, item 1.
689. *See* the Health Insurance Law, Art. 174, para. 1, item 2.
690. *See* the Health Insurance Law, Art. 174, para. 1, item 3.

With no regard as to the fact whether we are faced with parallel, additional or private health insurance, the insurer may not provide for voluntary health insurance for an identical type, content, extent, standard, manner and procedure of right assertion covered by compulsory health insurance regulated by the Health Insurance Law or other enactments passed for its implementation.[691]

386. According to the types of risk covered, voluntary health insurance contracts (either additional or private) may be divided into insurance against severe illnesses including their consequences and insurance against surgical interventions (operations). Special conditions are applicable to both of these insurance types regularly delivered and updated by Serbian insurance companies active within the field of voluntary health insurance.

387. Apart from the above, travel insurance has a significant role as a special type of voluntary health insurance present in the offers of Serbian insurance companies.[692] Such insurance provides coverage to persons travelling to foreign countries in the course of their journeys and stays abroad. By means of such an insurance contract, the insurer incurs the obligation to provide certain services to the insured, such as reimbursement of expenses, or provide the stipulated services of assistance during the insured's journey or stay abroad. Insurance companies normally have special terms of insurance pertaining to this insurance type representing the basic source of regulation of relationships stemming from this type of insurance.[693]

388. Finally, according to the number of persons covered by insurance, there are individual and collective voluntary health insurance contracts. By means of collective contracts coverage is provided to a larger number of persons. The insurance contractor may be any legal entity concluding a contract on the additional health insurance of its employees and/or its members, irrespectively of the fact whether the premiums are paid by the contractor directly or withheld from the insured's salary. Therefore, by means of such an insurance employees or members of certain organizations may be insured usually under more preferential conditions than in case of individual health insurance (e.g., payment of lower premiums per insured compared to the amount of insurance, the employees or members may be covered by insurance regardless of their age, medical condition, etc., that is, the circumstances otherwise having an effect to the increase of the premium and the decrease of the amount of insurance).

691. *See* the Health Insurance Law, Art. 171.
692. Such insurances are sometimes referred to as visa insurance within offers of Serbian insurance companies due to the fact that the conclusion of such an insurance contract is often a prerequisite for the issuance of visas, that is, permits to travel to particular countries.
693. *See* the Health Insurance Law, Art. 174, para. 4.

Chapter 4. Life Insurance

389. Generally, life insurance contracts within the Serbian legal system are contracts where the insurer, in consideration of the paid premiums, incurs the obligation to pay the insured or a nominated person (the insurance beneficiary) a particular amount or as an annuity in recurring regular payments in the event of a certain person's death (the insured or the insured persons) or his/her survival of a particular moment. The basic division of life insurance is into individual and group life insurance.

§1. Individual Life Insurance

390. Individual life insurance is contracted by individuals, whereby the insured object within the scope of one contract may be the life of one or, rarer, a greater number of persons (the case of mutual insurance). As opposed to group insurance, in case of insurance of a larger number of persons the membership in a particular group is not important for the persons covered to become insured persons. Serbian insurance companies offer different types of individual life insurance satisfying the various needs of their customers.

391. According to the type of risk, there are death insurances, insurances for the event of survivorship of a particular moment (a certain age or an event) and combined insurances covering both risks (death and survivorship).

392. Insurance for the case of death is a type of insurance where the insured event occurs at the moment of the insured person's death. Life insurance contracts for the case of death may be entered into for a particular term (e.g., five, ten, fifteen, twenty years) or for an undetermined period of time, that is, the whole life of a person. In the latter case, it is irrelevant when the insured event occurs. It is certain that the heirs or the beneficiary will be paid the insured amount upon the insured person's death, for the insured event's occurrence is inevitable. Whole life insurance has certain elements of savings characterized by the formation of a mathematical reserve, as well as rights stemming from such formation. Namely, in permanent, that is, whole life insurance the insurance premium should increase constantly in the course of time due to the fact that the risk covered also increases with the insured's older age. In order to omit permanent premium increase, the amount of premium is established as a constant value for the whole duration of insurance. Therefore the premium is in the first years of insurance higher than the real value of risk, but will later be lower than that. The premium surplus accumulated in the first years of insurance represents the mathematical reserve. There is a special interest towards these assets of the insurance contractor due to the fact that they do not represent only means of risk coverage but they are also savings vehicles. Accordingly, insurance contractors will have certain rights in the mathematical reserves. These rights may have different forms: (1) the right to seek payment of the mathematical reserve in case of risk exclusion;[694] (2) decrease of the insured amount; (3) the right to insurance repurchase; and (4) the right to claim an advance payment of the insured amount. The insured amount is going to be decreased in instances where the insured, after a given period of time upon contract conclusion and the payment of a certain number of premiums (for two or three[695] years) stops the payment of insurance premiums.[696] The only consequence to the insurance relationship even if the premiums are no longer being paid is the decrease of the insured amount according to a specially defined table. In order for an insurer to decrease the insured amount to the policy repurchase value (if at least two or three annual premiums have been paid) or cancel the agreement (if at least two or three annual premiums have not been paid), it is necessary that a subsequent time limit is established in advance for insurance payment. This time limit may not be shorter than one month from serving the pertaining notification along with a warning as to the consequences of premium non-payment upon expiry of the afforded time limit. Should the insured event occur after notification but before the expiry of the afforded time limit for premium payment, the foreseen consequences shall automatically take effect (decrease of the insured amount of contract cancellation, depending on the fact whether the insurance premiums were being paid in the above time periods). An insurance contractor that paid at least two or three annual premiums not having further interest for the insurance contract to be effective, may request the insurer to pay out the policy repurchase value. The policy is repurchased upon request of an authorized person (the insurance contractor or sometimes his/her creditors or the insurance beneficiary). Such a right is usually not afforded to the insurance contractor's creditors (apart from situations when a creditor received the policy as security, if the claim supported by security has not been settled at maturity),[697] nor to insurance beneficiaries (unless his/her appointment is irrevocable).[698] Payment of the policy repurchase price is the insurer's obligation. The insurance policy shall include terms and conditions under which the authorized person may request payment of the policy repurchase value, as well as an indication of the method of calculation of that value, in accordance with the insurance terms and conditions.[699] The obligations from the insurance contract shall cease to be effective from the moment of submitting the request of premium repurchase value payment by the authorized person. This means that if the insured event occurs after the repurchase request but before the policy repurchase value payment, the beneficiary will not be entitled to seek the insured amount, but only the amount of the policy repurchase value. Finally, upon request of the contractor of life insurance concluded for the insured's lifetime, the insurer

694. Risks usually excluded from life insurance in Serbia are the insured's suicide, malicious cause of the insured's death by the beneficiary, as well as death as a consequence of war manoeuvres.
695. The LO provides for three years, while the general terms of life insurance of Serbian insurers usually lay down a term of two years.
696. Should the insured stop the payment of premiums before the above time limit, it shall be deemed that he/she has withdrawn from the contract, the contract ceases to exist, while the paid premiums shall be retained. This has sense if taken into account that in case of a shorter period of payments, upon deduction of the insurer's expenses (e.g., costs of contract conclusion), as well as the price of risk coverage, the remaining amount would be insignificant.
697. *See* LO, Art. 954, para. 4.
698. *See* LO, Art. 954, para. 3.
699. *See* LO, Art. 954, para. 2.

may pay in advance a part of the amount insured, up to the policy repurchase value, which part may subsequently be restored by the insurance contractor.[700] Consequently, the advance payment is the insurer's right rather than obligation. The insurance contractor shall be obliged to pay interests for the advance payment received.[701] Should the insurance contractor delay with the payment of due interests, it shall be deemed that he/she requested the policy repurchase. The policy needs to provide for the terms of advance payment, the possibility to return the advance payment to the insurer, the interest rate, the consequences of interest non-payment, all in accordance with the terms of insurance.

393. Survivorship insurance is a type of insurance where coverage is provided against the risk of surviving a certain moment (achievement of an age, a determined event – e.g., childbirth, marriage). The insurer incurs the obligation to pay the insured amount at a particular moment or if a previously determined event occurs even if the insured is still alive. In this type of insurance, it is usually contracted that the insured amount shall be payable to the insured or the insurance beneficiary as an annuity rather than as a lump sum, that is, a capitalized amount. In accordance with the above, annuity policies differ in practice from capitalized amount policies. Annuity insurance may have different forms. According to the period of payment such insurances may be life-long (until the insured's death) or temporary (limited to a particular term). The annuities may be the same in the course of the whole period of payment or variable depending on money real value fluctuations or other causes diminishing their contracted value.

394. Combined insurance represents a type of life insurance where the insured is provided coverage simultaneously against two types of risks, that is, against death and for the case of surviving a certain moment (usually the achievement of a particular age). The insurer will be obliged to pay the amount of insurance to the insured (or exceptionally to the beneficiary) if the insured survives a particular moment, or to the heirs and/or beneficiaries in case of death. This form of insurance is beneficial both for an insured wishing to secure a certain sum for old age and to provide security to the heirs or another beneficiary[702] in case of death. A particular type of combined insurance is insurance with a determined payment maturity, in which coverage is provided against two risks, death or surviving a particular age, but the payment of compensation by the insurer is made at the stipulated moment, regardless of the moment of the insured event's occurrence (e.g., if the insured dies before the established date of payment, the insured amount shall be paid only at the moment contracted).

395. According to the conditions of contract conclusion there are life insurance contracts with or without the necessity of a previous medical examination. Insurance under the condition of medical examination is common in cases of contracting

700. *See* LO, Art. 955, para. 1.
701. *See* LO, Art. 955, para. 2.
702. Regarding the rules pertaining to the determination of insurance beneficiaries *see* LO Art. 957.

large amounts of insurance. The medical examination represents in fact the establishment of circumstances relevant for risk assessment. Smaller insurance amounts are contracted for without medical examinations, and the purpose of such rules is to make the contract conclusion as simple as possible and available for the widest range of potential contractors. General terms of insurance of Serbian insurance companies usually provide for the following solution: Should the insured event in life insurance contracts (exclusively in case of death) concluded without a medical examination occur in the first six months of insurance, the insurer shall be obliged to pay only 50% of the insured amount; should, however, the insurance contract be entered into upon medical examination, the total insured amount shall be payable regardless of the duration of insurance.[703]

396. Although individual insurance normally covers the life of one insured, a modality is possible where coverage of two or more persons' lives is provided, but where, as opposed to collective life insurance, membership in a particular group is irrelevant for the persons to become insureds in the insurance relationship at hand. Such types of insurance are usually entitled survivorship (or second-to-die) insurance of two persons. For instance, the insurance of two lives (mutual insurance) contracted by spouses, relatives, and so on where in case of the death of one the amount of insurance shall be payable to the other – the survivor. In case of mixed insurance, where apart from the risk of death the risk of surviving a particular moment is covered and both persons survive the given moment, the insured amount shall be payable to both insureds in equal amounts, unless otherwise provided.

397. Irrespectively of the fact whether we are faced with individual or group life insurance, and whether the insurance is for a particular period of time or for the insured's entire life, insurance payment is always facultative. Within life insurance the insurer is not entitled to judicially seek payment of due premiums.[704] However, there are other sanctions for non-fulfilment of the insurance contractor's basic obligation. These are contract rescission and the reduction of the insured amount by the insurer depending on the period of paid premiums and whether the case at hand is a life insurance for a particular term or the insured's entire life. Furthermore, the insurer may set off the amounts of unpaid premiums with the compensation owed to the insured or the beneficiary in case of insured event occurrence. Premium payment is optional in life insurance contracts primarily out of economic reasons. Life insurance contracts are long-term legal transactions. Insurance contractors oblige themselves to pay the premium over a longer period of time. After a certain number of years pass, circumstances may be altered, and the contractor may decide that the life insurance contract once concluded became economically unprofitable (due to lack of funds, descendants covered in another manner, etc.) Therefore, it would be unfair if the insurance contractor could in such instances be judicially forced for premium payment.

703. Šulejić, *Pravo osiguranja* (*Insurance Law*), 473.
704. *See* LO, Art. 954, para. 1.

§2. GROUP LIFE INSURANCE

398. Group life insurance contracts are contracts where the object of insurance are the lives of more people from a particular group of persons (syndicates, professional organizations, associations, legal entities, etc.).[705] For the purposes of such insurance already existing circles of persons with a common element of stability shall be understood under the term 'group'. For instance, a number of persons uniting for the sole purpose of insurance contract conclusion may not be considered as a group in the above sense. Within Serbian insurance law rights and obligations of the beneficiaries (members of an association, employees, etc.) are directly established although the insurance contractor is their association, their legal entity, and so on. Upon conclusion of group life insurance contracts between an insurer and an insurance contractor, no individual insurance contracts are entered into by the insurer and the particular beneficiaries. However, due to an imperative provision of the LO, the validity of contract depends on insured's written consent, indicated on the face of the insurance policy, or in a separate letter at the moment of signing the insurance policy, with an indication of the insured amount.[706] Such a consent is not necessary in accident insurance contracts despite the fact that one of their possible consequences may be the insured party's death. The obligation of premium payment is a duty of the insurance contractor (e.g., a legal entity), which may be paid from its own assets or from the insured party's assets. Compensation from insurance is payable directly to the insurance beneficiary.[707]

399. Group life insurance has the same forms as individual insurance (for the case of death, survivorship or mixed insurance). The general rules provided for by the LO pertaining to individual insurance are equally applicable in group insurance, such as the provisions on mathematical reserve formation,[708] the rule on the optional being of premium payment, and so on. However, there are certain special rules provided for by special terms of group life insurance passed by Serbian insurance companies providing such insurance services.

400. As in group insurance generally, group life insurance has numerous advantages in comparison with individual insurance. By means of group insurance equal or related objects of insurance are covered, a faster and simpler operation of insurance companies is secured, so that the conclusion of such contracts is more profitable for the insurance contractor, while simultaneously being cheaper for the insured. The advantages, however, are not only of an economic but also a legal nature. The conclusion of a group life insurance is more beneficial for the insureds regarding the conditions of contract conclusion. For instance, by means of a group insurance of employees against accident consequences the employees of a certain

705. For instance, group insurance of retired persons: the insurance contractor is a pensioners' association to which the common policy is issued, while each beneficiary is issued an individual document on the insurance containing data on the insured amount, the monthly premiums and the insurance beneficiary.
706. *See* LO, Art. 946, para. 3.
707. Šulejić, *Pravo osiguranja* (*Insurance Law*), 79.
708. *See supra* n. 136.

employer are covered regardless of their age, sex, health condition, and so on. The insurance premium is calculated based on the majority of the insureds' sex and the average age of employees. In individual insurance contracts, the above features have as their consequence the increase of premiums and the decrease of the insured amount. Furthermore, in group insurance it is possible to subsequently include additional persons in the insurance (e.g., new employees) or replace existing insureds by others (e.g., replacement of a former employee by a new one).

Chapter 5. Pension Funds

401. In the Republic of Serbia there is a state-owned institution, the Republic Fund for Pension and Disability Insurance[709] on the one hand and certain private voluntary pension funds on the other hand.

402. The Republic Fund for Pension and Disability Insurance provides mainly for rights of insureds within the system compulsory statutory insurance. The Pension and Disability Insurance Act provides for three categories of compulsory insurance: employees, entrepreneurs and agriculturers. In respect of persons simultaneously fulfilling the requirements for insurance on several of these bases, a priority system according to the above order has been established, meaning that the existence of employment excludes the insurance based on entrepreneurship or agricultural activities Persons not within the framework of compulsory insurance may enter the system and acquire pertaining rights from the age of 15. The Pension and Disability Insurance Act[710] provides for the following rights to a pension: in case of old age – the right to a retirement pension, in case of disability – the right to a disability pension, in case of the insured's death – the right to a widow's (or other family member's) pension, as well as the right to the reimbursement of funeral costs.

403. The voluntary pension fund is a type of investment fund serving for the collection of voluntary pension contributions and their investment for the purpose of generating returns of the invested funds and the later payment of private pensions. Private pension funds have a role to provide for the saving and value increase of invested contributions and the subsequent payment of private pensions. Compulsory separations for the purpose of acquiring pensions from the state-owned fund are not in any way connected with investments into voluntary pension funds. The state-owned fund in the Republic of Serbia is becoming weaker and weaker due to the reforms based on current financing, and there is a tendency of constant decrease in the amounts of state pensions, which tendency is likely to persist in the following years according economic and other indicators. Therefore, the role of voluntary pension funds is to overcome the grim perspective of the state-owned fund and enable the citizens a decent source of income for their old age.

404. The legal status of voluntary pension funds is regulated by the Voluntary Pension Funds and Plans Act.[711] Voluntary pension funds are administered by companies for the administration of voluntary pension funds that may exclusively be established in the form of joint stock companies. The legal status of companies administering voluntary pension funds is regulated by the Voluntary Pension Funds

709. From 1 Jan. 2008 three prior funds are united within this fund – the Fund for Pension and Disability Insurance of Employees, the Fund for Pension and Disability Insurance of Entrepreneurs and the Fund for Pension and Disability Insurance of Agriculturers.

710. OJ RS, 34/2003, 64/2004, 84/2004, 85/2005, 101/2005, 63/2006, 5/2009, 107/2009, 101/2010, 93/2012, 62/2013, 75/2014, 142/2014, 73/2018, 46/2019, 86/2019 and 62/2021.

711. *See* the Voluntary Pension Funds and Plans Act, OJ RS, 85/2005 and 31/2011, Arts 44–45.

and Plans Act (Articles 4–27) as well as the provisions of the LCC that are subsidiarily applicable in all matters not regulated by the above Act. Voluntary pension funds are special funds, that is, special assets without the status of legal entities.[712] The assets of voluntary pension funds are the property of their members in the proportion of their parts in the fund's assets.[713] They are separated from the assets of the company administering the fund.[714] Therefore, members of a fund may at any time, under certain conditions, transfer their assets, that is, their accounts from one to another voluntary pension fund.[715] The assets of voluntary pension funds are obligatorily held on accounts with custody banks[716] and may not be subject to enforced collection, pledge, mortgage; they may not be parts of the liquidation or bankruptcy estate of the administration company or other persons, nor be used for the payment of the voluntary pension fund members' or other persons' debts towards third parties.[717] The rules pertaining to the investment of voluntary pension fund assets are provided for by the Voluntary Pension Funds and Plans Act, as well as the terms and conditions of investments provided for by the NBS having a supervisory function over the business operations of companies administering voluntary pension funds and the investment of their assets.[718]

405. Fund members may be domestic or foreign natural persons. It is possible that one person is a member of more voluntary pension funds. As opposed to the investment into state-owned pension funds, the savings within voluntary ones are not conditioned on the existence of a beneficiary's employment relationship. It is possible that an unemployed person pays contributions into a voluntary pension fund from other resources. Fund members do not even have to correspond to the persons paying the contributions. For instance, employers may pay the contributions on behalf of their employees; spouses may do the same for each other; or parents may pay contributions for their children while unemployed. Fund membership is acquired by means of entering into a membership contract with the voluntary pension fund. Investment units mirror the value of the funds invested into the fund in a manner that the number of investment units held by a member is multiplied by the investment unit value published by the fund on its website and in a daily newspaper on a daily basis. The value of investment units is an indicator of profits generated by the fund. The higher the increase of the fund's investment units, the higher the private pensions of its members.

406. The withdrawal of assets from a voluntary pension fund is possible upon accomplishment of the age of 57 but up to the age of 70. It is also possible to withdraw funds earlier than that but only in extraordinary situations (medical treatment costs and permanent disability).[719] Assets may be withdrawn from a fund in a couple

712. *See* the Voluntary Pension Funds and Plans Act, Art. 28, para. 3.
713. *See* the Voluntary Pension Funds and Plans Act, Art. 29, para. 1.
714. *See* the Voluntary Pension Funds and Plans Act, Art. 29, para. 2.
715. *See* the Voluntary Pension Funds and Plans Act, Art. 44.
716. *See* the Voluntary Pension Funds and Plans Act, Art. 29, para. 3.
717. *See* the Voluntary Pension Funds and Plans Act, Art. 29, para. 4.
718. *See* the Voluntary Pension Funds and Plans Act, Arts 67–71.
719. *See* the Voluntary Pension Funds and Plans Act, Art. 62.

of manners: by means of lump sum payment, annuity purchase from an insurance company, programmed payment or the combination of the above three methods. Payment of a lump sum means the withdrawal of all accumulated assets within a single payment upon an order issued to the company administering the fund. The paid amount is subject to capital gains tax currently amounting to 10%. Programmed payment is carried out in accordance with the agreement concluded by the fund member and the company. It may entail monthly, quarterly, half-yearly or annual payments. Each particular payment is subject to capital gains tax. The transfer of assets onto an insurance company's account for the purpose of annuity purchase is not subject to tax payment. The combination of the above three methods may consist of, for instance, a payment of 50% of accumulated assets, 40% of assets payable on a quarterly basis and 10% for the purchase of annuities with an insurance company.

Part VI. Social Security

407. The social security system within the Republic of Serbia is a system where insureds and insured persons (employees and their family members, as well as retired persons and other insured persons) are provided security based on material investments of employees and other insured persons into the social security funds against: (1) sickness and temporary inability to work due to illness; (2) unemployment; (3) old age and permanent inability to work (disability); and (4) death of a family's breadwinner.[720] According to its organization and financing, the Serbian social security system is primarily of a public (state-owned) and compulsory nature. However, in the last few years, a legal framework has been established providing for the development of private social security as a system independent from or supplementary to compulsory (public) social security. The funds necessary for the materialization of rights from public (state-owned) social security are secured by means of compulsory contribution payments by insureds, as well as from the budget of the Republic of Serbia if it is in the common interest (financing of particularly endangered citizen categories). Public social security services are provided by public institutions. Each branch of social security has a specialized institution. According to the risks covered there are three types of social security in the Republic of Serbia: (1) health insurance; (2) unemployment insurance; and (3) retirement and disability insurance.[721]

408. The domain of health protection and health insurance is regulated in the Republic of Serbia by the Health Protection Law[722] and the Health Insurance Law.[723] Health protection is defined as an organized and comprehensive activity of a company with the primary purpose of reaching the highest possible level of health protection of citizens and their families.[724] Health protection comprises the introduction of measures aimed at the protection and advancement of health, the prevention, control and early detection of diseases, injuries and other health hazards, as well as timely and efficient treatment and rehabilitation. Each citizen of the Republic of Serbia is entitled to health protection, as well as other persons (foreigners) having an approved residency or temporary stay in the Republic of Serbia.[725] The

720. Senad Jašarević, *Socijalno pravo* (*Social Security Law*) (Novi Sad: Pravni fakultet u Novom Sadu, 2009), 190.
721. *Ibid.*
722. OJ RS, 25/2019.
723. OJ RS, 25/2019.
724. Jašarević, *Socijalno pravo* (*Social Security Law*), 208.
725. *Ibid.*

Republic Health Protection Fund is responsible for the implementation of health protection. Individual health protection activities are carried out by health services comprising health institutions and private practices. The financing of health protection is secured in two manners: from the budget of the Republic of Serbia as well as based on health insurance. Health protection of particularly sensitive and socially endangered citizen categories (especially exposed to morbidity), the treatment of diseases of higher social-medical importance, as well as the achievement of health protection in the general interest are budget-financed.[726] Health protection and other rights of employees and other persons financed by labour, as well as the rights of their families are financed by means of compulsory health protection contribution payments. Apart from compulsory health insurance, private insurance is also possible for persons not covered by compulsory insurance or persons wishing to accomplish a greater extent of rights. The basic rights guaranteed to insureds and their families based on compulsory health insurance are the right to a health protection, the right to a compensation of salaries in course of temporary inability to work and the right to a reimbursement of travel expenses incurred in connection with health protection.[727]

409. The domain of unemployment insurance is regulated by the Law on Employment and the Affairs of Unemployment Insurance.[728] This law in fact represents a modified version of the Law on Employment and the Affairs of Unemployment Insurance of 2003[729] regulating the fundamentals of the present system of unemployment insurance. The Law of 2003 rationalized the system of unemployment insurance by means of motivating unemployed persons to actively seek employment (an active employment policy has been introduced),[730] avoiding the possibility of abusing material rights, as well as harmonizing the entire system with the most important standards of the International Labour Organization, and especially the regulation of the EU and the Council of Europe.[731]

410. Unemployment insurance is compulsory in the Republic of Serbia for employed and self-employed persons. These categories are obliged to pay unemployment insurance contributions. Based on the above insurance, they acquire the right to a pecuniary compensation in case of unemployment along with health insurance, retirement insurance and disability insurance rights in accordance with the pertaining statutory provisions. In order for an insured person to acquire entitlement to compensation, the condition of prior insurance needs to be fulfilled – the person at hand needs to be continuously insured for a period of at least twelve months or for eighteen months with interruptions. Continuous insurance shall also comprise an interruption of insurance shorter than thirty days.[732] Compensation shall be due in case of labour relationship termination by the employer in compliance with the

726. *Ibid.*
727. *Ibid.*, 209.
728. OJ RS, 36/2009, 88/2010, 38/2015, 113/2017, 113/2017 and 49/2021.
729. OJ RS, 71/2003.
730. Jašarević, *Socijalno pravo* (*Social Security Law*), 235.
731. *Ibid.*
732. The Law on Employment and the Affairs of Unemployment Insurance, Arts 66–77.

labour provisions, as well as in other instances of insurance cancellation (termination of a labour relationship for a determined period of time, occasional and seasonal jobs, cessation of a title, transfer of founders' rights, etc.).[733] The basis for establishing the amount of compensation is the average income (salary or salary compensation) in the six months preceding the month of employment or insurance termination. The compensation amounts to 50% of the base. Insureds shall be entitled to compensation from the first day of compulsory insurance termination. The pecuniary compensation is payable on a monthly basis, always for the month preceding the month of payment. The law also provides for the possibility to pay a lump sum if this is required for the beneficiary to permanently solve the problem of unemployment by means of self-employment.[734] The duration of payments depends on the term of insurance, so that an unemployed shall receive payments in the course of at least three but maximum twenty-four months. In the period of compensation payment, a beneficiary is obliged to report the National Employment Service[735] to acquire information on the possibilities and conditions of employment, as well as employment intermediation within thirty-day period, in accordance with the individual unemployment plan.[736] The insured shall be entitled to health, pension and disability insurance in the course of compensation payment. Furthermore, health insurance is provided to the beneficiary's family members too, unless they are covered in another manner.

411. Pension and disability insurance has as a purpose to provide the beneficiaries with a stable and certain income in situations of their inability to acquire funds by means of their own labour.[737] Insurance is provided against the risk of old age, permanent inability to work (disability), as well as the death of a family's breadwinner. As the title itself may suggest, there are two branches of social security in the Republic of Serbia: pension and disability insurance functioning in a united manner. The Pension and Disability Insurance Act provides for the establishment of the Republic Pension and Disability Fund. It is the organ competent for the materialization of the rights of persons covered by means of statutory compulsory insurance.[738] The Pension and Disability Insurance Act provides for three categories of compulsory insurance: employees, entrepreneurs and agriculturers. In respect of persons simultaneously fulfilling the requirements for insurance on several of these bases, a priority system according to the above order has been established, meaning that the existence of employment excludes the insurance based on entrepreneurship or agricultural activities. Persons not within the framework of compulsory insurance may enter the system and acquire pertaining rights from the age of 15. The Pension and Disability Insurance Act provides for the following rights to a pension: in case of old age – the right to a retirement pension, in case of disability – the right to a disability pension, in case of the insured's death – the right to a widow's pension (or family pension in case of other family members), as well as the right to the

733. Jašarević, *Socijalno pravo* (*Social Security Law*), 251.
734. *Ibid.*, 252.
735. *Ibid.*
736. *Ibid.*
737. Jašarević, *Socijalno pravo* (*Social Security Law*), 195.
738. Regarding voluntary pension funds within the Republic of Serbia *see supra* nn. 402–405.

reimbursement of funeral costs, in case of bodily injury caused by work place accident or occupational illnesses – the right to compensation of bodily injury.[739]

412. Retirement pension[740] is payable to a person upon a certain length of service. The basic condition is an adequate pensionable length of service (thirty-five to forty years), that is, the payment of contributions over a certain period of time. Apart from the above, all conditions for acquiring a retirement pension are connected with the achievement of a certain age, unless the employee works long enough to have the maximum length of service. The age required to attain pension rights is usually between 60 and 65, although, due to population aging, the above limit has an upward tendency in the Republic of Serbia. The amount of pension depends on the length of service and the amount of contributions paid. A full length of service (currently amounting to thirty-five years in women and forty years in men) will lead to a maximum pension (established by means of coercive provisions), while a shorter length of service will have a lower amount of pension as a result.[741] For the purpose of protecting the existential level of employees with lower wages or persons that are unemployed for a longer period of time, the Republic of Serbia guarantees a minimum pension financed by the Republic budget. In order to maintain the real value of pensions, as well as the existential standard of pensioners, the pensions are adjusted to the costs of life, the inflation and the fluctuation of wages, while the adjustment formula is sometimes a combination of the above three elements.[742]

413. Disability pension is payable for persons with a permanent (either full or partial) inability to work. Should the person be partially capable to work, the difference between the previous and the new salary (in case it is lower) shall be payable from the funds of insurance. Should the insured (the disabled worker) need assistance within the framework of performing basic life necessities, an extra payment for third-party care and help shall be afforded.[743] Disability pension functions primarily in accordance with the principle of solidarity[744] due to the fact that in case of work injuries or occupational illnesses such pensions are not conditioned on the length of service, nor the insured's age, while the conditions in case of an injury or an illness sustained outside of the workplace are substantially less strict (e.g., one to five years of service is required depending on the insured's age). Furthermore, the amount of payments is not always connected with the amount of paid contributions, especially in case of disabled young persons.[745]

414. In case of a breadwinner's death, a survivor's pension is payable to the members of his/her family (children, spouses, eventually certain closer relatives living in the same household). The conditions of this type of pension pertain to both the deceased insured, as well as the beneficiaries themselves. It is required that the

739. Jašarević, *Socijalno pravo* (*Social Security Law*), 195.
740. For details *see* the Pension and Disability Insurance Act, Arts 19–20.
741. Jašarević, *Socijalno pravo* (Social Security Law), 196.
742. *Ibid.*
743. Jašarević, *Socijalno pravo* (*Social Security Law*), 195–196.
744. For details *see* the Pension and Disability Insurance Act, Arts 21–26.
745. Jašarević, *Socijalno pravo* (*Social Security Law*), 197.

insured has a certain length of service, while no length of service is required in case of workplace accidents or occupational illnesses. The family members need to have been supported by the insured, while the possibility to work on their own, the family relationships (duration of marriage, conclusion of another marriage), other incomes, potential support from relatives, and so on are all taken into account when determining the amount of pension. The pension is payable as a percentage of the insured's salary or pension at the moment of death, while the proportion depends on the number of family members too.[746]

415. The person organizing a pensioner's funeral shall have the right of funeral cost reimbursement.[747]

416. Compensation for bodily harm sustained as a consequence of a workplace injury or an occupational illness shall be payable to an insured with a physical impairment of at least 30%.[748] Physical impairment as well as the pertaining percentage points is established by the minister competent for issues of pension and disability insurance, as well as the minister competent for health affairs upon proposal of the Republic Fund for Pension and Disability Insurance.[749] Physical impairments are categorized according to their severity into eight levels.[750]

746. For details *see* the Pension and Disability Insurance Act, Arts 27–36.
747. *See* the Pension and Disability Insurance Act, Art. 41.
748. *See* the Pension and Disability Insurance Act, Art. 37.
749. *See* the Pension and Disability Insurance Act, Art. 38.
750. *See* the Pension and Disability Insurance Act, Art. 39.

Part VII. Insurance Intermediaries

Chapter 1. Establishment and Supervision

417. Within Serbian insurance law, there is a clear distinction between insurance brokerage and insurance agency activities. In accordance with the above, there is a difference between subjects active within the field of brokerage and those carrying out agency operations.

418. Insurance brokerage activities include insurance and reinsurance brokerage activities.[751]

419. Insurance brokerage activities shall be activities related to introducing the insured and/or policyholder to an insurance/reinsurance undertaking for the purpose of negotiating the conclusion of an insurance/reinsurance contract, preparation for the conclusion of these contracts, as well as providing help in exercising the rights arising from such contracts, in particular in settlement of claims for damages.[752] Insurance brokerage activities shall be carried on, as an exclusive activity, by an insurance brokerage undertaking with its head office in the Republic, registered with the competent authority based on its licence to carry on such business issued by the NBS.[753] Insurance brokerage companies may usually not carry out insurance agency activities.[754] Insurance brokerage companies are incorporated as joint stock companies or limited liability companies, subject to the law determining the legal status of companies.[755] There are only a few specific provisions different compared to the incorporation of 'classical' joint stock or limited liability companies. These are provided for by the LI. The distinctive provisions pertain to the minimum amounts of the share capital's pecuniary portion, the business name (it must include the activity description 'insurance brokerage'), the obligatory conclusion of a contract against liability for damages arising from insurance brokerage activities or unconditional bank guarantees accepted by the NBS and the licensing conditions of the NBS for carrying out insurance intermediary activities.[756] In parts not regulated by special norms, the provisions of the LI regarding joint stock insurance companies apply

751. *See* LI, Art. 85, para. 1.
752. *See* LI, Art. 85, para. 2.
753. *See* LI, Art. 86, para. 1.
754. *See* LI, Art. 86, para. 2.
755. *See* LI, Art. 88, para. 2.
756. *See* LI, Art. 88, paras 3–6.

accordingly to issues relating to the licensing and approval granted to insurance brokerage companies by the NBS. Regarding contractual relationships established by means of insurance intermediation contracts, the provisions of the LO shall be applicable.

420. Insurance agency activities shall be the activities of initiating, proposing or carrying out the tasks of preparation and conclusion of insurance contracts on behalf and for the account of an insurance undertaking.[757] Insurance agency activities are conducted by legal entities (insurance agencies) or natural persons (insurance agents) pursuant to insurance agency agreements on behalf of insurance companies, under the condition that they obtained a licence to engage in insurance agency activities.[758] As an exception, insurance agencies and/or agents can represent more than one insurance company based on their written consent. Insurance agency, as an exclusive activity, shall be carried on by:

(1) an insurance agency undertaking with its head office in the Republic, registered with a competent authority based on its licence to carry on insurance agency activities issued by the NBS;
(2) a natural person – entrepreneur (hereinafter 'insurance agent') with its head office in the Republic, registered with a competent authority based on its licence to carry on insurance agency activities issued by the NBS.[759]

421. A bank, with its head office in the Republic and established in accordance with the law Governing banks (hereinafter 'the Bank), a financial leasing provider with its head office in the Republic and established in accordance with the law governing financial leasing and the public postal operator with its head office in the Republic and established in accordance with the law governing postal services may, as a supplementary activity, carry on insurance agency business on the basis of prior approval of the NBS for carrying on these activities.[760]

422. An insurance agency undertaking shall not engage in insurance brokerage activities.[761] There are only a few specific provisions differing from the establishment of a 'classical' joint stock company or limited liability company. These are provided for by the LI. The distinctive provisions pertain to the minimum amounts of the share capital's pecuniary portion that needs to be paid up upon incorporation, the business name (it must include the activity description 'insurance agency/agent') and the licensing conditions of the NBS for carrying out insurance agency activities.[762] In parts not regulated by special norms, the provisions of the LI regarding joint stock insurance companies apply accordingly to issues relating to the

757. *See* LI, Art. 97, para. 1.
758. *See* LI, Art. 97, para. 2.
759. *See* LI, Art. 98, para. 1.
760. *See* LI, Art. 98, para. 2.
761. *See* LI, Art. 98, para. 3.
762. *See* LI, Art. 99–102.

licensing and approval granted to insurance agencies by the NBS. Insurance representatives (agents) are entrepreneurs, that is, a natural person – entrepreneur (hereinafter 'insurance agent') with its head office in the Republic, registered with a competent authority based on its licence to carry on insurance agency activities issued by the NBS. Their legal status is regulated by the LCC (Articles 83–92). There are only a few specific provisions regulated by the LI. According to one, at establishment, insurance agent must hold the cash amount in RSD equivalent of EUR 1,500 calculated at the middle exchange rate of the NBS on the date of payment, originating from the applicant's own funds, and in the course of the insurance agent's business must maintain the liquid assets (cash assets, short-term securities and other short-term investments and receivables) at the level of at least 75% of that amount.[763] Other specific provisions pertain to the application for a licence by the NBS for the provision of insurance agency services.[764]

423. Insurance agencies and/or agents must remit to the insurance company all monies, other payment instruments and collaterals collected and/or taken over from policyholders and/or insurance contractors on behalf of the insurance company, by the following workday from the date of collecting or taking over the latest.[765] They are furthermore obliged to hand over other payment instruments or collaterals to the insurance company within the same time limit. Insurance agencies and/or agents collect insurance premiums according to the insurance company's rules and regulations.[766] Until the day of payment and/or remittance to the insurance company, insurance agencies and/or agents are obliged to keep at a safe place the collected monies, payment instruments and collaterals.[767]

424. The insurance company or the insurance agent is liable for the acts performed in the course of insurance agency activities.[768] The insurance agency and/or agent is liable towards the policyholder for damages caused by false impersonation or malpractice of the insurance agency and/or agent, and/or due to the fact that the insurance agency and/or agent failed to inform the policyholder on their acting in the capacity of representatives.[769] The general manager of the insurance company and/or the specially authorized official signing the agency contract is liable towards the insurance company for damages caused by such contracts.[770] The provisions of the LO are applicable regarding the contractual relationships established by insurance agency contracts.

425. The supervision over subjects active within the field of insurance in its widest possible sense, including insurance brokerage and agency operations is performed by the NBS.

763. *See* LI, Art. 103, para. 4.
764. *See* LI Art. 105.
765. *See* LI Art. 106, para. 1.
766. *See* LI Art. 106, para. 2.
767. *See* LI Art. 106, para. 3.
768. *See* LI, Art. 107, para. 1.
769. *See* LI, Art. 107, para. 2.
770. *See* LI, Art. 107, para. 3.

Chapter 2. Insurance Intermediaries and the Insurance Contract

§1. Brokers and the Insurance Contract

426. An insurance contract may be concluded upon the engagement of a broker. In practice brokers provide information on the terms of insurance, collect offers for the conclusion of insurance contracts. By a brokerage contract in general, the broker shall assume the obligation to try to find and connect the principal with a person willing to negotiate the conclusion of a specific contract, while the principal shall assume the obligation to pay the broker a particular fee should such contract be concluded.[771] The broker is obliged to seek a possibility of contract conclusion with the care of a prudent businessman and indicate such a possibility to the principal.[772] If such obligation is expressly assumed, the broker shall be the intermediary in course of negotiations and do his/her utmost for the contract to come about.[773] The broker shall not be liable in case of unsuccessful intermediation performed with the highest possible level of engagement.[774] The brokerage order does not automatically contain an authorization for the broker to accept performance of the contract concluded upon intermediation on the principal's behalf (e.g., receiving the insurance premiums). A special power of attorney is necessary to the above effect. A broker shall acquire the right to remuneration at the moment of entering into a contract he/she has mediated, unless otherwise stipulated.[775] The broker's interest for the conclusion of the mediated insurance contract follows from the above provision. A broker shall not be entitled, unless stipulated to the contrary, to reimbursement of expenses incurred in carrying out the order.[776] Should, however, the broker's right to reimbursement of expenses be recognized by the contract, the broker shall be entitled to such reimbursement even if the insurance contract has not been concluded.[777]

427. It is a general rule that the broker is liable for loss eventually sustained by one or the other party involved in his/her mediation, which occurs because of his/her mediation on behalf of a person without business capacity, whose incapacity was known, or should have been known to him/her, or on behalf of a person of whose incapacity to meet the contractual obligations he/she was aware, or should have been aware, and shall generally be liable for all loss caused through his/her fault.[778] A broker shall be liable for loss sustained by the principal if the broker, without the principal's permission, discloses to a third party the substance of the order, the commenced negotiations, or terms and conditions of a contract concluded.[779] Apart from the general rules on the liability of brokers from the LO, the

771. *See* LO, Art. 813.
772. *See* LO, Art. 813, para. 1.
773. *See* LO, Art. 813, para. 2.
774. *See* LO, Art. 813, para. 3.
775. *See* LO, Art. 823.
776. *See* LO, Art. 824, para. 1.
777. *See* LO, Art. 824, para. 2.
778. *See* LO, Art. 820, para. 1.
779. *See* LO, Art. 820, para. 2.

LI provides for a couple of special rules pertaining to insurance brokerage companies. Based on a broker's basic obligation to perform brokerage activities pursuant to the insured's order in good faith and in a professional manner and to explain to and advise the insured on the circumstances relevant to the conclusion of the insurance contract, the law provides for a series of special duties:[780] to draft an appropriate risk analysis and suggest suitable coverage, to draft a solvency analysis of the insurance company, to mediate in the conclusion of insurance contracts with the insurance company, to inform the insurance company on the insured's intent to conclude the insurance contract and to offer the insured the conditions of insurance and provide them with information on the method of premium calculation, to check the insurance policy contents, to monitor the execution of the insurance contract by the insured concluded through his/her mediation, to draft a proposal to amend the concluded insurance contract for the purpose of ensuring a higher level of safety to the insured.[781] For the purpose of preserving the broker's impartiality towards the insured, the LI provides for the broker's obligation to inform the insured on potential conflicts of interest (for instance, in case of contractual relationships with particular insurers to mediate solely for them or in case of stipulating higher than regular commissions for mediating in certain classes of insurance).[782] Due to the brokers' widely defined liability, the LI provides for an obligation to submit in the course of establishing an insurance brokerage company a concluded preliminary contract on the broker's insurance against liability for damages caused in the course of performing insurance brokerage activities. It is interesting that the above contracts may be substituted by unconditional financial bank guarantees accepted by the NBS for the insured sum and/or the sum not less than EUR 200,000 in its RSD counter-value according to the middle exchange rate of the NBS on the day of payment.[783]

§2. Agents and the Insurance Contract

428. Insurance contracts are often entered into through agents. An insurance agent is a person authorized by means of the law or a contract to undertake legal transactions pertaining to the insurance contract and perform other insurance services for and on behalf of the person represented.[784] Agency in its widest sense comprises legal transactions (usually contract conclusion) for and on behalf of third parties. Both the insurer and the insurance contractor may enter into insurance contracts through agents. However, it is more common for the insurer to conclude contracts through agents. In the course of carrying out insurance operations, insurers set up a wide network of agents in order to make their services closer to potential customers.

780. Šulejić, *Pravo osiguranja* (*Insurance Law*), 164.
781. *See* LI, Art. 94.
782. *See* LI, Art. 95.
783. *See* LI, Art 89, para. 3.
784. Šulejić, *Pravo osiguranja* (*Insurance Law*), 159.

429. Insurance agency activities are regulated by means of general provisions of contract law (Articles 84–98 LO), the LCC (Article 25), as well as by a special provision of the LO (Article 906) pertaining exclusively to insurance agency. At this point, a couple of special rules within insurance agency operations shall be presented. Should an insurer authorize someone to represent him/her, while not specifying the scope of his/her powers, such agent shall be entitled to conclude, on behalf and for the account of the insurer, insurance contracts, to negotiate and conclude contract modifications or extend their validity, to issue insurance policies, to collect premium payments, and to accept statements communicated to the insurer,[785] as well as to perform activities of consultancy and assistance in processing claims, as well as risk and damage assessment. Should the insurer limit his/her agent while this fact is not known to the insurance contractor, such limitations shall be considered as non-existent.[786] Insurance agencies and/or agents may normally engage in agency activities for one insurance company only. Only exceptionally may insurance agencies and/or agents represent more than one insurance company based on their written consents.[787] Insurance agencies and/or agents are obliged to have the name of the insurance company they represent placed in a prominent position in their business premises.[788] Regarding other matters please refer to the general rules on agency provided for by the LO and the LCC. They regulate questions such as: the effects of agency, transfer of rights, excess of authorization, conclusion of contracts by unauthorized persons, legal transactions of commercial company agents entered into outside of the company's scope of business activities, and so on.

785. *See* LO, 906, para. 1.
786. *See* LO, Art. 906, para. 2.
787. *See* LI, Art. 99, para. 1.
788. *See* LI, Art. 100.

Part VIII. Reinsurance, Coinsurance, Pooling

Chapter 1. Reinsurance

430. Reinsurance is a type of insurance activity. According to the LI reinsurance activities entail the conclusion and execution of contracts on the reinsurance of risks surpluses exceeding the self-retention insurance amount of an insurance company with another insurance company licensed to conduct reinsurance activities.[789] Therefore, by means of reinsurance a legal relationship is established between two insurance companies, one of which shall take on the insured's role while the other that of the insurer (i.e., the reinsurer). Reinsurance is concluded by entering into a reinsurance contract. A reinsurance contract is an agreement where one party (the reinsurer) incurs the obligation to pay to the other party (the insurer – being entirely liable towards all of its insureds with whom it has valid insurance contracts) whole or part of the amount paid or payable to insureds, while the insurer assumes the obligation to pay a certain premium to the reinsurer. Reinsurance enables insurers to incur in their portfolios risks that would normally not be allowed due to the fact that they exceed the scope of their capacity. By means of reinsurance, legal relationships are established exclusively between the insurer not being able to independently cover the risk incurred by the insurance contract and the reinsurer assuming the obligation to pay whole or part of the amount paid or payable to insureds. Insureds, however, remain outside of the legal relationships established by the reinsurance contract. As opposed to coinsurance contracts where risks are horizontally divided between two or more (co)insurers being in a direct legal relationship with the insured, reinsurance provides for a vertical risk division between the insurer and the reinsurer, whereby the latter does not establish a direct legal relationship with the insured. This means that the insured is not entitled to claim anything directly from the reinsurer. Should the insured event occur, the insured may seek compensation only from the insurer. Insureds usually are not even familiar of the fact that the insurer entered into a reinsurance contract for the purpose of dispersing the risks incurred by means of the insurance contract. It is thereby legally irrelevant whether the insurer pays the compensation from its own assets or partially from the assets received from the reinsurer. However, despite the fact that the insured and the reinsurer are not in a legal relationship because the insurance contract and the reinsurance contract are two completely separated legal transactions, the existence of an insurance contract is a prerequisite of the reinsurance contract's full legal effect. The insurer would otherwise not have an insurable interest for concluding a reinsurance

789. *See* LI, Art. 7, para. 1.

contract. Interest as a conscious relationship between the necessity and the manner of its fulfilment does exist in reinsurance regardless of the fact whether it is a postulate of property or personal insurance.[790] The reason for the above is that insurers need in both cases certain safety from eventual material loss in case that the insured event occurs. Namely, the insurer incurs damage in both cases by payment of compensation or the insured amount. Risk within reinsurance is the uncertainty as to the fact whether the insurer is going to be obliged to pay the insured amount or compensation due to the occurrence of the insured event (from the underlying insurance contract).

431. The provisions of Chapter XXVII LO pertaining to insurance contracts are not applicable to relationships based on reinsurance contracts.[791] Within Serbian insurance law reinsurance contracts are not regulated by means of Acts of Parliament, but exclusively by autonomous sources of law (contracts and general terms and conditions representing their constituent parts). The above is justified by the specificities of such contract types. Reinsurance contracts usually provide for the type of reinsurance,[792] the commencement of its effects and the term of contract. Furthermore, matters such as the insurance transactions to which the contract's effects are extended, the insurer's self-retention, the maximum liability of the reinsurer, the deposit to which the insurer is entitled,[793] are also regulated by means of reinsurance contracts.

432. There are various types of reinsurance contracts. The most important division of reinsurance contracts is into reinsurance contracts against proportional parts of risk (proportional reinsurance), risk surplus reinsurance contracts, damage surplus reinsurance contracts and loss surplus reinsurance contracts.[794]

433. By means of proportional reinsurance contracts, the insurer assumes the obligation to pay the reinsurer part (a percentage) of the premium received from the insured, while in consideration of the above the reinsurer is going to be obliged to pay a percentage (a proportion) of the compensation paid to the insured in case the insured event occurs.[795] Such type of reinsurance is beneficial to the insurer not having sufficient funds and experience in risk selection[796] due to the fact that a certain proportion of risks is transferred into the reinsurance leading to the simultaneous

790. Šulejić, *Pravo osiguranja* (*Insurance Law*), 516.
791. *See* LO, Art. 899, para. 2.
792. *See infra* n. 267.
793. Reinsurance contracts normally provide for the insurer's right to a deposit, that is, part of the premium as a security that the reinsurer is going to perform, should the insured event occur.
794. Šulejić, *Pravo osiguranja* (*Insurance Law*), 517.
795. *Ibid.*
796. This reinsurance type is rarely employed by insurers having a developed insurance portfolio due to the fact that such companies usually keep coverable risks for themselves (so-called good risks), while only risks deemed uncoverable are reinsured.

coverage of both large and small risks by the reinsurance. A rule is applicable in this reinsurance type in that the reinsurer is not permitted to further reinsure the part of the assumed risk.[797]

434. As opposed to proportional reinsurance, risk surplus reinsurance does not pertain to all contracts covering a certain risk (fire, burglary, etc.) but only to those where the amount of insurance or the insured object's value exceeds a certain limit, that is, the insurer's self-retention. Should the insured event occur, the reinsurer's obligation is going to come about only if the insurer's self-retention limit is exceeded.[798]

435. Damage surplus reinsurance contracts are contracts where the insurer transfers damage surpluses to the reinsurer by laying down in the contract that damage up to a certain value shall be covered by the insurer, while damage exceeding the contracted amount shall be compensated by the reinsurer.[799] This type of reinsurance differs from risk surplus reinsurance in that the limit of the insurer's obligation is determined exclusively by the extent of damage, which, if exceeded, shall be compensated by the reinsurer.[800] Damages up to a certain amount are indemnified by the insurer, while above that the reinsurer is the one obliged to compensate. Within damage surplus reinsurance, there is a difference between second risk reinsurance and pure damage surplus reinsurance.[801] In second risk reinsurance, the reinsurer assumes the obligation to repair damages stemming from a particular insurance contract concluded between the insurer and the insured. Damages above the established amount (but only from the precisely defined insurance contract) shall be repaired by the reinsurer, while the premiums are payable only from the amounts received based on that very contract.[802] Other contracts between the insurer and the insured party are irrelevant for the reinsurer. In pure damage surplus reinsurance, the situation is just the opposite due to the fact that the reinsurer assumes the obligation to repair all damages exceeding the determined value from several insurance contracts, under the condition that such damages were incurred as a consequence of the same insured event (fire, lightning, etc.).[803] Premiums are paid according to the same principle. As opposed to second risk reinsurance, they are payable from all contracts covered by reinsurance. The reinsurer's obligation pertains to all contracts, rather than being limited to damages from a particular contract between the insurer and the insured party.[804]

797. Šulejić, *Pravo osiguranja* (*Insurance Law*), 517.
798. *Ibid.*
799. *Ibid.*, 518.
800. *Ibid.*
801. *Ibid.*
802. *Ibid.*
803. *Ibid.*
804. *Ibid.*

436. By means of loss surplus reinsurance contracts, the reinsurer assumes the obligation to compensate the insurer against losses incurred in a particular insurance type in a certain period (for instance, within a year).[805] In this type of reinsurance, the reinsurer's obligations are determined at the end of the contracted period by means of comparing the total premiums received and compensations paid in the given period. Should the amount of compensations in the period exceed the amount provided for by the reinsurance, the reinsurer incurs the obligation to compensate them. The difference between this type of reinsurance and damage surplus reinsurance lies within the fact that loss surpluses over a particular time period in one insurance type are taken into account rather than damage surpluses from one or more policies.[806]

805. Šulejić, *Pravo osiguranja* (*Insurance Law*), 518.
806. *Ibid.*

Chapter 2. Coinsurance and Pooling

437. Coinsurance contracts are contracts where the same object of insurance against the same risk and for the same interest is simultaneously insured with more insurers by means of one contract, whereby an agreement on the collective exposure to and division of risks is entered into between the different insurers. Such contracts were created due to various practical reasons, the most important of which is the division of 'high' risk coverage between several insurers. Due to the fact that the independent coverage of such risks would mean a great burden for the insurer, instead of rejecting the offer to enter into the insurance contract, insurers opt for offering other insurers to divide their obligations regarding risk coverage. Although the aim of such contracts is similar to reinsurance, there are substantial differences between the two contract types.

438. Two essential features are characteristic of coinsurance contracts. First, that the same object of insurance against the same risk and for the same interest is simultaneously insured with more insurers, and second, that there is an agreement on the collective exposure to and division of risks between the different insurers.[807]

439. By means of coinsurance contracts, the same object of insurance against the same risk and for the same interest is simultaneously insured with more insurers by means of one integral contract. As opposed to multiple insurance where the insurer is simultaneously in multiple independent insurance relationships with several insurance contractors, in coinsurance contracts there is only one contractual relationship between the insurance contractor on the one hand and two or more insurers on the other hand.[808] While in multiple insurance, the insurance relationships are independent of one another, coinsurance contracts pertain to one particular insurance realized by entering into an insurance between the insurance contractor and one or more insurers. The fact that a greater number of insurers primarily participate in the insurance by covering particular risks, that is, that each of the participants is in a direct legal relationship with the insurance contractor or another person (the insured, the beneficiary or a third-party claimant) does not mean that in coinsurance contracts there are more existing insurance relationships.[809] In case of a concluded coinsurance contract, there is one contractual relationship irrespective of the fact that the insurers may assume obligations towards the insured exclusively in the capacity of partial debtors. Therefore, in coinsurance contracts, there is one debtor-creditor relationship, while the obligation of a contracting party (the insurer) may be precisely divided between several entities. Consequently, in case that the insured amount exceeds the value of insured interest, the rules on overinsurance shall be applicable rather than those pertaining to double insurance. Therefore, the possibility of the insured amount exceeding the value of insured interest is a feature

807. Vladimir Marjanski, 'Ugovor o saosiguranju' (Coinsurance Contract), *Pravni život* 11 (2008): 901.
808. Marjanski, 'Ugovor o saosiguranju' (Coinsurance Contract), *Pravni život* 11 (2008): 901.
809. *Ibid.*

that renders coinsurance different from the institute of multiple insurance.[810] In multiple insurance the total aggregate amount of insurance never exceeds the value of insured interest. For all of the above reasons, the coinsurance contract is not to be treated as a special type of multiple insurance. Furthermore, coinsurance contracts are also different from reinsurance contracts. Coinsurance contracts, as well as reinsurance contracts serve as a vehicle of risk atomization, but in coinsurance contracts, as opposed to reinsurance, each co-insurer primarily participates in the insurance against particular risks, whereby each of them is in a direct legal relationship with the insured. In reinsurance contracts, however, there is no direct legal relationship between the reinsurer and the insured party. Apart from the above, it needs to be pointed out that coinsurance is also possible within the domain of reinsurance.[811] Thus, for instance, proportional reinsurance represents a modality of coinsurance entered into by the insurer in the capacity of the reinsured on the one hand and a greater number of reinsurers on the other hand. Examined from the viewpoint of the insured's rights, the difference between classic insurance contracts and coinsurance contracts is exclusively of a quantitative nature. In both cases, the legal relationships are of the same nature with the only difference that in coinsurance contracts there is a number of insurers on the insurer's side that agreed upon the collective coverage and division of risks.[812] The same nature of insurance and coinsurance has as its consequence that the relationships between the insurance contractor (the insured, the beneficiary or a third-party claimant – hereinafter collectively referred to as 'other parties') and the particular co-insurers established by an integral coinsurance contract are regulated by the rules applicable to the particular type of insurance contract.

440. Apart from the integrated being of the contractual relationship, coinsurance contracts have another important characteristic. The other essential element of coinsurance contract is the existence of an agreement between the co-insurers on the collective coverage and division of risks. Namely, the consent of an insurer to assume obligations towards the insured or certain other parties together with other insurers means that there is an agreement between the insurers on the collective exposure to and division of risks pertaining to the object of insurance. Such an agreement on the collective coverage and division of risks is already existing at the point of entering into the coinsurance contract by all of the co-insurers and the insurance contractor under the conditions laid down in the coinsurance contract and represents a prerequisite for the conclusion of such a contract.[813] Thereby the proportion of risk coverage of each of the co-insurers may or may not be precisely determined. The system of liability of co-insurers towards the insured or certain other parties, as well as the internal relationship of co-insurers regarding the division of risks is going to be discussed at a later point.

810. *Ibid.*
811. *Ibid.*, 902.
812. *Ibid.*, 902.
813. Jovan Slavnić, *Ugovor osiguravača o zajedničkom snošenju i raspodeli rizika putem saosiguranja i njegovo sprovo enje (The Agreement of Insurers on the Collective Coverage and Division of Risks by means of Coinsurance and its Implementation), Pravni život* 11–12 (1993), 1546.

441. Apart from the above two important features, coinsurance contracts are characterized by other properties not having an essential effect on the conceptual definition of such contracts. One of the so-called unimportant features of coinsurance contracts is that they often contain a 'lead clause'. The advantages of this manner of contracting are underscored by means of laying down a clause on the lead insurer. A lead (co)insurer established by such a provision is entrusted with various authorizations. If provided for, lead clauses represent constituent parts of coinsurance contracts. They regulate not only the internal relationships between the lead and the other co-insurers, but also the external relationships between the insurance contractor and/or other parties on the one hand and the co-insurers on the other hand. Due to the fact that such clauses are constituent parts of coinsurance contracts, they require the insurance contractor's consent. Such a consent of the insurance contractor is expressed by means of entering into the coinsurance contract containing a lead clause. Apart from the above, the insurance contractor may have an influence on the selection of the lead (co)insurer. In practice, however, the most common way to choose the lead (co)insurer is according to the amount of coverage. The lead (co)insurer will usually be the one providing for the largest part of coverage according to the agreement concluded between the (co)insurers. Of course, it is also possible to stipulate otherwise. The lead needs to be one of the (co)insurers. If a lead (co)insurer is determined, it needs to be clarified that such an insurer is entering into an agreement with the insurance contractor only as one of the participants covering part of the insured amount rather than independently, and who will, in case of a lead clause, have the authorization of the other (co)insurers regarding certain matters.[814] The advantages of this manner of contracting are emphasized by means of laying down a clause on the lead insurer. Such clauses primarily make it easier for the insurance contractor to perform his/her obligations. For instance, it may be sufficient that the insurance contractor notifies or submits a declaration of intent only to the lead (co)insurer or pays him/her the whole amount of premium, so that it will be deemed that such obligations were performed towards all of the (co)insurers.

442. A lead clause may have various contents. In this regard, it may be of substantive, procedural or mixed nature.[815] Substantive authorizations of the lead (co)insurer may also be diverse. In case of providing for a lead clause, some of the substantive authorizations are deemed to exist, while others need to be expressly stipulated. Thus, for instance, the right and obligation of having certain authorities shall be deemed without express provisions to that effect should the insurance contract contain a lead clause.[816] By means of providing for a lead (co)insurer, he/she will be authorized to represent the other (co)insurers within the contractual relationship. Thereby it is assumed that the lead insurer received from the others the rights of insurance agents the scope of authorities of which have not been contractually determined.[817] These are: to enter into an insurance contract for and on behalf of

814. Marjanski, *Ugovor o osiguranju* (*Insurance Contract*), 116.
815. Marjanski, 'Ugovor o saosiguranju' (Coinsurance Contract), *Pravni život* 11 (2008): 906.
816. *Ibid.*
817. *Ibid.*

the insurers (in accordance with the agreement on the joint coverage and distribution of risks), to conclude contract amendments or prolong their term, to issue insurance policies, to collect premium payments, to present and clarify declarations of intent and the explanations of insurance contractors (and/or insureds, beneficiaries, etc.) towards the other (co)insurers,[818] to notify the other (co)insurers on the occurrence of the insured event, to receive statements directed both to him/her or to the other insurers.[819] In the course of declarations of intent made by insurance contractors and/or other parties, these need to demonstrate at all times that such declarations of intent are not meant only for the lead (co)insurer. A declaration of intent or a notification communicated to the lead insurer will have an effect to all of the other insurers.[820] However, certain substantial authorizations need to be expressly stipulated and pointed out within the lead clause so that it may be deemed that the lead insurer had those authorizations. Such are, e.g., statements on the termination of contract or extra-judicial settlements, and so on. Lead clauses may also contain certain procedural authorizations. As lead clauses provide for certain substantial authorizations for the (co)insurer, procedural clauses also need to be expressly stipulated. However, the procedural authorizations of a lead (co)insurer are going to be of relevance only in case of a dispute.[821] Therefore, a claim at law directed towards the lead (co)insurer shall be deemed to have been made towards all of the insurers, while a potential final judgment shall be binding upon all of the (co)insurers. By means of providing for a procedural clause, other (co)insurers in fact consent to the compensatory nature of the final judgment rendered against the lead (co)insurer or a settlement entered into by him/her.[822] Thus, substantial influence is exercised on procedural efficiency and economy. A claim at law eventually made towards other (co)insurers not having a lead status may be dismissed by the court if the subject (co)insurer invokes the procedural clause. Therefore, a procedural clause, apart from the rights afforded to the insurance contractor and other parties, has as a consequence an obligation to abstain from directing claims towards other (co)insurers, for on the contrary they will be liable for damages caused (e.g., the procedural costs will be borne by him/her).[823] There is a partial exception to the rule *pactum de non pretendo*, according to which the insurance contractor (or another party) is obliged to abstain from directing claims towards other (co)insurers. Should the risk coverage part of the lead insurer not amount to the sum claimed by the claimant, the insurance contractor or the other participants shall have the right (and the obligation if so requested by the lead (co)insurer) to divide and broaden the claim onto the other (co)insurers up to the claimed amount. The insurance contractor may in such instances choose against which (co)insurers to direct his/her claim. Procedural clauses, however, do not provide for the representation of other (co)insurers by the lead before courts. The lead insurer has the same procedural rights as all other parties in the procedure. Only regular procedural actions may be undertaken by him/

818. Declaration of intent given by the insurance contractor to the lead insurer shall be deemed to have be communicated to all of the other co-insurers.
819. *See* LO, Art. 906.
820. Marjanski, 'Ugovor o saosiguranju' (Coinsurance Contract), *Pravni život* 11 (2008): 906.
821. *Ibid.*, 907.
822. *Ibid.*, 907.
823. *Ibid.*, 907.

her. Due to the influence of the state of affairs established by means of a judgment on the status of other (co)insurers, the lead has the right to settle and recognize the claim at law only if the express consent of the other (co)insurers has been procured to that effect. The lead is obliged to inform the other (co)insurers on the litigation and to procure their consents regarding settlement, the recognition of claims, and so on. Should the lead (co)insurer settle or recognize a claim without the express consent of the other (co)insurers, he/she shall be liable towards them within the framework of their internal relationship. A rendered judgment (even if delivered according to admittance or settlement) shall always be effective in the external relationship between the claimant and all of the (co)insurers. In other words, should the lead (co)insurer fail to perform the obligation laid down in the judgment, the claimant shall have the right to seek enforcement against any of the (co)insurers based on the coinsurance contract, the procedural clause and the judgment delivered against the lead (co)insurer. In such instances other (co)insurers may only raise objections and seek the potential proportionate reduction of payment obligations if in the case at hand the system of several liability is applicable and if the amount claimed from the (co)insurers is higher than their part of risk coverage established by means of the coinsurance contract. Due to the fact that within the framework of granted substantial and procedural authorizations the lead (co)insurer acts as a sort of a proxy of the others, pursuant to the general rules of contract law and the above-mentioned lead clause, he/she is entitled to a fee and a reimbursement of necessary and useful costs incurred in connection with the performance of the above authorizations. Without providing for a lead clause (a regular and/or a procedural one), there would be no existing legal relationship between the (co)insurers apart from the agreement on the joint coverage and distribution of risks. An insurance contractor or other participants would in such case need to perform their obligations separately towards each of the (co)insurers (such as, premium payment, communication of various notifications, declarations of intent), while they would need to address each of them separately for the fulfilment of their substantive and procedural claims.

443. In respect to the (co)insurer's liability, two types of relationships need to be differentiated. One is the relationship between the (co)insurers themselves (an internal relationship), while the other is the relationship between each of the (co)insurers individually and the insured (or another party – an external relationship). In case of internal relationships, an express or implied agreement on the joint coverage and distribution of risk may exist between the (co)insurers. In other words, their parts of coverage may be precisely and expressly provided for (in particular percentage points, in absolute amounts) or remain undetermined. Should the (co)insurers fail to lay down the coverage parts, a legal assumption shall be applicable according to which they implicitly agreed that they shall be liable towards the insured or another person in equal parts. A potential agreement or the above legal assumption, however, is applicable only regarding their internal affairs. The other group of relationships is the one between each of the (co)insurers individually and the insured.[824] There are two systems (co)insurer liability towards the insured. According to one, (co)insurers are jointly and severally liable. According to the

824. Marjanski, 'Ugovor o saosiguranju' (Coinsurance Contract), *Pravni život* 11 (2008): 907.

other, (co)insurers are only severally liable towards the insured. Within Serbian law, both systems of liability are applicable depending on the type of insurance contract in respect of which a coinsurance has been entered into.

444. Should the (co)insurers be jointly and severally liable towards the insured, the insured may address any of them with the claim for payment of the whole compensation or the contracted insured amount. If a (co)insurer makes payment of the whole compensation to the insured, the burden is going to be subsequently divided between the (co)insurers according to their internal agreement.[825] Such a system is provided for by the LO. Should a contract of insurance be concluded with several insurers who agree on joint coverage and distribution of risk, each insurer designated in the insurance policy shall be liable to the insured person for the entire compensation.[826] Such a provision is applicable to all insurance contract types, apart from those regulated by means of special laws. The provision is of a coercive nature and may not be deviated from according to the (co)insurers' will. An eventually different agreement on the risk coverage and distribution would be effective only within the (co)insurer's internal relationships. A provision to the contrary within the coinsurance contract (i.e., in the relationship towards the insured) would be ineffective and the above coercive statutory provision applicable instead. The system of joint and several liability of (co)insurers is more beneficial for the insured. Its importance is especially emphasized in case of a (co)insurer's bankruptcy. The risk of a (co)insurer's insolvency is in such instances covered by the other (co)insurers instead of the insured, due to their joint and several liability towards the insured.[827]

445. However, the system of several liability corresponds more to the economic purposes of concluding coinsurance contracts. According to the system of several liability, a divided debt relationship exists between the (co)insurers. This means that the insured may claim from particular (co)insurers only their pertaining part of coverage. In case of a bankruptcy the other (co)insurers shall not be liable for the bankruptcy debtor's part of coverage.[828] Such a system enables the distribution of risk at the moment of insured event occurrence due to the fact that each (co)insurer shall be liable towards the insured only up to his/her pertaining part of risk coverage. The system of several liability is adopted by the LMIN. Should in case of an insurance contract concluded by several insurers their special parts of coverage be determined, each of the insurers shall be liable for indemnification only proportionally to their part of coverage.[829] This provision is applicable to all insurance types within the domain of transport insurance.

---

825. Šulejić, *Pravo osiguranja* (*Insurance Law*), 70.
826. *See* LO, Art. 935.
827. Blagojević–Krulj, *Komentar Zakona o obligacionim odnosima, knjiga II* (*Commentary to the Law on Obligations, Book II*), 511.
828. Predrag Šulejić, *Pravo osiguranja* (*Insurance Law*) (Belgrade: Pravni fakultet u Beogradu, 1992), 70.
829. *See* LI, Art. 765.

446. Everything said regarding to the relationship of the (co)insurers and the insured also pertains to insurance beneficiaries (if the coinsurance contract is entered into on behalf of a third party), as well as third-party claimants (in case of liability insurance contracts).

447. Insurance pools represent business associations of two or more insurance companies for the purpose of carrying out insurance or reinsurance transactions covering risks of large damages. The former Basic Law on the Property and Personal Insurance System of the SFRY[830] provided in principle for a special type of association within the domain of insurance: the possibility of insurance or reinsurance pooling was afforded. Article 33 of the said law laid down that two or more insurance organizations may establish a pool for carrying out property or personal coinsurance or reinsurance transactions. Although the presently applicable LI does not provide expressly for the possibility of establishing coinsurance and reinsurance pools, there are no hindrances to contractually create such relationships between a larger number of insurance companies. Failing express provisions of the LI regarding insurance pools, the regulations on business associations shall be accordingly applicable in their regard.[831]

830. OJ SFRY, 17/1990, 82/1990 and OJ FRY, br. 31/1993, 24/1994.
831. *See* LCC, Arts 578–580.

Part IX. Taxation of Insurance

Chapter 1. Taxation of Insurance Companies

448. In accordance with the general rules established regarding all legal entities, insurance companies in the Republic of Serbia are obliged to pay corporate tax imposed by the Corporate Profit Tax Law.[832] The corporate tax base is the legal entity's taxable profit.[833] The principle that the business balance sheet governs the tax balance sheet is applicable to the determination of the taxable profit, which means that the tax base is calculated by adjusting the profit posted in the profit and loss statement in a manner that incomes and expenditures are recognized in the amounts established in the profit and loss statement, in accordance with the International Accounting Standards and the Accounting and Auditing Law, apart from incomes and expenditures for which the Corporate Profit Tax Law provides another type of determination. The principle of accrual accounting is usually used for the purpose of determining business results and the taxable profit, according to which it is deemed that profit is generated upon the creation of the right to receive income, while costs are created when the obligation for their payment is incurred.[834] The taxable period in which corporate tax is accounted is a business year. This usually corresponds to a calendar year. The corporate tax rate amounts to 15%.[835]

832. OJ RS, 25/2001, 80/2002, 43/2003, 84/2004, 18/2010, 101/2011, 119/2012, 47/2013, 108/2013, 68/2014, 142/2014, 91/2015, 112/2015, 113/2017, 95/2018, 86/2019, 153/2020 and 118/2021.
833. *See* the Corporate Profit Tax Law, Art. 6, para. 1.
834. *See* Popović, *Poresko pravo* (*Tax Law*), 5 for details regarding incomes and expenditures within the profit and loss statement, adjustments within the tax balance sheet, the tax law treatment of business losses, as well as the tax base in case of the taxpayer's liquidation or insolvency. Regarding exceptions, *see* the Corporate Profit Tax Law, Arts 38 and 34, paras 3–4.
835. *See* Corporate Profit Tax Law, Art. 39, para. 2.

Chapter 2. Taxation of Insurance Proceeds

449. Life insurance premiums are exempted from tax payment. Furthermore, taxes are not payable for the following non-life insurances: (1) accident insurance; (2) workplace accident and occupational disease insurance; (3) voluntary health insurance; (4) motor vehicle insurance covering the damage to self-propelled vehicles and/or the loss of such vehicles owned by persons with a disability established by competent authorities; (5) housing loan insurance; (6) export credit insurance; (7) insurance of citizen's credits payable in instalments; (8) agricultural credit insurance.

450. Taxes are, however, payable for several non-life insurance types. Such taxes fall into the category of special service taxes affecting the consumption of particular goods. As all other consumer taxes, these are indirect charges. Taxes for non-life insurance premiums shall be accounted and paid for the following types of insurance: (1) motor vehicle insurance (apart from types exempted); (2) railroad vehicles insurance, aircraft insurance and vessels insurance; (3) insurance of goods in transport; (4) property insurance against fire or other perils (explosion, storm or other natural disasters, nuclear power, landslides and land settling, etc.); (5) other property insurance (covering the damage to property caused by machine breakdown, burglary, glass shattering, hail, frost or other perils); (6) motor vehicle liability insurance due to vehicle usage; (7) aircraft and vessel liability insurance due to usage, (8) general liability insurance; (9) credit insurance (apart from types exempted), (10) guarantee insurance; (11) financial loss insurance (covering losses due to loss of employment, insufficient income, bad weather, loss of profit, unplanned general expenses, unplanned business expenses, etc.); (12) legal aid insurance (judicial costs, attorney's fees and other procedural costs); (13) travel assistance insurance; (14) other types of non-life insurance.[836]

451. The taxpayer of non-life insurance premium taxes is the insurance company entering into such contracts and directly or indirectly (through brokers or agents) collecting premiums.[837] In non-life insurance premiums, the tax obligation comes about at the moment of entering into the contract.[838] The tax base is the total amount of non-life insurance premium.[839] The non-life insurance premium tax rate amounts to 5%.

452. Non-life insurance premium tax is assessed by means of self-taxation. The taxpayer is obliged to pay taxes until the tenth day in the month for insurance contracts concluded in the previous month. The Non-life Insurance Premium Tax Act provides for the obligation of the taxpayer to calculate the non-life insurance premium tax until the tenth day in the month in respect of contracts concluded in the

836. *See* LI, Art. 10.
837. *See* the Non-life Insurance Premium Tax Act, Art. 4.
838. *See* the Non-life Insurance Premium Tax Act, Art. 7, para. 1.
839. *See* the Non-life Insurance Premium Tax Act, Art. 4.

previous month and submit such calculation in the prescribed form to the competent tax authority regardless of the fact whether in the subject month a tax payment obligation occurred or not.[840]

840. *See* the Non-life Insurance Premium Tax Act, Art. 7, para. 2 and the Procedural Rules on the Methods of Non-life Insurance Premium Tax Assessment and the Contents and Methods of Registration providing for Supervision over Non-life Insurance Premium Tax Calculation and Payment, Art. 4, OJ RS, 140/04.

Part X. Risk Management and Prevention

453. Risk management entails actions having an effect on risk materialization in insurance. There are five risk management methods. These are avoidance, retention, transfer, sharing and reduction. The method of avoidance means non-performance of the risk-carrying activity. The method of risk retention is performed by not doing anything aimed at the avoidance, reduction or transfer of risk. Risks are thus consciously retained due to the fact that only small losses are sustainable upon their eventual materialization. The method of risk transfer means outsourcing the risk from one subject to another that has the possibility of covering it. Risk sharing means a distribution of losses between a large number of subjects. Risk reduction is performed in two manners: preventing risk occurrence and risk control. Risk prevention exists, e.g., when fire-protection measures, measures aimed at securing objects against burglary, health care of persons suffering from a particular disease, and so on are undertaken.

454. Risk management within insurance has been gaining relevance in Serbia in the last couple of years. Based on a strategic plan (NBS, 2004), as well as the framework of supervision, in the summer of 2005 a new system started functioning at full capacity. The NBS strictly supervises whether insurance companies follow the mandatory requirements that are mostly in compliance with international standards. The extensive mandatory reporting in electronic formats enables the supervisor to detect and respond quickly to deficiencies in the insurer's books.[841] All of the above resulted in significant developments in the affirmation of risk management within the Serbian insurance sector. Different forms of intermediaries – both natural persons and legal entities – are obliged to be licensed by the NBS, which eliminated hundreds of ill-equipped market players. Voluntary pension insurance (based on accumulation) is transformed into a separate, strictly regulated and triple-controlled system – with an investment fund as a central object. Greater transparency of the sector is supported through the NBS' website that offers numerous up-to-date data. However, despite the encouraging initial results, certain problems become visible or start appearing on the horizon. As the system is still in its introductory phase, these difficulties could threaten it as a whole.[842]

---

841. Dragiša Martinović, Nikola Uzelac, *Strategic View on Banking and Insurance Risk Management in Serbia*, Časopis Strategijski Mendžment 1–2 (2007): 75 and 77.
842. For details *see* Martinović, Uzelac, *Strategic Wiew on Banking and Insurance Risk Management in Serbia*, Časopis Strategijski Mendžment, 75–79.

Selected Bibliography

Antić, Oliver, et al. *Leksikon građanskog prava* (*Civil Law Lexicon*). Belgrade: Nomos, 1996.

Arsić, Zoran. 'Dejstva otvaranja stečajnog postupka na dvostrano obavezne ugovore' (Effects of the Initiation of Bankruptcy Proceedings to Mutually Binding Contracts). *Glasnik advokatske komore, Vojvodine* 2 (1982): 1–12.

Blagojević, Borislav & Vrleta Krulj. *Komentar Zakona o obligacionim odnosima, knjiga II* (*Commentary to the Law on Obligations, Book II*). Belgrade: Savremena administracija, 1980.

Carić, Slavko, et al. *Me unarodno privredno pravo* (*International Commercial Law*). Novi Sad: Centar za privredni konsalting, 2000.

Jakaša, Branko. *Pravo osiguranja* (*Insurance Law*). Zagreb: Informator, 1972.

Jankovec, Ivica & Miladinović Zoran. *Pravo osiguranja* (*Insurance Law*). Niš: Pravni fakultet u Nišu, 2006.

Jankovec, Ivica. *Obavezno osiguranje za štete od motornih vozila* (*Compulsory Insurance of Motor Vehicles against Damages*). Belgrade: Naučna knjiga, 1977.

Jankovec, Ivica. *Privredno pravo* (*Commercial Law*). Belgrade: Službeni list SRJ, 1999.

Jankovec, Ivica. *Ugovor o reosiguranju* (*Reinsurance Contract*). Belgrade: Institut za uporedno pravo, 1968.

Jašarević, Senad. *Socijalno pravo* (*Social Security Law*). Novi Sad: Pravni fakultet u Novom Sadu, 2009.

Jovanović, Vladimir. *Osiguranje u privredi* (*Commercial Insurance*), nos 11–12. Zagreb: Informator, 1962.

Jovanović, Vladimir. *Prava osiguravača prema trećem odgovornom licu* (*The Insurer's Rights towards Third party Responsible Persons*) doctoral dissertation. Belgrade: Pravni fakultet u Beogradu, 1956.

Marjanski, Vladimir. 'Funkcije polise osiguranja' (Insurance Policy Functions'). *Pravni život* 12 (2009): 879–891.

Marjanski, Vladimir. 'Interes u odštetnom osiguranju' (Interest within Damage Insurance). *Pravo i privreda* 5–8 (2006): 823–833.

Marjanski, Vladimir. *Ugovor o osiguranju* (*Insurance Contract*). Novi Sad: Pravni fakultet u Novom Sadu, 2007.

Marjanski, Vladimir. 'Ugovor o saosiguranju' (Coinsurance Contract). *Pravni život* 11 (2008): 899–910.

Marović, Boris & Slobodan Jovanović. *Reosiguranje (Reinsurance*). Novi Sad: DDOR Novi Sad, 2004.

Martinović, Dragiša & Nenad Uzelac. 'Strategic Wiew on Banking and Insurance Risk Management in Serbia'. *Časopis Strategijski Mendžment* 1–2 (2007): 75–79.

Nikolić, Dušan. *International Encyclopaedia of Laws – Tort Law, Serbia and Montenegro.* Alphen aan den Rijn: Kluwer Law International, 2007.

Pak, Jasna. *Osiguranje od nuklearnih rizika* (*Nuklear Risk Insurance*), magistrate thesis. Belgrade: Pravni fakultet u Beogradu, 1982.

Pavić, Drago. 'Osigurljiv interes' (Insurable Interest). *Svijet osiguranja* 6 (2004): 39–48.

Pavić, Drago. *Ugovorno pravo osiguranja – Komentar zakonskih odredaba* (*Contractual Insurance Law – Commentary to the Statutory Provisions*). Zagreb: Tectus, 2009.

Perović, Slobodan. *Komentar Zakona o obligacionim odnosima* (*Commentary of the Law on Obligations*). Belgrade: Savremena administracija, 1995.

Perović, Slobodan & Dragoljub Stojanović. *Komentar Zakona o obligacionim odnosima, knjiga II* (*Commentary to the Law on Obligations, Book II*). Kragujevac: Kulturni centar, 1980.

Popović, Dejan. *Poresko pravo* (*Tax Law*). Belgrade: Pravni fakultet u Beogradu, 2008.

Radović, Zoran. 'Mesto osiguranja u dokumentarnom akreditivu' (The Place of Insurance within Documentary Letters of Credit). *Pravni život* 10 (2002): 1003–1011.

Schimikowski, Peter. *die Skripte für Versicherungsvertragsrecht* (*Lecture Notes on Insurance Contract Law*). Köln: Institut für Versicherungswesen, 2003.

Schimikowski, Peter. *Versicherungs-vertragsrecht* (*Insurance Contract Law*). München: Verlag C.H. Beck, 2004.

Slavnić, Jovan. 'Ugovor osiguravača o zajedničkom snošenju i raspodeli rizika putem saosiguranja i njegovo sprovođenje' (The Agreement of Insurers on the Collective Coverage and Division of Risks by means of Coinsurance and its Implementation). *Pravni život* 11–12 (1993): 1545–1570.

Šogorov, Stevan. *Bankarsko pravo* (*Banking Law*). Novi Sad: Poslovni biro, 2004.

Sokal, Vladimir. *Osiguranje u korist trećeg* (*Insurance for the Benefit of Third Parties*). Belgrade: Dunav osiguranje, 1976.

Šulejić, Predrag. *Osiguranje od građanske odgovornosti* (*Civil Liability Insurance*) *doctoral dissertation*. Belgrade: Pravni fakultet u Beogradu, 1967.

Šulejić, Predrag. *Pravo osiguranja* (*Insurance Law*). Belgrade: Pravni fakultet u Beogradu, 2005.

Šulejić, Predrag. *Pravo osiguranja* (*Insurance Law*). Belgrade: Pravni fakultet u Beogradu, 1992.

Tomašić, Veljko. *Pravna priroda pomorske izvozne police* (*The Legal Nature of Marine Export Policies*). Belgrade: Institut za uporedno pravo, 1961.

Index

The numbers here refer to paragraph numbers.

Index

www.ingramcontent.com/pod-product-compliance
Ingram Content Group UK Ltd.
Pitfield, Milton Keynes, MK11 3LW, UK
UKHW020140290926
15471UKWH00003B/612

9 789403 507361